THRESHOLD TO VALLEY FORGE

THRESHOLD TO VALLEY FORGE

The Six Days of the Gulph Mills Encampment

SHEILAH D. VANCE

BROOKLINE books
Havertown, Pennsylvania

Brookline Books is an imprint of Casemate Publishers

Published in the United States of America and Great Britain in 2025 by
BROOKLINE BOOKS
1950 Lawrence Road, Havertown, PA 19083, USA
and
47 Church Street, Barnsley, S70 2AS, UK

Copyright © 2025 Sheilah D. Vance

Paperback Edition: ISBN 978-1-955041-31-7
Digital Edition: ISBN 978-1-955041-32-4

A CIP record for this book is available from the British Library

All rights reserved. No part of this book may be reproduced or transmitted in any form or by any means, electronic or mechanical including photocopying, recording or by any information storage and retrieval system, without permission from the publisher in writing.

Printed and bound in the United Kingdom by CPI Group (UK) Ltd, Croydon, CR0 4YY
Typeset in India by DiTech Publishing Services

For a complete list of Brookline Books titles, please contact:

CASEMATE PUBLISHERS (US)
Telephone (610) 853-9131
Fax (610) 853-9146
Email: casemate@casematepublishers.com
www.casematepublishers.com

CASEMATE PUBLISHERS (UK)
Telephone (0)1226 734350
Email: casemate@casemateuk.com
www.casemateuk.com

Front cover image: *Troops' Retreat Through Gulph Mills toward Valley Forge* by Robert Knight, 2000. (© Collection of the Lower Merion Historical Society, Inc.; Courtesy of the Lower Merion Historical Society, Inc.)

All images are in the public domain or from the author's collection unless otherwise stated.

Contents

Dedication and Acknowledgments		vi
Note to the Reader		viii
Map		ix
Introduction		xi

1	The Continental Army and the New Nation: In Search of a Way Forward	1
2	Leaving Whitemarsh, December 10	19
3	The Battle of Matson's Ford, December 11	29
4	The Army is on the Move Again, December 12	53
5	The March into Gulph Mills, December 13	65
6	Hardships at the Gulph, December 14	81
7	The Army Settles Down, December 15	95
8	Tents Arrive, Skirmishes with the British, and the Army Waits, December 16	107
9	Washington Announces the Move to Winter Quarters, December 17	121
10	Thanksgiving, December 18	135
11	The Army Leaves the Gulph and Marches to Valley Forge, December 19	149
12	Gulph Mills During the Valley Forge Encampment	163

Appendix	173
Endnotes	183
Bibliography	215
Index	225

Dedication

To all of the people I grew up with on Rebel Hill and in Gulph Mills.

Acknowledgments

I would like to thank the following organizations, their staffs, and their members for their help and contributions to this book: the King of Prussia Historical Society; the Lower Merion Historical Society; the Library of Congress Manuscript Room; the Library of Congress Reading Room; the Historical Society of Pennsylvania; The Society of the Cincinnati and its American Revolution Institute; the American Philosophical Society and its Sol Feinstone Collection of the American Revolution; the Library Company of Philadelphia; the Montgomery County Historical Society; the Archives of the City of Liverpool, England; the University of Michigan Clement Library; the Radnor Historical Society; the Tredyffrin Easttown Historical Society; and the Commonwealth of Pennsylvania Archives.

Special thanks to Cheryl Hardy, Esq., my trusted editor and friend; to Barbara Eunice, for always encouraging me; and to my children, Hope and Vance, for their love and support.

Thanks to my editors at Brookline Books and Casemate Publishers for their skills and effort: Jennifer Greene, Ruth Sheppard, and Lizzy Hammond.

Proceed, great chief, with virtue on thy side,

Thy ev'ry action let the goddess guide.

A crown, a mansion, and a throne that shine,

With gold unfading, Washington! be thine.

—Phillis Wheatley, Poet and Author[1]

There are some topics of local history which are purely local and nothing else, and there are those which, while no less important to the history of the locality, are also of significance with respect to the larger one of the nation.

—John Franklin Jameson, Ph.D., LL.D.[2]

Note to the Reader

These are the Registers,

the chronicles of the age.

They were written in, and speak the truth of History

Better than a hundred of your printed Communications.

—Shackerley Marmion's *The Antiquary*

The Bradford Club used the quote from Shackerley Marmion's play, *The Antiquary*, to explain their issuance of "curious manuscripts or documents worthy of notice" and "unpublished journals of correspondence containing matter worthy of record."[3]

This book features a number of original documents and manuscripts, in the language of those who wrote them. They vividly told the tale of and the significance of the Gulph Mills Encampment far better than anyone else could. For many of these soldiers, grammar and spelling were not their strong suits. Further, some of the language that was used in 1777 was very different than the language that we use today. Yet, their words get the point across far better than paraphrasing. So, hopefully you will read the words in their accounts in the spirit in which they wrote them.

One of the Revolutionary War soldiers explained this to the readers of his narrative book on his experiences during the war:

> The critical grammarian may find enough to feed his spleen upon, if he peruses the following pages; but I can inform him beforehand, I do not regard his sneers; if I cannot write grammatically, I can think, talk, and feel like other men. Besides, if the common readers can understand it, it is all I desire; and to give them an idea, though but a faint one, of what the army suffered that gained and secured our independence, is all I wish. I never studied grammar an hour in my life, when I ought to have been doing that, I was forced to be studying the rules and articles of war.
>
> As to punctuation, my narrative is in the same predicament as it is in respect to the other parts of grammar. I never learned the rules of punctuation any farther than just to assist in fixing a comma to the British depredations in the State of New York; a semicolon in New-Jersey; a colon in Pennsylvania, and a final period in Virginia;—a note of interrogation, why we were made to suffer so much in so good and just a cause; and a note of admiration to all the world, that an army voluntarily engaged to serve their country, when starved, and naked, and suffering every thing short of death, (and thousands even that,) should be able to persevere through an eight years war, and come off conquerors at last!
>
> —Joseph Plumb Martin, 12th Connecticut Regiment[4]

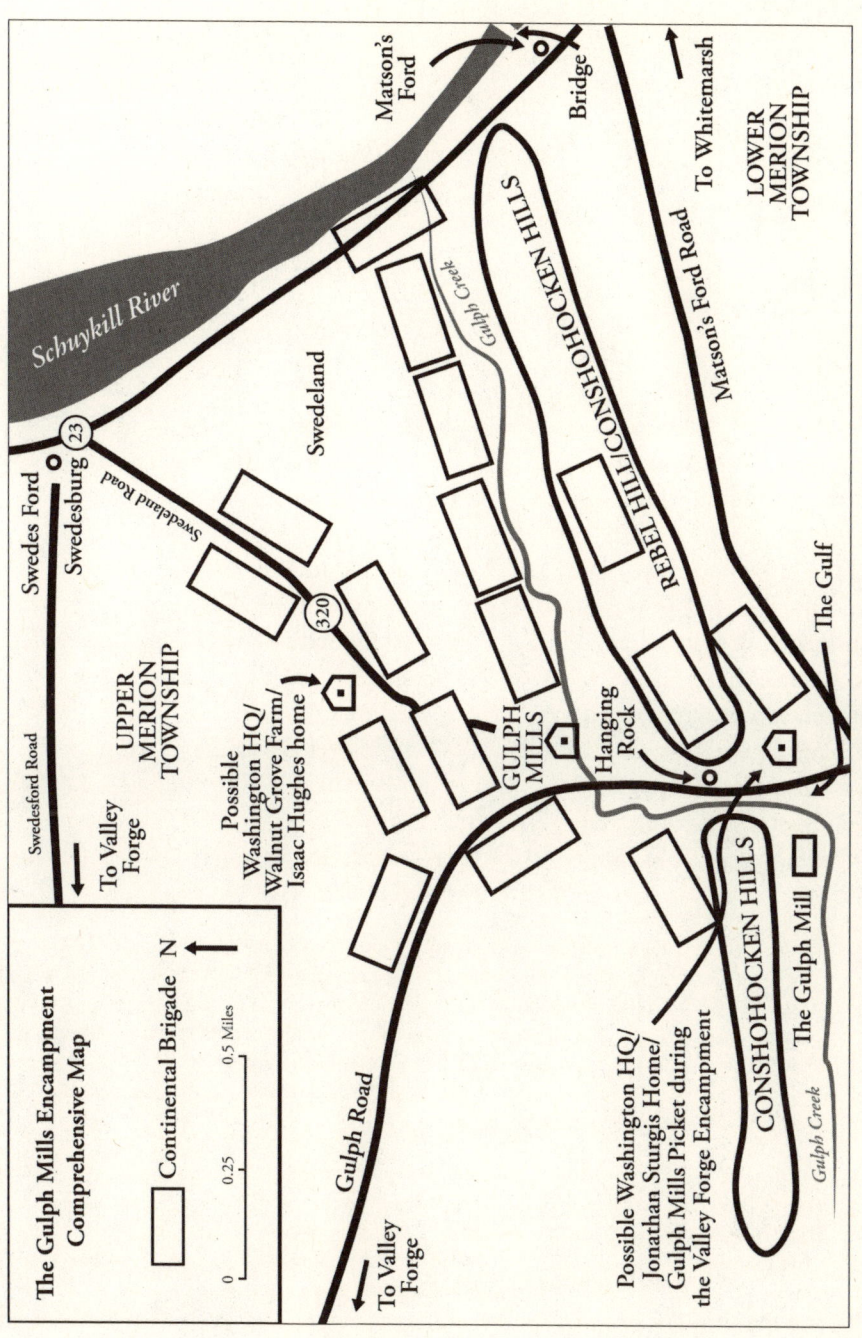

Comprehensive map of the Gulph Mills Encampment, December 12–19, 1777.

Introduction

We are standing on historic soil. Yonder hills, one hundred and sixteen years ago, witnessed the privations and sufferings of a band of heroes,—the soldiers of the Revolution. The old Gulph Mill, its walls grim and gray with age, still guards the spot, a faithful sentinel. Here have passed and repassed men whose names are history itself, whose deeds are a cherished inheritance. Washington, modest as virtuous; Greene, wise as brave; Knox, gallant as true; Lafayette, the friend of America; Sullivan, Stirling, De Kalb, Muhlenberg, Maxwell, Huntington, and Wayne! Anthony Wayne! Pennsylvania's soldier and patriot. These grounds were the threshold to Valley Forge, and the story of that winter—a story of endurance, forbearance, and patriotism which will never grow old—had its beginning here, at the six days encampment by the old Gulph Mill. The memorial which we dedicate to-day in remembrance of this encampment—rough, unchiselled, nature's monument—is a fit emblem of the dreary days of December, 1777.

So said William S. Baker when he spoke in 1893 at the Pennsylvania Sons of the Revolution ceremony that dedicated a 9-foot, rough memorial stone to mark the site of the Continental Army's encampment in Gulph Mills, Pennsylvania from December 13 to 19, 1777. The 20-ton stone, which was carved out of the surrounding hills and situated by the old Gulph Mill, was inscribed:

GULPH MILLS. THE MAIN CONTINENTAL ARMY COMMANDED BY GENERAL GEORGE WASHINGTON ENCAMPED IN THE IMMEDIATE VICINITY FROM DECEMBER 13 TO DECEMBER 19 1777 BEFORE GOING INTO WINTER QUARTERS AT VALLEY FORGE. ERECTED BY THE PENNSYLVANIA SONS OF THE REVOLUTION 1892. THIS MEMORIAL TO THE SOLDIERS OF THE REVOLUTION STANDS ON GROUND PRESENTED BY HENDERSON SUPPLEE OWNER OF THE GULPH MILL ERECTED IN 1747.[1]

Baker, like this author, believed that the historical importance of the Gulph Mills Encampment of General George Washington and 11,000 members of the Continental Army has been sorely overlooked, leaving the world without an understanding of the many significant matters that occurred during those six days. As Baker put it, "it is curious to note that this fact has been passed over by most historians, or, if alluded to at all, spoken of in very brief mention."[2]

The Gulph Mills Encampment of the Continental Army occurred in the middle of that part of the Revolutionary War that is called the Philadelphia

Campaign,[3] which ran from the Battle of Brandywine on September 11, 1777, to the march out from Valley Forge on June 19, 1778. Gulph Mills, a village about 17 miles from the city of Philadelphia, but then also a part of Philadelphia County,[4] was like many other areas of Pennsylvania at the time: sparsely populated, rural, with large farms, plantations, and quarries to extract stone. The area also had a fast-flowing creek, called Gulph Creek, that ran through the community and powered various mills that harnessed the creek's power. Among those mills was a grist mill to make flour and corn meal, which was called the Gulph Mill; a sawmill to cut logs into lumber, a powder mill to manufacture gun powder, a textile mill to produce cloth, and a paper mill.

Yet, Gulph Mills was distinguished from a lot of other small towns by its location in a range of hills called the Conshohocken[5] Hills that ran for

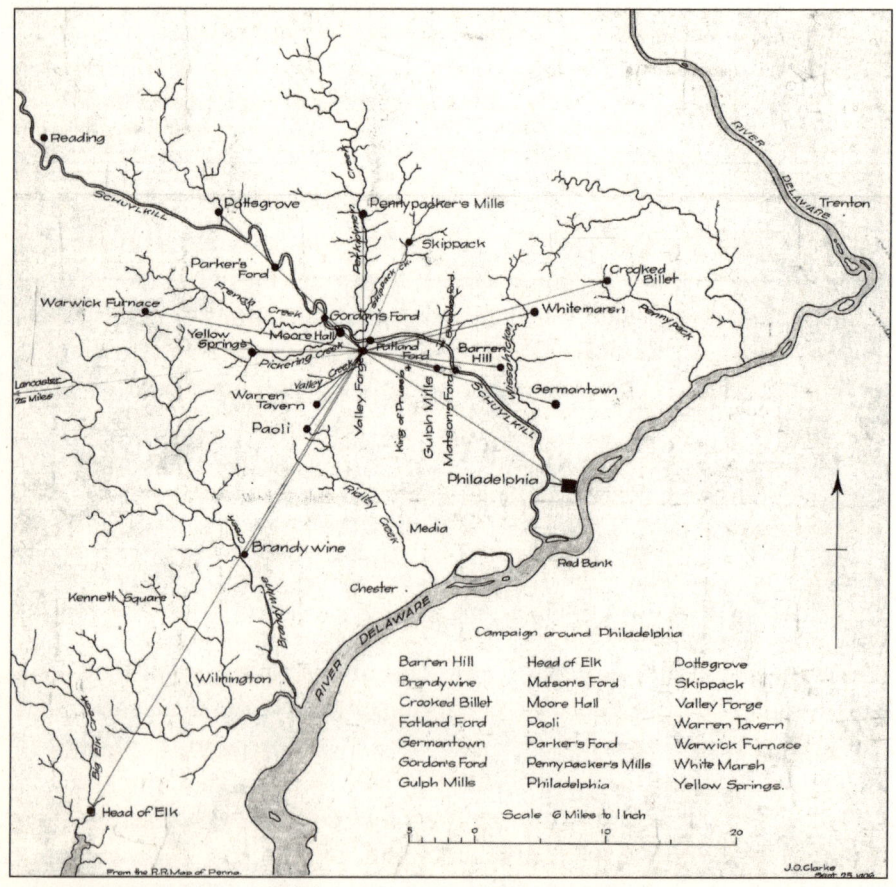

A 1906 map of significant locations in the Philadelphia Campaign of the Revolutionary War, September 11, 1777 to June 19, 1778, showing Gulph Mills. (Courtesy of King of Prussia Historical Society)

two miles from the Schuylkill River at one end of Gulph Mills to a defile called the Gulph at the other end. The highest point, about 400 feet,[6] came to be known as Rebel Hill, due to the rebel Continental Army soldiers who encamped there in December 1777. From those high hills one could see as far as Philadelphia. One could also see who was attempting to cross into Gulph Mills from the eastern banks of the Schuylkill River on the Matson's Ford, one of two main routes to cross the Schuylkill in that part of Philadelphia County. The hills also gave anyone on them a good view of the other Schuylkill River crossing point in that area, which was the Swedes Ford, only about four miles further north.

The Matson's Ford today is marked by the Fayette (named after Continental Army Major General Marquis de Lafayette) General Street Bridge, also known as the Matsonford Bridge, which spans the Schuylkill River, with Conshohocken, Plymouth Whitemarsh Township, on the east side and West Conshohocken, Upper Merion Township, on the west side. The Swedes Ford is marked today by the DeKalb (named after Continental Army Major General Baron de Kalb) Veterans Memorial Bridge across the Schuylkill River, with Norristown, a large non-township municipality, on the east side and Bridgeport, Upper Merion Township, on the west side.

The length of the Conshohocken Hills in Gulph Mills was cut in half in the 1950s for the construction of the Schuylkill Expressway, which runs from Philadelphia to Valley Forge. The cuts on the rocks on either side of the road are very visible to anyone who drives near the expressway's Gulph Mills exit. Yet, the highest points on those hills remain, and their importance can never be diminished.

General references to the Continental Army in this book include both the soldiers in the formal Continental Army and those in the state militias. The formal Continental Army, which was under the jurisdiction of the Second Continental Congress (which from here on I'll abbreviate to Congress), the legislative governing body of the new United States, included the more regular and professional soldiers who enlisted in the Continental Army for a period of one to three years. The soldiers in the various state militia units were more of the volunteer, short-term and part-time citizen soldiers who were under the jurisdiction of the various states and whose roles had been primarily fighting in and protecting their individual states. The militia units joined in fighting the British with the Continental Army units, and they were all under the overall command of the Commander in Chief of the Continental Army, General George Washington.

The leadup to the Philadelphia Campaign began in August 1777 when the Commander in Chief of the British Army in America, General William Howe,

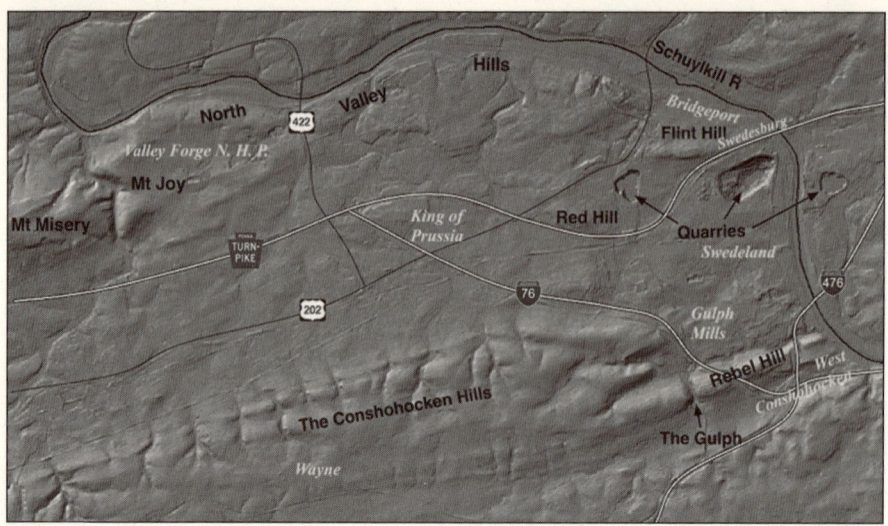

Relief map of Upper Merion Township area, showing Rebel Hill, Conshohocken Hills, Gulph Mills, and Valley Forge. (Courtesy of King of Prussia Historical Society)

sailed from his outpost in New York City and landed at the Head of the Elk, in Elkton, Maryland, with 15,000 troops. Howe's goal was to capture the rebel city of Philadelphia, which was the capital of the new United States and the most populous city in the 13 states at 40,000 residents. Philadelphia was also the seat of the United States' fledgling government, the Continental Congress, which met in the center of the city of Philadelphia at the Pennsylvania Statehouse, which was also the meeting place of the Pennsylvania General Assembly and Supreme Executive Council. That Statehouse is now called Independence Hall.

Washington marched about 11,000 members of the Continental Army from New York to Pennsylvania to defend Philadelphia. The first major head-to-head battle in the Philadelphia Campaign occurred on September 11, 1777, on the banks of the Brandywine Creek, in Chadds Ford and Kennett Square, Chester County, in the Brandywine Valley, about 44 miles from Philadelphia. As explained by the organization that supports the Brandywine Battlefield, "The Battle of Brandywine was the largest single day engagement of the American Revolution where nearly 30,000 soldiers (not including civilians, teamsters, servants, and other members of the army) squared off on a ten square mile area of roughly 35,000 acres."[7]

The British surprised Washington's forces, who luckily received a last-minute warning from a local farmer. Nevertheless, the battle was chaotic and resulted in a defeat for Washington's forces, who hurriedly retreated from the field of battle and moved closer to Philadelphia. The American forces incurred 1,300 casualties to the British's 587.[8]

The British stayed on the patriots' tails and pursued them throughout the western Pennsylvania outskirts of Philadelphia. They caught up with the rebels on September 16 in Chester County, and both sides prepared for a major battle near West Whiteland and East Goshen Townships, about 32 miles west of Philadelphia. Some parties from both armies skirmished, but before the bulk of both armies, in just about the size that they were at the Battle of Brandywine, could fully engage, there was a violent thunderstorm that wet the gunpowder, the muskets, and the ground so that neither side could fire their guns or hardly move about in the now muddy fields.

Washington moved his army further west of Philadelphia to Yellow Springs, about 35 miles away, and then to Reading, some 64 miles away, while the British encamped in Tredyffrin Township, about 24 miles west of Philadelphia in Chester County. While in Tredyffrin, the British raided the Valley Forge, which was owned by Pennsylvania Militia colonel William DeWeese. The Forge made and stored munitions for the Continental Army. With Washington's army miles away, Howe and his army attacked the Valley Forge, captured "upwards of 3,800 barrels of flour, soap, and candles; 25 barrels of Horse Shoes; several thousand tomahawks and kettles; intrenching tools; and 20 hogshead of resin," and then destroyed all of the forges and dams there.[9]

To surveil the British and harass them if possible, Washington sent General Anthony Wayne and his Pennsylvania Division of about 2,000 men, down toward Tredyffrin, which was only a few miles from Wayne's home, Waynesborough, in Paoli, Easttown Township, Chester County. Wayne's forces encamped near the Paoli Tavern in the area of Malvern, about four miles from the British camp. Washington had also sent General William Smallwood's Maryland Militia to join Wayne in an attempt to capture part of the British Army's baggage train.

Howe received information about where Wayne's forces were located and planned to attack. Howe sent out Major General Charles Grey and about 1,200 men late in the evening of September 20. Grey ordered his men to use their bayonet only, not to fire their rifles, so that Wayne's troops would be surprised. This tactic worked, and Wayne's largely sleeping and unaware troops were badly injured and killed by the bayonets in what has been called the Paoli Massacre. Smallwood's troops made it to Wayne's location while the tail end of the battle was underway, but the British troops still had the upper hand. The Americans had 272 casualties, including some 58 dead, while the

British only had 11 casualties.[10] Grey was then known as "No Flint" Grey. The patriot battle cry at the next major engagement against the British was "Remember Paoli!"

The British then moved east, closer to the Schuylkill River, to cross it to enter Philadelphia. Washington's troops followed the British, harassing and skirmishing when they could. As the British Army moved closer to Philadelphia, Washington made the strategic decision based on the number of American troops, their condition, and their training, to not engage in a battle to stop the British from entering Philadelphia. On September 26, some 17,000 to 20,000 British troops marched into Philadelphia and claimed the capital of the United States without one shot being fired.

Regrouped, Washington thought that he had a strategic advantage, so the two armies met again, essentially in full, on October 4 in the Germantown area of Philadelphia, which was 7 miles northwest of the center of the city. Washington thought that he could strike a decisive blow against the British. The army fought fiercely at the Battle of Germantown, but a thick fog caused chaos among the American troops, so much so that at one point they were even shooting at each other. There were heavy losses on both sides, and the battle was considered a draw. General Wayne's forces again led the American troops in cries of "Remember Paoli!"

Washington's forces retreated about 15 miles further north of Philadelphia to Whitemarsh Township, a small farming community on the banks of the Schuylkill and Wissahickon rivers, like many others on the outskirts of Philadelphia. Washington and the 11,000 members of the main Continental Army began the Whitemarsh Encampment on November 2, and they were still encamped there when December 1777 unfolded.

While Washington was in the Philadelphia area with the main branch of the Continental Army, a smaller branch, the Northern Department of the Continental Army, also referred to as the Northern Army, under the command of General Horatio Gates, was encamped in New York. Gates and his forces scored one of the major victories of the Revolutionary War for the Americans in October 1777 in the Battle of Saratoga. Gates and his army captured British General William Burgoyne and 5,000 of his troops on October 17, 1777. Gates was lauded as a hero all over the United States, and internationally, for this great military achievement.

Washington and the 11,000 members of the Continental Army forces faced December 1777 as a number of existential questions about the Revolutionary War swirled around them and in their camp. Those questions formed the context and the themes of the Gulph Mills Encampment.

There were five main themes of significant events during the Gulph Mills Encampment (GME):

What problems would arise from the British Army's continued occupation of Philadelphia, the new United States' capital city, and the largest in the new nation with about 40,000 residents? Philadelphia was only about 17 miles from Gulph Mills.

What were General George Washington and the Continental Army's plans for the winter? Washington started December 1777 grappling with two main decisions about the winter. One, where would the army go for winter quarters? At that period in history, armies went into winter quarters, which was basically a period of seasonal respite when armies did not fight because of the difficulties of moving around when roads were frozen, and fields did not yield the food or forage that the armies needed to survive. Two, could the Continental Army in its current state, which lacked food, clothing, provisions, and weapons for the troops, not to mention the absence of recent battlefield victories during the Philadelphia Campaign, successfully mount another battle against the British?

Could the Second Continental Congress, which was the body composed of representatives of the 13 states that was then governing the new United States, implement a victorious way forward for the Continental Army while also formulating the new government that the army was fighting for?

What would be the fate of Benjamin Franklin and the then two other members of the Committee for Foreign Affairs, also known as the Committee of Secret Correspondence, which was appointed by the Continental Congress to conduct international diplomacy to garner support for the United States from foreign nations? Would they succeed in their efforts to secure from French King Louis XVI his nation's formal and open recognition of the United States as an independent country, with increased military and financial aid, after over a year of informal and clandestine military and financial support?[11]

Would the people and government of the Commonwealth of Pennsylvania provide the necessary support to the Continental Army, which was now in their backyards?

This is the backdrop that existed at the beginning of the Gulph Mills Encampment.

The resolution of these questions would help the United States solidify the motto that the Continental Congress adopted on July 4, 1776, at the suggestion of Benjamin Franklin, Philadelphia's most famous citizen—*E pluribus, unum.* Out of many, one.[12]

First, the British occupation of Philadelphia. This military takeover of Philadelphia on September 26, 1777, created hardship, deprivation, and anxiety for most Philadelphians. Earlier in September, the Continental Army had already passed through Philadelphia, causing hardship to its inhabitants by taking or burning provisions or supplies that they thought would support the British when they arrived in Philadelphia.

British General Howe hoped that by seizing the prize of Philadelphia, the war would end shortly because the rebels and its capital city would feel the full force of the British Army. The British also believed that there were many loyalists in the city who supported the British, wanted the Crown's forces to come and quell the patriots' rebellion, and who would rise up to support the British.[13] The occupation of Philadelphia deviated from the British plan early in 1777 to first conquer New England, but that proved to be very difficult. The New Englanders, who comprised the bulk of the newly formed Continental Army, led by its newly appointed Commander in Chief George Washington, surprised the British with the strength of their military prowess against the British Army during the Siege of Boston in 1775. The Continental forces drove the British out of the area, up to Canada, and back down to New York. Since that time, the British Army's ill-conceived military strategy had led to the failure of their plan to cut New England off from the rest of the colonies and to the growing prowess of the Continental Army.

Sarah Logan Fisher, a Philadelphia resident, recalled the British Army's triumphal entry as follows:

> First came the light horse, led by Enoch Story and Phineas Bond, as the soldiers were unacquainted with the town and the different streets, nearly two hundred, I imagine, clean dress and their bright swords glittering in the sun. After that came the foot, headed by Lieutenant General Lord Cornwallis. Before him went a band of music, which played a solemn tune, and which I afterwards understood was called "God Save Great George Our King." Then followed the soldiers, who looked very clean and healthy and a remarkable solemnity was on their countenance, no wanton levity, or indecent mirth, but a gravity well becoming the occasion seemed on all their faces. After that came the artillery and then, the Hessian grenadiers, attended by a large band of music but not equal fitness or solemnity to the other. Baggage, wagons, Hessian women and horses, cows, goats and asses brought up the rear.[14]

The nation's largest city of about 40,000 grew even larger with the occupation of about 20,000 British soldiers. They were all fighting for food and supplies that were often limited due to blockades of the rivers that carried supply ships, land battles that blocked roads and destroyed supplies, and local roads that the Continental Army soldiers monitored and limited traffic on to deprive the British of needed supplies. The British soldiers, based in a large city with comfortable stone and wood housing that they occupied when they were not out in the field for battle, surveillance, or foraging, were able to stay in better shape than the Continental Army soldiers, who were regularly in smaller towns with limited housing and often forced to stay out in the field in huts or wigwams, which were lean-tos built of branches and leaves. No one knew how long the British were going to occupy Philadelphia, but just about everyone knew that, because the cold December weather had already started freezing roads and rivers, the British would likely make their winter quarters in the city and stay there until the spring.

Second, on December 10, 1777, General George Washington readied approximately 11,000 soldiers in the Continental Army to march out of their headquarters in the area around Whitemarsh Township about 13 miles northwest of Philadelphia.[15] This encampment lay along the Wissahickon Creek, on the east side of the Schuylkill River, one of two main rivers that traverse Philadelphia and southeastern Pennsylvania, the other being the Delaware River. As was the case with most townships in Pennsylvania at the time, Whitemarsh was a sparsely populated farming community with a number of mills of all types by its waterways, some quarries, and craftsmen, such as blacksmiths and carpenters. The Whitemarsh Encampment also included present-day Springfield Township, Upper Dublin Township, and Fort Washington, where Washington established his headquarters at the Emlen House.

Washington's goal was to have his army cross the Schuylkill into an area called Gulph Mills, a small hilly village about 15 miles from Philadelphia, but on the west side of the Schuylkill. It was named Gulph Mills because of a defile, or narrow path, called "the Gulph" that existed at the end of the highest of the Conshohocken Hills. The defile was created when a large piece of overhanging rock, named the Hanging Rock, split the Conshohocken Hills where the Gulph Creek flowed through it. Gulph Road, as it went by the Hanging Rock, was an extremely narrow road, but it was a main thoroughfare from the city of Philadelphia and surrounding townships that was laid out in 1713 and opened in 1726. One writer described the area this way:

> A dozen miles northwest of Philadelphia, the road leading then to Valley Forge threads a miniature mountain pass. On either hand, the wooded slopes rise steeply to a height of more than two hundred feet. At the left ripples the stream on its downward course. Midway of the pass, a threatening mass of rock, overhanging the highway on the right, appears the remnant of some great portal that once spanned the road.[16]

The highest point on the Conshohocken Hills at about 400 feet was a hill that the locals designated as Rebel Hill because of the rebelling patriots who lived there.[17]

It seems that only Washington knew whether he was marching the army to Gulph Mills to establish winter quarters there or just moving them further away from the British Army, who had just marched out of Philadelphia and engaged the Continental Army in a battle called the Battle of Whitemarsh, on December 5–8.

The Continental Army suffered the deaths of about 100 men at the Battle of Whitemarsh,[18] but the losses were not as great as they could have been, because British Commander in Chief General William Howe unexpectedly withdrew his forces on the 8th rather than engage in the all-out battle that Washington had been warned about and had expected. The tired, barely clothed, and hungry Continental Army knew that they would likely soon go into winter quarters and would have some much-needed time until the spring to rest, rebuild, and refresh.

At the same time, the Continental Congress was trying to formulate the government that the army was fighting for and to muster the resources of the 13 former colonies as the United States to support the Continental Army. The Continental Congress, which was composed of a proportionate number of delegates from all 13 states, met in Philadelphia from May 1775 to September 1777, except for December 1776 to February 1777, when British forces then in New York moved on Philadelphia, and the Congress moved to the Baltimore, Maryland, home of Henry Fite.[19] When the British Army later triumphantly marched into Philadelphia to capture it, with nary a shot fired, the Continental Congress moved about 100 miles away to the Court House in York, Pennsylvania, also referred to as Yorktown, which was the first Pennsylvania town to be sited west of the Susquehanna River.

On November 15, 1777, the Continental Congress passed the Articles of the Confederation to

Charles Thomson, Secretary of the Continental Congress.

organize the 13 new states, which had largely functioned independently in so many governance matters, into a unified, fully functioning national government. The Congress then sent the Articles to each state, requesting that each state legislature pass a resolution that adopted the Articles and that directed its representatives at the Continental Congress to vote the Articles into law.

The Continental Congress had the responsibility of supporting the Continental Army financially and in every other way, with such items as clothes, weapons, and food. Congress had created the Continental Army on June 14, 1775. The next day, they voted as Commanding Officer of the new Continental Army, their fellow Congress member from Virginia—the soldier, officer, and plantation owner named George Washington, who immediately headed to Boston to join the mostly New England states' militia units then under siege by the British, and who had just fought the British at Bunker Hill, Lexington, and Concord, and had taken Fort Ticonderoga in New York.[20]

In 1777, the Continental Congress passed constant resolutions regarding the Continental Army, and it communicated regularly with Washington, and vice versa. The Congress was concerned about the many losses or draws in the battles of the Philadelphia Campaign. All of these losses occurred in engagements of the main army, which was directly under Washington's command. General Gates's victory at the Battle of Saratoga in October 1777 contrasted greatly with Washington's losses. As a result, Washington gained a number of detractors who thought that Gates, not Washington, should be the Commander in Chief of the Continental Army.

One historian's view of the situation facing Washington was that "there was secret and almost malignant censure on every act" and omission, whether real or apparent, but definitely attributed to Washington.

> A cabal consisting of a few members of Congress, of discontented and disappointed officers of the army, and of others still more worthless and better suited to the purposes of secret slander, had been formed, whose end and aim seemed to be the defamation of the Commander-in-Chief. Every unavoidable disaster was a Subject of ill-natured comment. The most unworthy and transient popular resentments were stimulated and directed against him, and it was with the greatest difficulty that this secret hostility was prevented from an outbreak before which even Washington with all his power and dignified self-reliance might have sunk. The machinations of the conspiracy were on full display after Gates' victory at Saratoga, and during Washington's apparently helpless inaction in the neighborhood of Philadelphia.[21]

The Continental Congress had even sent a Continental Congressional Camp Committee (CCCC) of three of its members to the army's camp in Whitemarsh on December 3.[22] The CCCC was charged with determining whether the army should engage in one or more battles with the British before going into winter quarters, to discuss with Washington where the army would go into winter quarters, and to essentially assess Washington's abilities and capabilities.

Congress's doubts about Washington were real. Colonel Elias Boudinot was a Philadelphia lawyer who served as an intelligence officer and prisoner-of-war commissary. Despite being named in November 1777 as a delegate from New Jersey to the Second Continental Congress, he did not serve until May 1778 because of his Continental Army duties. He was still in camp on December 5, when British General Howe moved his troops out for the Battle of Whitemarsh.

Boudinot recalled that one evening during the Battle of Whitemarsh, "Washington was informed of some very harsh and severe speeches made by a Committee from Congress for not attacking the British and putting an End to the War at once." Boudinot observed that Washington was "exceedingly hurt" by the statements from Congress, to the point where Washington was determined to launch an attack and let the Committee deal with the consequences of a possible loss. He dispatched General Anthony Wayne and his brigade to march into the valley between the American and British, "near the foot of Chestnut Hill," and to be ready for action the following morning.[23]

The CCCC issued its recommendations to Washington on December 10 before they left camp. They had to wait at camp beyond their earlier scheduled departure date of December 5 because of the British attack on the camp December 5 to 8.

Third, the Revolutionary War being in their backyards was difficult, draining, and a hardship for the residents of the Commonwealth[24] of Pennsylvania and their government. Pennsylvania was then governed by a unicameral legislature known as the General Assembly that had representatives from 11 counties[25]—Philadelphia, Chester, Bucks, Lancaster, York, Cumberland, Berks, Northampton, Beford, Northumberland, and Westmoreland—and the city of Philadelphia itself.[26] The administrative functions of state government were carried out by the Supreme Executive Council, which had 12 members. The President of the Supreme Executive Council, a position that is likened to being the governor, was Thomas Wharton, whose full title was "President of the Supreme Executive Council of Pennsylvania, Captain-General and Commander-in-Chief in and over the same." Wharton was a staunch patriot and member of the original Pennsylvania Committee of Safety that was appointed in 1775 after the Battle of Bunker Hill and charged with raising and managing a Pennsylvania militia. Wharton also ran a successful import business.[27] The supreme legislative power was vested in the General Assembly, while the supreme executive power was vested in the President and Council.

The Pennsylvania General Assembly and Supreme Executive Council were rightfully very concerned about the impact of the war on its citizens—their safety, and how they were expected to personally support the Continental Army. They also were anxious that the Continental Army and the Congress being in the Commonwealth of Pennsylvania would rely more on the Pennsylvania General Assembly to support the Continental Army financially and logistically, as opposed to the Congress itself. They were troubled by the extraordinary demands that the war's presence in Pennsylvania made on its Pennsylvania Militia, which, like most other state militias, they knew was too often loosely organized, supplied, and trained. Further, they were increasingly consumed with fear about how the Continental Army was going to protect Pennsylvania during the winter of 1777/78.

Thomas Wharton, President of the Supreme Executive Council of the Commonwealth of Pennsylvania, Captain General and Commander in Chief in and over the same.

There was regular and constant communication between the Pennsylvania Supreme Executive Council, Washington, other officers in the Continental Army, and the Congress. The Pennsylvania governmental bodies and the Congress often fought over which government was responsible for supplying and funding what activities. These fights began long before the Gulph Mills Encampment, but they continued during it.

Relationships between the federal and state governing bodies were so concerning earlier in 1777 that on April 14, 1777, the Continental Congress passed a resolution recognizing even then that "Whereas the State of Pennsylvania is threatened with an immediate invasion; and, from the adjournment of the Legislative and Executive Authorities of the Commonwealth it is impracticable to carry into immediate execution many measures of the utmost importance, not only to the safety of this Commonwealth, but likewise to the general welfare of the United States."

The resolution also called for the establishment of a committee where bodies could confer "in order that proper measures may be pursued for the

1777 map showing Gulph Mills and Valley Forge; Map L2022LA1ff, "The Province of New Jersey: Divided into East and West, Commonly Called the Jerseys." (Courtesy of The Society of the Cincinnati, Washington, DC)

defense of the "Commonwealth."[28] The Committee had an agreeable meeting on April 15, 1777. It decided that the Congress would care for the safety of the people of Pennsylvania until its General Assembly could reconvene. The Committee explained that the Commanding Officer of the Continental Forces in the city and the Congress would be "facilitating every measure which may be deserved conducive to the safety of the State."[29] Even though Congress gave those assurances in April 1777, by December 1777, the Pennsylvania General Assembly and its Supreme Executive Council still sought further assurances from Congress that the burden of the current Philadelphia Campaign would not fall on Pennsylvania alone.

Across the Atlantic Ocean, in France, members of the Committee for Foreign Affairs, known as the American Commissioners, appointed by the Continental Congress, continued working to get the French King, Louis XVI, to recognize the United States as an actual nation. Committee members included Pennsylvania's and, due to his groundbreaking achievements with electricity and other scientific matters, the world's citizen extraordinaire Benjamin Franklin; Virginia's Arthur Lee, a merchant who had been living in London; and Silas Deane, who had represented some of the colonies in France since March 1776. The perspectives of these Commissioners, who all went to France with different backgrounds and constituencies, yet firm in one goal for the new United States, will be included in this recounting of these important December days. It is important to understand how they handled the monumental task before them with diplomacy, daring, and delicacy.

The Commissioners had convinced the French Foreign Minister, Charles Gravier, Comte de Vergennes, to secretly support the new United States with guns, cannons, and funds. The French

Etching of Benjamin Franklin's reception at the Court of Versailles (by Daniel Chodowiecki, 1784), showing Franklin before the French King Louis XVI. (Courtesy of The Society of the Cincinnati, Washington, DC)

looked to exact revenge on their long-term arch enemy and rival, Great Britain, to which they had just lost territory in America during the French and Indian War, which began in 1754 and ended in 1763 when the French were expelled from America.

Colonel Elias Boudinot recalled a conversation that he had with Commissioner Silas Deane. It was about how, in 1776, the Comte de Vergennes had to conceal France's provision of "Warlike Stores, from a flint to a Thirty Six pounds Great Gun" for the Continental Army through "a Man under the name Monsieur Beaumarchais whom Mr. Deane considered as sent by Count De Vergennes."[30]

Monsieur Pierre-Augustin Caron de Beaumarchais was a great and colorful supporter of the American Revolution. He was a successful French businessman, author of the famous operas *The Barber of Seville* and *The Marriage of Figaro*, and a classic Renaissance man. He was also thought to be a polymath—a "person of encyclopedic learning."[31] Beaumarchais, who had performed various duties, official and unofficial, for Kings Louis XV and XVI, created a stealth company called Roderigue Hortalez et Cie, with 40 ships, to surreptitiously ship money, arms, uniforms, and other supplies from the French and the Spanish to America. He was instrumental in swaying the French foreign minister, Comte de Vergennes, and the French King Louis XVI himself to support the United States in its revolution against their mutual, bitter enemy, England.

Boudinot recalled that an "old frigate" was quickly loaded with everything that Deane "bought," but the British minister to France found out about it "and made a spirited memorial to the King, A Violent Proclamation was the Consequence, threatening death and destruction to all concerned in so wicked an Attempt, and ordering the frigate be immediately unloaded in the day." Not to be stopped, Beaumarchais had three of his sailors reload the ship under cover of night. The war cargo safely hidden, the ship sailed in a few days and arrived safely in the United States, "to the great relief of the American Army. All this was a profound secret, but was well understood by Congress to be a present from the King of France."[32]

Boudinot noted that the author Thomas Paine, as the Secretary of the Secret Committee of Correspondence, who was under an oath of secrecy, nevertheless "divulged the Whole business in one of his publications." This suggestion that the French minister and France itself was supporting this new nation called the United States required the French minister, diplomatically, to repudiate the whole business in writing to the Continental Congress, "Who found themselves obliged to deny the King of France having anything to do with the Transaction, declaring it to be a common Mercantile contract with Beaumarchais." Like the businessman that he was, Beaumarchais "took advantage of this acknowledgment" and "called on Congress to pay the whole purchase money with interest."[33]

Franklin was extremely popular in France due to his experiments in electricity, inventions, and general demeanor.[34] Franklin and the other American Commissioners constantly engaged in diplomatic activities for the United States while in France regarding their clandestine support and relationships with the British and other European countries, such as Spain and the Netherlands, from which the Commissioners also sought support. The French were reluctant to come right out and diplomatically support the United States until they believed that the Continental Army could actually win.

The Old Gulph Mill and Memorial Stone. (Samuel Castner Scrapbook, The Free Library of Philadelphia)

On December 4, Franklin received notice that the Continental Army had brilliantly and valiantly defeated Burgoyne at Saratoga and captured 5,000 of his British soldiers. Franklin immediately wrote to King Louis XVI of this great news. A few days later, Louis XVI invited Franklin and the American Commissioners to resubmit a request for a formal alliance.[35] This news energized the American Commissioners, the French people, the French King, and the French government as they started thinking that the Americans might actually defeat the British, and the American ideals of democracy and a "republican" government by and for the people might actually become a reality.

So, in early December 1777, and during the six days of the Gulph Mills Encampment, December 13 through December 19, these five major concerns were on the minds of George Washington, the Continental Army, and their countrymen:

- How long would the British occupy the capital of the United States, its largest city, Philadelphia, and what did that mean?
- Where and when was the Continental Army going for winter quarters, and would it mount a winter campaign against the British in Philadelphia?

- Would the Continental Congress come together and truly support the Continental Army in every way and create a government that the people would continue to fight for?
- How would the people and the government of the Commonwealth of Pennsylvania react to the Continental Army now that the war had come to their backyards?
- Could the American Commissioners in France convince the French King Louis XVI to diplomatically recognize the United States as a true, foreign country, and openly provide financial and military support through a treaty of alliance?

The answers to all of these questions were exceedingly uncertain.

CHAPTER 1

The Continental Army and the New Nation: In Search of a Way Forward

As December 1777 began, George Washington and the Continental Army, in their encampment in Whitemarsh, Pennsylvania, were at a crossroads and in search of a way forward. On December 10, that way forward came into better focus. To understand the state of Washington and his army on December 10, one must first look more closely at what happened in the early days of December 1777.

Washington grappled with two major decisions: 1) whether to engage in another battle with the British before going into winter quarters, and 2) where to go for winter quarters. Unbeknownst to Washington when the month began, he would also have to fight against one more attack on the Continental Army by British General William Howe, but more on that later.

On November 30, Washington met with his Council of General Officers, made up of the generals and brigadier generals with him at the Whitemarsh Encampment, and asked each of them to provide him with a letter by December 1 detailing where they thought the army should go into winter quarters. Although all officers, except one, were physically together at the Whitemarsh Encampment, Washington usually asked his officers to put their important thoughts in writing for his military and personal records, to share with others, and for posterity.

These officers were Washington's band of brothers.[1] Washington served with several of them when he was in the First Continental Congress in 1774–75. He had been Commander in Chief of many of the other officers since 1775, when he went to Boston to take command of the newly created Continental Army and fight with them at the Siege of Boston. Washington knew many of the generals from their previous joint service in the French and Indian War in 1754–63. Additionally, he had interacted with many of them simply as a large, successful, Virginia plantation owner. Further, Washington was a

General George Washington and his generals. (A. H. Ritchie, 1870; Library of Congress)

Key identifying the generals in the photo. (A. H. Ritchie, 1870; Library of Congress)

member of the Freemasonry, a brotherhood of men of similar socioeconomic status, as were seven of the 20 generals with him at Whitemarsh on November 30. The officers' ages and backgrounds varied, but many of them, too, were not strangers to each other. Washington was 45, and the other officers' ages ranged from their 20s to their 60s.[2]

Washington asked the generals to give their opinions on three alternatives for the location of their winter quarters. One option was Wilmington, Delaware, some 32 miles from Philadelphia. The second option was to locate the army further north and west in Pennsylvania, farther away from Philadelphia, to towns like York or Lancaster, where the Continental Congress and Pennsylvania legislative bodies had escaped to when the British invaded Philadelphia. The third option was to position the army in a location not far from Philadelphia, where the American forces could keep an eye on the British, someplace close enough for the Americans to move on the British if necessary, and somewhere the American army could protect the bulk of Pennsylvania's population—meaning someplace west of the Schuylkill River, like Gulph Mills, Tredyffrin or Easttown Township, or other towns west of Philadelphia.

Washington received responses from Major Generals Nathanael Greene, John Clark, Jr., Johann de Kalb, Marquis de Lafayette, William Alexander (who referred to himself as Lord Stirling due to his family's royal Scottish background), and John Sullivan. Also communicating their thoughts were Brigadier Generals Louis Duportail, James Irvine, Henry Knox, William Maxwell, Peter Muhlenberg, Enoch Poor, James Potter, Casimir Pulaski, Charles Scott, William Smallwood, James Varnum, Anthony Wayne, George Weedon, William Woodford; as well as Henry Emanuel Lutterloh, who was Deputy Quartermaster of Forage, and Lieutenant Colonel Robert Hanson Harrison, military secretary and aide-de-camp to General Washington.

The opinions of these men were as wide-ranging and divergent as the generals themselves. It is important at this point to understand these men, who had such an influence on Washington and the Revolutionary War, and what impact their counsel had on his final decisions.

General William Alexander, 51, referred to himself as "Lord Stirling" because he was the senior male heir of his paternal grandfather, the Scottish Earl of Stirling. His claim to the title was granted by a Scottish court in 1759, but the House of Lords denied him the title in 1762 when it overruled Scottish law. Still, Alexander continued to call himself Lord Stirling. Stirling distinguished himself at the Battle of Long Island on August 27, 1776, although he was captured. He was released in a prisoner exchange and became one of Washington's most trusted advisors.[3]

Alexander's response to Washington's request was, "Upon the Whole, I should be for hutting the Army somewhere in or Near [Tredyffrin Township, in the Great Valley] especially if it is so fine and Rich a Country as has been represented."[4] He added, "I think it is also of high importance to Cover as much of the Country as we can; and that the position in the Valley will Cover as much or more of the country than any other that can be pointed out."[5]

Major General John Armstrong, 60, was in charge of the Pennsylvania Militia. He had been a brigadier general in both the Pennsylvania Militia and the Continental Army. He was born and educated in Ireland as a civil engineer.[6] Armstrong opposed the army establishing winter quarters in "the back villages" of the state because that would leave much of the state open to British plundering.

He said that good people throughout all of the states were "depressed," and the people in Pennsylvania, where the war now was, were depressed even more so because of their great sacrifice. He felt that if the army moved too far away from where the British were, fewer Pennsylvanians would take the Oaths of Allegiance to the new government or join Pennsylvania's militia. "The hearts of good-men thro' all the States depressed, and this state in particular, little less than Sacrificed to the whole without real necessity! Amongst the innumerable evils resulting from that Situation, the impossibles of the Oaths of Allegiance & the end to Government, & the future aids of the Militia thro a great part of the State, must inevitably follow."[7]

Brigadier General Louis Lebegue DePresle Duportail, 34, was Chief Engineer of the Continental Army. He was a French soldier who was secretly sent to America in March 1777 under an agreement between American Commissioners Ben Franklin and Silas Deane with King Louis XVI as part of his secret support of the new United States, in response to an expressed need for experienced military engineers. Duportail planned the fortifications for many battles and laid out the encampments. When enlisted by Franklin, Duportail was a member of the Engineering Corps of the French Army.[8]

Duportail did not give an opinion about where the army should establish winter quarters because he was "ignorant of the country." However, he felt that it would be better for the army to lose men during battle than to lose them due to the disorder and desertion that would result from their idleness and the misery caused by poor clothing, shelter, and provisions. "Misery destroys part of an Army and leaves it without Vigor, without Courage, and without good Will." He wrote that if that misery was allowed to continue unchecked, "We should find ourselves then in the Spring with a Body of an Army incapable of anything, and consequently, have no right to expect a successful campaign."[9]

Major General Nathanael Greene, 35, from Rhode Island, was with Washington early on in Washington's command of the Continental Army, at the Siege of Boston in 1775, and he was one of Washington's most trusted generals. Greene felt that the army should establish winter quarters in Wilmington with also a brigade of Continental Army troops stationed in "the Jerseys,"[10] with about 1,000 militia troops stationed between the Delaware and Schuylkill rivers, another 1,000 militia troops at or near "the Gulph," and an advance post of Continental Army troop near Chester, a borough in southeastern Pennsylvania, about 19 miles from Philadelphia on the Delaware River.

Greene wrote that it was essential to get into winter quarters to address "the general discontent among the officers of almost all ranks" and to reorganize for the spring. He noted that, curiously, "the fatigues and hardships of the campaign and the want of rest and relaxation are not the great sources of discontent that prevails." In fact, he wrote, the officers were discontented because the low or non-existent pay they received was not enough for them to support their families in dignity. He warned, "This is the great evil, and this must be remedied or else this army must and will dissolve."[11]

Brigadier General James Irvine, 42, was awarded this rank in the Pennsylvania Militia, after having been a colonel in the Continental Army. Born in Philadelphia, he well knew the Commonwealth of Pennsylvania.[12] His opinion of where to locate the army for winter quarters was just about what Washington ultimately decided on: "the weak and infirm be immediately collected together and quartered between Lancaster & Reading, that the residue of the army take a strong position on the other side [of the] Schuylkill, where wood is plenty, out of surprising [by the British] distance, and there hut themselves for the winter." Irvine felt that it would hurt Pennsylvania and the patriot cause to leave much of the state uncovered by the army. He said that it would "have a very unhappy effect upon the minds of the inhabitants, and render it extremely doubtful whether much, if any assistance could be drawn from this state [for] the ensuing campaign." He added that "few men have a less opinion of the importance of the militia in the present state than myself, but I am apprehensive that should our friends be disgusted as it is highly probable they would be, the executive powers would not be able to make drafts therefrom to fill up the thirteen regiments raised in the state which form no inconsiderable part of the Continental Army."[13]

Major General Johann de Kalb, 56, was a former German officer who moved to France after marrying a French heiress. In 1768, he "traveled to North America on a covert mission from the Etienne Francois de Choiseul, Duc de Choiseul, the Foreign Minister of War of France, to determine the level of discontent among colonists towards Great Britain." While there he "gained respect for the colonists and their 'spirit of independence'" and produced "detailed reports to the French government; upon his return to Europe, he expressed a strong desire to go back to colonial America and join the nascent fight against the British, a French adversary. He returned to the United States in July 1777 with his protégé, the Marquis de Lafayette."[14] Kalb favored winter quarters between Lancaster and Reading with the army partly in huts.[15]

Brigadier General Henry Knox, 27, was formerly a bookseller in Boston who witnessed the 1770 Boston Massacre and was one of the guards who made sure that no tea was unloaded from the British ship, the *Dartmouth*, one of the boats involved in the Boston Tea Party. Knox expressed a preference for a place "about 30 miles distant from & North or NW of Philadelphia." He felt that the army could not sufficiently cover Pennsylvania if it located winter quarters in between Lancaster and Reading, so he favored hutting the army somewhere that was about 10 or 12 miles from the Schuylkill River.[16]

Deputy Quartermaster Colonel Henry Emanuel Lutterloh also wrote to Washington with his opinion about winter quarters. Lutterloh was in favor of having quarters at Pottsgrove, a town about 39 miles west of Philadelphia. He said that the right-wing militia could locate themselves over the Schuylkill River near the Matson's Ford and upwards because he found "the Country very advantageous with hills where No Surprise could happen to them."[17]

Major General Marie-Joseph Paul Yves Roch Gilbert du Motier de Lafayette, referred to as the Marquis de Lafayette, 20, was a wealthy French officer who caught the fever of the American Revolution for liberty and for the creation of a country that was a republic of the people, not a monarchy of a few. He sailed to America in 1777, on his own ship and at his own expense, to serve without pay in the Continental Army. He arrived in the United States in June 1777. Lafayette was part of a wave of young Frenchmen who often could not speak English or had little military experience, but who were recruited by American Commissioner Silas Deane. After George Washington met Lafayette in August 1777, he bonded with him and took Lafayette under his wing. Lafayette distinguished himself at the Battle of Brandywine in September 1777. After he was shot in the leg, he still managed to rally the American troops, who were outnumbered and losing, to achieve a more orderly retreat. Lafayette preferred Lancaster for winter quarters after outlining in his letter a number of inconveniences that would arise from other choices.[18]

Brigadier General William Maxwell, 44, was born in Ireland but was raised in New Jersey. After commanding the New Jersey Brigade in the

Continental Army, he commanded the provisional corps of light infantry. Maxwell opined that if covering the countryside was Washington's chief objective, he recommended that the army be moved to the west side of the Schuylkill at about 30 miles from Philadelphia, with the army's left side near the Schuylkill and a party of observation on the east side. But, he said, if Washington's aim was to refresh the army, then the Reading–Lancaster line seemed best.[19]

Pennsylvanian General Peter Muhlenberg, 31, a member of the Lutheran Church clergy, was born in Pennsylvania but lived in Virginia in the early 1770s. He commanded the 8th Virginia Regiment of the Continental Army's Virginia line. He knew the area because he was raised in Trappe, Pennsylvania, close to where the army was currently headquartered. Muhlenberg favored "Lancaster for the Right of the Cantonment & Reading for the left."[20]

Brigadier General Enoch Poor, 41, was born and raised in Massachusetts, but he was a ship builder and merchant from New Hampshire. He was at the Battle of Saratoga before he joined Washington with the main army. He noted that although he was not acquainted with that part of the country, based on what information he had, he favored the Lancaster–Reading line.[21]

Brigadier General James Potter, 48, was the commander of the Pennsylvania Militia. Born in Ireland, he lived in Cumberland County, in central Pennsylvania, about 127 miles from Philadelphia. He was very familiar with the Commonwealth of Pennsylvania. His militia was often assigned to go here and there around the Commonwealth to successfully harass the British or to be the first line of the Continental Army's advance.

Potter knew Gulph Mills. He wrote "from near Gulph Mills" to Washington on October 16. He told Washington then that he heard that there were 1,300 British troops in Wilmington. Of his troops, Potter wrote, "My party is so small, & I am Obliged to keep them on such hard duty that they will soon be wore out. My men killed four of the enemy yesterday, and one Hessian officer the other day."[22] He also noted that he did his "positive duty" against a loyalist. "I have sent off to your Excellency (Washington) a number of Cattle the property of Sheriff Vernon & John Roberts Miller both of them Aiding and Assisting the enemy."[23]

Vernon was the Sheriff of Chester County and Roberts was a successful Quaker mill owner in Lower Merion, a few miles from Gulph Mills, who was thought to be a loyalist. The captured livestock list that was attached to the letter included 10 cattle from Vernon, 21 from Roberts, six from two local butchers, 26 sheep from Roberts, and two horses. Potter noted that he kept two of Roberts's horses and six of Vernon's cattle.[24]

Potter did not send Washington his letter until December 4. Since December 1, Potter had been out of camp, following Washington's instructions to harass the British up and down on both sides of the Schuylkill River. When he had time to write Washington on the 4th, Potter recommended winter quarters be located in Wilmington or Newport, both in Delaware, and "what other Houses we could find in a convenient place in Chester county and raise huts for the remainder of the troops, to prevent the enemy from foraging in that country." Potter felt that the backcountry had too many people who had escaped from Philadelphia. He questioned what would be done with those people if the army came to town: were the people to be turned out to make room for the soldiers? However, Potter did believe that the army should engage in a winter campaign against the British.[25]

General Casimir Pulaski, of Poland, 32, came to the United States from France, where he fled after unsuccessfully fighting among those who tried to stop Russian forces from seizing Poland's territory, on the recommendation of Ben Franklin in July 1777. An accomplished cavalryman, Pulaski was credited with saving Washington's life during the retreat at the Battle of Brandywine. Franklin recommended Pulaski as "an Officer famous throughout Europe for his Bravery and Conduct in defence of the Liberties of his Country against the three great invading powers of Russia, Austria and Prussia...may be highly useful to our Service."[26] Pulaski did not offer an opinion on the location of winter quarters because he said that he was not well acquainted with the country. He did state his opinion that he was not in favor of going into winter quarters. "Our continuing in a state of activity will give counsel to our Friends, be an antidote to the Effeminacy of Young Soldiers, and enure them to the fatigues which veterans undergo," and he added, "the activity of winter quarter, will ruin the Army, discourage the County, leave a extent of Territory for the Enemy to ravage and depopulate."[27]

General Joseph Reed, 36, was a Philadelphia lawyer who went on to serve as a colonel, secretary, aide-de-camp to George Washington, and Adjutant General.[28] Reed proposed that Washington disperse the troops and march them into New York and New England, surprise the British, and attack that part of their Northern Army. "Do not, my dear Sir, be discouraged at the Distance or length of March your Troops will think nothing of it when they see the Prize before them—& the calling the New England Brigades down with in Case of Success be deem'd a Stroke of Generalship to deceive the Enemy & weaken the Post you meant to attack."[29]

Washington wrote to Reed, a trusted adviser, on December 2 and asked him to meet with him to discuss the opinions that he would be receiving from the other generals. Washington explained:

I am about fixing the Winter cantonments of this army, and find so many, & such capitol objections to each mode proposed, that I am exceedingly embarrassed, not only by the advice given me, but in my own judgment, and should be very glad of your sentiments on the matter without loss of time. In hopes of seeing you, I shall only add that from Reading to Lancaster Inclusively, is the general Sentiment, whilst Wilmington and its vicinity, has powerful advocates. This however is mentioned under the rose—(meaning in confidence)—forever convinced in my own opinion, that if the enemy believed we had this place in contemplation they would possess themselves of it immediately.[30]

Brigadier General Charles Scott, 38, of Virginia's 5th Regiment, commanded the light infantry. Scott favored Wilmington in a short and sweet letter.[31]

Maryland's Major General William Smallwood, 45, was a planter, farmer, and plantation owner. He recommended sending the sick somewhere between Bethlehem and Lancaster with "the hail and active part of the Army" going to Wilmington "to awe, & perhaps Annoy the Enemy."[32]

Major General John Sullivan, 37, was a lawyer and miller from New Hampshire who was a delegate to the First and Second Continental Congress. In 1775, he left Philadelphia with Washington to join the Continental forces at the Siege of Boston.[33] Sullivan thought that if there was to be a winter campaign, Germantown, on the outer northwest edge of the city of Philadelphia, would be a good location because the Continental Army could keep an eye on the enemy, which was in Philadelphia proper, and keep a "strong party of Pennsylvania Militia on the west of the Schuylkill and one of the Jersey Militia on the east of [the Delaware River]." If there was not going to be a winter campaign, Sullivan recommended the Lancaster–Reading line.[34]

Rhode Island's General James Varnum, 29, was an attorney who served in the siege of Boston in May 1775 with his Varnum's Regiment, later the 9th Continental Regiment. Varnum wrote that he was in favor of "that Position which will give them the greatest check, consistent with the Ease of the Troops" as the best position. He thought that was "that part of Pennsylvania which lays between the Delaware and the Schuylkill."[35]

Brigadier General Anthony Wayne was a surveyor and farming plantation owner from Pennsylvania. He resided in Easttown Township, some 26 miles from Philadelphia, in Paoli, Chester County. Wayne was very familiar with Pennsylvania as a resident and as a professional surveyor of the land of many Pennsylvanians. Due to his temperament, he was called "Mad Anthony" Wayne. Wayne favored Wilmington, getting the Continental troops out of his state of Pennsylvania and away from his people.[36]

Brigadier General George Weedon, 43, of Virginia's 3rd Regiment, was in favor of hutting the troops somewhere. He wrote that "the chain of cantonments from Reading to Lancaster" were "the most likely to cover the troops & afford them rest thro' the winter."[37]

Lastly, Virginia's William Woodford, 43, of the 2nd Virginia Regiment, was among the officers and soldiers that drove Virginia's Royal Colonial Governor, Lord Dunmore, from the Norfolk Peninsula in the Battle of Great Bridge on December 9, 1775. Woodford thought the best protection for winter quarters would be in the villages of Reading to Lancaster with some huts.[38]

Lieutenant Colonel Robert Harrison, born in Maryland, was a Virginia attorney who had represented Washington in several legal matters before the Revolutionary War. Washington appointed Harrison as an aide-de-camp in 1775 and his military secretary the following year, essentially functioning as a chief of staff. Harrison was one of Washington's most trusted aides. Harrison wrote a memorandum, endorsed by Washington, titled, "Opinions summed up." It showed that six generals were in favor of Wilmington—Greene, Lafayette, Armstrong, Smallwood, Wayne, and Scott; nine were in favor of the Lancaster–Reading line—Sullivan, de Kalb, Maxwell, Knox, Poor, Muhlenberg, Varnum, Weedon, and Woodford; that Lord Stirling favored "the Great Valley" area; that Duportail and Irvine were for hutting "in a strong position," and Pulaski favored a winter campaign.[39]

The second major question facing Washington was whether there should be a winter campaign against the British. On November 24, Washington received from Brigadier General John Cadwalader a plan for attacking Philadelphia.[40] Washington was not sure that such an attack was warranted or whether his army was in shape to mount such an attack. While Washington contemplated whether to mount another attack before going into winter quarters, the Continental Congress wanted its say.

On November 28, the Continental Congress passed a resolution to send a committee to Washington's camp to make other inquiries:

> Resolved, unanimously, That a committee of three be appointed forthwith to repair to the army, and, in a private confidential consultation with General Washington, to consider of the best and most practicable means for carrying on a winter's campaign with vigor and success, an object which Congress have much at heart, and on such consultation, with the concurrence of General Washington, to direct every measure which circumstances may require for promoting the public service. The members chosen were Robert Morris, Elbridge Gerry, and Joseph Jones.[41] This committee became known as the Continental Congress Camp Committee (CCCC).

The Continental Congress also passed another resolution on November 28 that could be read as second-guessing Washington's leadership and judgment. The resolution:

> Resolved, That an enquiry be made into the causes of the evacuation of Fort Mercer, on the river Delaware, and into the conduct of the principal officers commanding that garrison; and that a committee be appointed to report the mode of conducting the enquiry.

> Resolved, That an immediate enquiry be made into the causes of the failure of the late expedition against Rhode Island, and into the conduct of the principal officers conducting such expedition; and that a committee be appointed to report the mode of conducting such enquiry.
> Resolved, That an enquiry be made into the loss of Forts Montgomery and Clinton, in the State of New York; and of Fort Mifflin, on the river Delaware, in the State of Pennsylvania, and into the conduct of the principal officers commanding those forts; and that General Washington be directed to cause this enquiry to be made, and to transmit the proceedings of the court to Congress with all possible dispatch.
> Resolved, That whenever any expedition which may be undertaken either by sea or land, by order, or at the expense of the United States, shall fail in the execution; or whenever any important post, fort, or fortress, garrisoned and defended at the expense of the United States, shall be evacuated, or taken by the enemy, it be an established rule in Congress to institute an enquiry into the causes of the failure of such expedition, or into the loss of such post, fort, or fortress, and into the conduct of the principal officer or officers conducting the expedition so failing, or commanding the post, fort, or fortress so evacuated or taken by the enemy; the enquiry so instituted, to be conducted in such manner as Congress shall deem best adapted for the investigation of truth in the respective cases.
> Resolved, That the committee for conducting the enquiry into the causes of the evacuation of Fort Mercer, and the failure of the expedition against Rhode Island, consist of three members.
> The members chosen, Mr. William Duer, Mr. Francis Dana, and Mr. Francis Lightfoot Lee.[42]

Around noon on December 3, the CCCC arrived at the camp at Whitemarsh. Washington met with the CCCC in the evening, and they discussed his general officers' opinions about a winter campaign and winter quarters that came out of Council of General Officers meetings in November. Washington then sent a circular to his officers to solicit their opinions on the question of whether to mount a winter campaign and/or an additional attack against the British before going into winter quarters. He requested that the officers respond by the morning of December 4.

Washington's Circular read:

> I wish to recall your attention to the important matter recommended to your Consideration sometime ago—namely—the Advisability of a Winters Campaign, & practicability of an attempt upon Philadelphia with the Aid of a considerable body of Militia to be assembled at an appointed time and place. Particular reasons urge me to request your sentiments on this matter by the Morning, and I shall expect to receive them accordingly in writing by that time.[43]

Washington received letters in response to his circular from Armstrong, Cadwalader, Irvine, Maxwell, Knox, Lafayette, Stirling, and Varnum on December 3. On December 4, letters came in from Armstrong, Irvine, Maxwell, Muhlenberg, Paterson, Poor, Potter, Reed, Scott, Smallwood, Sullivan, Wayne, Weedon, and Woodford. The majority of the generals, who were the people closest to their troops, felt strongly that their men were in no condition to wage another fight against the British.

General Stirling's responses to the winter campaign question echoed those of most of his colleagues—that the troops were in no condition to undertake another action. He specifically mentioned items of clothing that the soldiers needed but many did not have: two warm vests, two pairs of wool stockings and mittens, good shoes, wool overalls, a good blanket coat, and even just a blanket. Stirling also pointed out what Washington would have already known—that the troops were already worn out from the previous campaigns, and that too many were in hospital and "above one half of those in Camp are almost Naked, and are walking bare footed on the Ice or frozen 'round." In short, he warned Washington that, should another engagement occur, "the Army will be totally ruined."[44]

Pennsylvania's Major General Armstrong, who replied on December 4, was in favor of a winter campaign, in no small part to protect his fellow citizens. "…Pennsylvania is that moment a public Sacrifice, her spirits, her hopes & future exertions Civil & Military, are blasted at once! Unhappy State! & well if her diseases do not contaminate some of her neighbours—a mutilated victim cursed of the other twelve—and by Britain too, who for her manifold Services to Congress & to this Army, hath now made her the Capital Seat of War."[45]

General John Cadwalader, 35, favored a winter campaign. An ardent supporter of General Washington,[46] Cadwalader was a Philadelphia merchant and member of the American Philosophical Society, the

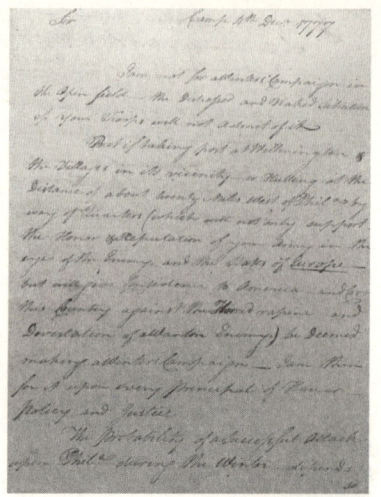

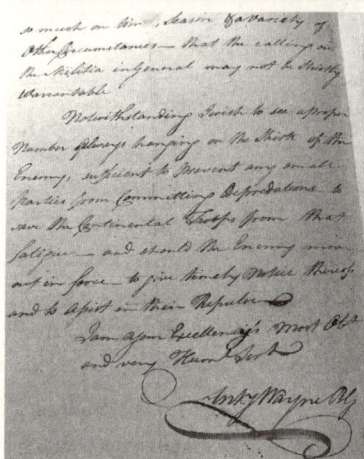

Letter from General Anthony Wayne to General George Washington, December 4, 1777, in response to Washington's December 3, 1777 letter to his generals soliciting their opinions on the advisability of a winter campaign and the practicability of an attempt on Philadelphia. (Anthony Wayne Papers, Historical Society of Pennsylvania)

august gathering of learned and financially successful men organized by Ben Franklin and notable Philadelphia men of the time.[47] Cadwalader thought that the soldiers would have the clothing that they desperately needed if they remained in the field, rather than not.

> Your men, I know, Sir, are in great want of cloathing, but I conceive they will be sooner equipped by remaining in the field than in winter Quarters—because by being in the field, the necessity will appear more evident, will endure those employed to provide cloathing to exert themselves, and will justify measures that otherwise would disgust & exasperate those from whom they are taken.[48]

Cadwalader also thought that Washington should mount another attack against the British before going into winter quarters. He argued that Pennsylvanians expected this new government and its army to protect them, but that they were sorely disappointed when British General Howe "penetrated thro' the country" and took possession of its state and nation's capital, Philadelphia. He said that the Continental Army's success in the north, notably Saratoga, enabled it to move down to Pennsylvania a great number of reinforcements from the troops that were stationed in the north and that gave the Pennsylvanians hope. He thought that although the Pennsylvanians may not expect an attack on Philadelphia in the winter, they expected to be protected nonetheless. "The withdrawing of your army to a great distance will not only magnify the enemy's strength [in the inhabitant's opinions] but will be construed into an acknowledgment of our own weakness."[49]

Brigadier General Louis Duportail, who was against a winter campaign, wrote, "it still appears to me too dangerous—the great Body of Militia with which we might be reinforced for this purpose does not give me any additional hope of succeeding—it is not the number of Troops which is of importance in this case, but it is the quality, or rather their nature and manner of fighting."[50] Many officers and government officials had a low opinion of the soldiers in the various state militias. Their beliefs, often grounded in experience, were that the men in the militia were usually untrained or barely trained volunteers with loose enlistments and too much of a tendency to not vigorously engage in the fight or exert or follow proper and strict military discipline, unlike the trained soldiers in the Continental Army.

Major General Nathanael Greene wrote, "However desirable the destruction of General Howe's army may be & however impatient the public may be for this desirable event; I cannot recommend the measure." He went on with, "Let any body examine the Condition of the troops, one half without breeches, Shoes, ofr stockings and some thousands without Blankets and judge how far men in this situation are capable of enduring the severity of a winter's

Campaign." Greene added, "The King of Prussia the greatest General of the age strongly protests against attacking troops by storm in villages much more, in large regular brick cities—He observes, it often proves the ruin of the best part of an army—this was verified in several attacks he made upon towns and villages last war—Philadelphia is a great object but I wish our reason may not be seduced from its importance to take measures to repossess it that are to warranted by history or our own observation."[51]

Pennsylvania's Brigadier General James Irvine wrote in support of a winter campaign:

> If posting the army in a position similar to that I advised in my last letter, be to form a winters campaign, the measure in my opinion is not only advisable, but absolutely necessary, as the more I think on the subject the more I am convinced that retiring into winter quarters and leaving the country uncovered will be followed with the ruin of our friends, give ease and plenty to our enemies, and do an irreparable injury to the cause we are engaged to defend." However, he did not think that it was advisable to gather a large number of militia for an attack on Philadelphia.[52]

Major General Johann de Kalb, in opposing the campaign, noted that a winter campaign "will ruin the army by Sickness and discontent perhaps too by desertion, and how will another almost new one be revise, except Congress take such measures as to oblige the Militia to serve constantly for two years, and to be put into the regulars to compleat the regiments..."[53]

Brigadier General Henry Knox was brief and direct in his opposition:

> I think a Winters Campaign, under the present circumstances, will be the inevitable destruction, if not of the Liberties of the Country, yet of the present Army; my opinion is founded on the following Reasons. Our entire want of Cloathing to keep the men from Perishing by the cold winters season. The improbability and impracticability of surprising 10,000 veteran troops in a well fortified city. The impossibility of our keeping the field to besiege their works and city regularly, and being almost totally deficient of any warlike apparatus for so arduous an enterprize. The uncertainty of obtaining such a sufficient number of Militia as to make the enterprize warranted by reason, or common Military knowledge.[54]

Major General Lafayette opposed a winter campaign. He said an attack on Philadelphia "seems to me attended with so many difficulties, inconveniences and bad chances, that if it is not looked upon as a necessary and almost [desperate] enterprize, tho' it is a very shining and highly pleasing idea, however, I cannot think it is a prudent and reasonable one." He then gave eight very lengthy reasons why he was opposed and six ways forward should Washington decide that a winter campaign was absolutely necessary.[55]

Brigadier General William Maxwell wrote in opposition, "The attack proposed on Philada Appears to me to be liable to so many Accidents that the success of it would be very doubtful and should it fail our Armey would be ruined waiting for it."[56]

Brigadier General Peter Muhlenberg wrote:

> A Winters Campaign to me, seems not only unadvisable, on account of our Situation, but impracticable, at least if I am to Judge of other Brigades by my own; One single Regt of mine have turn[ed] out Ninety Men unfit for duty, on Account of Shoes & other Necessary's. The Sick become Nauseous, & the Men, notwithstanding the utmost Care of their Officers, will be Frostbitten, & Subject to many other disorders, if they are to keep the Field, until the Militia can be Collected, which if we are to Judge From the past, cannot be done in less than two Months.[57]

Brigadier General John Paterson echoed Muhlenberg in opposing a winter campaign:

> The Attack on Philadelphia, from the best Knowledge I can obtain of the Strength of their Works I must think wou'd fail, the Consequences of which would be a universal Discouragement to the Country and Army, I find my Brigade falling Sick very fast, and am informed that others nigh me are equally unfortunate, should therefor think it advisable to retire to some convenient Place for the Winter, and recruit the Army as much as possible, that we may at an early Day in Spring take the Field & give Genl How the so much desired Defeat.[58]

Brigadier General Enoch Poor opposed a winter campaign: "[y]our men are much [fatigued] & numbers falling Sick every day for want of Clothing and Coumfertable habitations."[59]

In contrast, Pennsylvania's Brigadier General James Potter favored a winter campaign. He wrote that a winter campaign was practicable, but the very thought of a winter campaign in the army's current circumstances appeared dreadful. However, he wrote, like many other evils that befall us in this life, before we undergo them, we are ready to conclude that they are unsupportable. Yet, when they are over, we do not find them as dreadful as we apprehended. From his experiences of winter campaigns, he stated that he did not find it to "have so many evils attending to it" as other people represented. Nevertheless, if those evils were real, they would be remedied "by going into winter Quarters."[60]

General Joseph Reed reflected on how a winter campaign had brought mighty armies to near ruin. He wrote:

> There cannot be any Person, Sir, either on a publick or private Account, upon whom the Motives for a Winters Campaign can operate more forcibly. I have every Reason to wish

it—& yet in the State & Condition of our Army my Judgment is against it. The History of every Winters Campaign made in Europe clearly evinces how destructive they have ever proved: during the Course of the last War the allied Army under Prince Ferdinand was almost ruined tho' victorious, & pursuing the Enemy—Charles the 12th failed & fell from the very Summit of Victory, & Success by keeping the Field a part of the Winter.[61]

Brigadier General Charles Scott wrote, "after Your Excellency returned from Reconnoitering the Enemy's Lines and hearing your opinion with regard To their Strength, I lost every Idea of a Winters Campaign." Washington left his camp and stealthily examined the British lines in late November to get an idea of their strength. That visit alarmed Washington and made him think that his army should not undertake another attack before going into winter quarters.[62]

Brigadier General William Smallwood wrote:

> It will be unnecessary to point out the sufferings of the Continental Troops, from their various hard Duty, & distresses for want of Cloathing, particularly in the Article of Blankets, Shoes, Stockings, then most essential part to enable them to encounter the severity of a Winter Campaign, and the improbability of procuring those necessary Supplies, without which our prospect of success in an undertaking of this Nature must be unpromising & fruitless.[63]

Major General John Sullivan opposed a winter campaign, noting that most of the officers were in the same sad situation as the general soldier as regards to needing shoes, stockings, and other clothing. The officers also had great concerns about their pay and their commissions, and Sullivan urged Washington to address those issues as well. "I am fully Convinced and fear the Event will prove that more than half your officers will Leave you in a month unless Some Remedy is found out to Quiet their minds and relieve their Distresses—Under These circumstances a winters Campaign will in my opinion Dissolve the Army."[64]

Brigadier General James Varnum, in opposing a winter campaign, noted, "The salvation of America does not depend upon a successful victory this winter; but a severe defeat, would plunge us into difficulties, out of which we could scarcely extricate ourselves."[65]

Pennsylvania's Brigadier General Anthony Wayne's opposition was short and direct: "I am not for a Winters Campaign in the Open field—the Distressed and naked State of your Troops will not admit of it."[66]

Brigadier General George Weedon wrote eloquently that the troops, though brave, were mere mortals who could not endure a winter campaign:

> Your Excellency is perfectly acquainted with my Sentiments respecting this Army, it is Sir the Bulwark of America and should be nursed and Cherished as the salvation of her Liberties. The Troops that compose it are not more than Mortal, and cannot work miracles. The bravest

spirits may be exhausted by uncommon, and constant fatigue, And Sir, there is not in my opinion an Object on the Continent that justifies Subjecting them, at this particular time, to a winters Campaign, unless there was a moral certainty of obtaining that Object, and with it, a permanent and honorable end to any further Hostilities.[67]

Finally, Brigadier General William Woodford's letter summed up the majority opinions of the generals and, he assumed, the regular soldier:

> I have before given my reasons for being against [exposing] this army to a Winters Campaign in their present condition. I would add to them the present Temper of the Soldiery, who I am convinced are very generally against it. The practicability of an Attack upon Philadelphia I have look'd upon to be entirely out of the question since your Excellency's return from viewing the Enemy's Works.[68]

On December 4, Washington gave the Continental Congress Camp Committee (CCCC) his officers' responses to that December 3 circular. He began discussing the responses with them, but those discussions did not last long.

As much as the generals opposed another battle because of their troops' condition, they had to fight one. The British, with spies everywhere, likely knew of the American troops' weakened condition and wanted to take advantage. General Howe decided that he would take one last fight to the

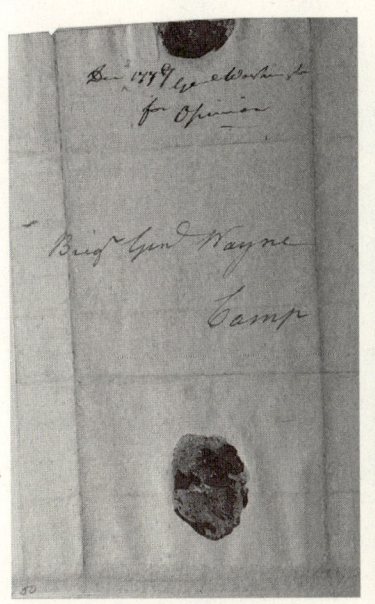

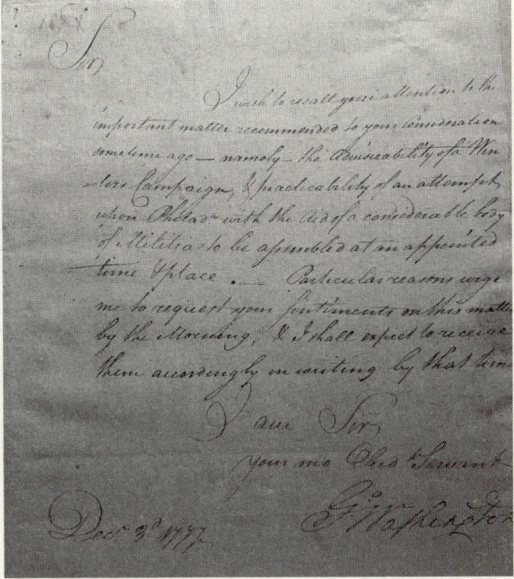

December 3 letter from General Washington to General Wayne. (Anthony Wayne Papers, Historical Society of Pennsylvania)

Continental Army before he put the British Army in winter quarters and, on December 4, he started marching his army out of center city Philadelphia up the Germantown Road towards Whitemarsh.

The CCCC stopped their deliberations with Washington during this Battle of Whitemarsh. Instead, it had a firsthand experience of the state of the Continental Army in battle.

The Battle of Whitemarsh made the two central questions facing George Washington even more critical as he looked for a way forward.

CHAPTER 2

Leaving Whitemarsh, December 10

Luckily, Washington had been warned that Howe was planning another attack, so the Continental Army was not completely surprised. Just two days earlier, a Quaker woman in Philadelphia named Lydia Darragh, whose son was in the 2nd Pennsylvania Regiment, felt that she had no other choice but to allow some British officers into her home, which was across the street from General Howe's headquarters, for a meeting. Like her son, she was a patriot. She overheard the British officers plan to attack Washington and the Continental Army. After the meeting, Darragh wrote down this information on a piece of paper. She obtained a pass from the British to leave the city, ostensibly to buy flour at the Frankford Mill, but really to warn Washington.

Fields and hills of Gulph Mills. (Radnor Historical Society)

On the way towards Washington's camp in Whitemarsh, Darragh ran into Colonel Thomas Craig, of the 3rd Pennsylvania Regiment, who has been described as a friend of Darragh's. She told him about Howe's plan and asked him to get that information to Washington. Darragh continued on and delivered the paper to Colonel Elias Boudinot—an intelligence officer and Commissary General of Prisoners, who was then trying to secure provisions at the Rising Sun Tavern at the Germantown Road and Old York Road. Boudinot immediately rode back to Whitemarsh and got the information to Washington.[1]

Washington also received information from other spies in the city that Howe was readying to march out.

In his journal, Boudinot described telling Washington about the attack.

> I was reconnoitering along the Lines near the City of Philadelphia.—I dined at a small Post at the Rising Sun about three miles from the City.—After Dinner a little poor looking insignificant Old Woman came in & solicited leave to go into the Country to buy some—flour—While we were asking some Questions, she walked up to me and put into my hands a dirty old needlebook, with various small pockets in it. Surprised at this, I told her to return she should have an answer—On opening the needlebook, I could not find anything till I got to the last Pocket. Where I found information that General Howe was coming out the next morning with 5000 Men—13 pieces of Cannon—Baggage Wagons, and 11 Boats on Waggon Wheels. On comparing this with other information I found it true, and immediately rode Post to head Quarters.[2]

On December 4, William Dewees, ironmaster and co-owner of the iron forge at Valley Forge, fresh from a British prison on November 14 after being captured on October 4, 1777, also warned Washington. He wrote Washington that he had just received information that the night before, the British Army packed up all their baggage, gave each man four days' provisions, got their horses and artillery, and planned to attack.[3]

Washington readied his troops for a major battle.[4] Some 10,000 British troops, led by British Commanding Officer Howe himself, marched out of the center of Philadelphia shortly before midnight on December 4. So, when Lieutenant General Lord Cornwallis's advance troops were seen marching up the Germantown Road, Washington was ready.

Brigadier General James Irvine, with 600 members of the Pennsylvania Militia; Brigadier General James Potter, with another 1,000 militia men; and Webb's 2nd Connecticut Regiment battled with the British around Chestnut Hill, a few miles down the road from the Whitemarsh Encampment. The British soon overpowered those troops, shooting off three of Irvine's fingers and capturing him when he fell from his horse.

Howe arrived as his troops advanced north and captured St. Thomas Episcopal Church on Germantown Avenue. Howe climbed the bell tower and observed strong American positions. He opted not to attack that night, but to give a barrage of artillery fire to the Continental Army. However, Howe's forces were not close enough for his guns to hit the patriots, so he held the troops in Chestnut Hill for the evening and devised a different plan of attack for the next day.

On December 6, both parties watched each other warily, waiting for the other to attack. Neither did. They essentially remained in their positions.

On December 7, several divisions of the Continental Army engaged in battle around Edge Hill, further down the roads towards Philadelphia. The Pennsylvania Militia and the 2nd Connecticut ended up fleeing back towards the camp at Whitemarsh in a chaotic retreat. Captain Morgan's Rifle Corps from West Virginia and the militia from Maryland were led by Colonel Mordecai Gist, whose forces distinguished themselves at the Battle of Long Island in 1776 by allowing the American army to escape encirclement. Gist's militia gave the British a good fight, but they, too, retreated back to camp after Cornwallis sent in the 33rd Regiment of Foot.

On the morning of December 8, the British generals and engineers again reviewed the position of the Continental Army. Howe decided to withdraw his troops and return to Philadelphia because their provisions and supplies were running low, they did not have tents, and his army had not made as much progress surrounding the Continental Army as they had hoped. Both the British and American armies were shocked when Howe withdrew back to Philadelphia without continuing the attack. Captain Morgan's troops harassed the British who were in General Charles Grey's column as they marched back down to Philadelphia before Morgan's men retreated when Hessian soldiers struck back at them. The British arrived back in center city Philadelphia that day, where they stayed for the winter.[5]

Washington, his troops, his generals, and the Continental Congressional Camp Committee (CCCC) made it through the Battle of Whitemarsh without the major confrontation that they all feared. Though no actual return of the damage that the battle did to the Continental Army has been found, various sources have pieced together information to largely conclude that there were 90 American troops killed or wounded and 32 missing or captured, and 19 British killed, "60 wounded, 33 missing, and 238 deserted."[6]

The personal experience of the battle, conversations with Washington, his officers, and the rank-and-file soldier undoubtedly influenced the CCCC. They resumed their deliberations on December 9. Before they left camp on

December 10 at around noon, they wrote Washington with their opinions about whether there should be a winter campaign and whether the army should go into winter quarters. They noted that their opinions, which, they wrote, were formed after conferences with Washington and reviews of the officers' letters regarding the winter quarters and winter campaign issues, were "as far as we can judge most consistent with the Public good."

Their letter read as follows:

> Among the many reasons offered against a Winters Campaign we were sorry to observe one of the most prevalent was a general discontent in the army and especially among the Officers. These discontents are ascribed to various causes and we doubt not many of them are well founded and deserve particular attention, and in the course of the present Winter, will be taken into consideration by Congress, and we hope effectually remedied.
>
> That a reform may take place in the army, and proper discipline be introduced, we wish to see the Military placed on such a footing as may make a Commission a desirable object to the Officer, and his Rank preserved from degradation & contempt.

To shore up the officers, the CCCC wrote that it would recommend to Congress that officers receive at least half pay if they did not receive full pay, that a pension for officers' widows be established, that there be a new regulation of rank, and that an equitable mode of payment of back rations be established. Their letter continued:

> Should these several regulations be approved and established by Congress (and we have reason to suppose they will) We trust the prevailing discontents will subside and a Spirit of emulation take place upon the Gentlemen of the army to promote the public service and introduce that order and discipline amongst the troops so essential to the Military character.
>
> Signed by Robert Morris, Elbridge Gerry, and Jos. Jones[7]

The CCCC also relayed this same decision to the Continental Congress on December 16. The Continental Congress acted on that report by issuing the following, in pertinent part:

> That an attempt on Philadelphia with the present Force under George Washington, either by storming the Lines and Redoubts, crossing the Schuylkill, or by regular approaches to the City is an enterprise, under the circumstances of the Army, attended with such a variety of difficulties as to render it ineligible.
>
> That the Season is so far advanced as to render very precarious, large reinforcements of the Militia from the distant States to cooperate with the regular Army in an attempt across the Schuylkill, and it is apprehended sufficient reinforcements, for the purpose, cannot be obtained from the neighbouring States.
>
> That there being time for Congress to determine on the most proper mode of reinforcing the Army before the intended Enterprise can be carried into execution, it is inexpedient for the Committee to adopt measures for that purpose.
>
> That until sufficient reinforcements can be obtained such a post should be taken by the Army as will be most likely to aggrieve the Enemy, afford supplies of provision, Wood, Water

and Forage, be secure from a surprize, and best calculated for covering the Country from the Ravages of the Enemy, and prevent their collecting Recruits and supplies for their Army; as well as afford comfortable Quarters for the officers and Soldiers.[8]

So, with the blessing of the Continental Congress to not undertake a winter campaign against the British, Washington prepared to move his army further away from the British, to the west side of the Schuylkill. On December 10, Washington issued this General Order and notified the 11,000 soldiers in the main body of the Continental Army that, after being stationary for over a month, they were leaving their encampment at Whitemarsh:

> The army to march at four o'clock from the right.—A Subaltern from each regiment and a Captain from each brigade, under the command of a Field Officer from the line, are to assemble at General Knox's quarters in the morning and remain 'till the Army moves off the ground, and then see that all stragglers in the camp, and its environs, are collected and marched after it—They are also to see that no baggage, entrenching tools or other articles are left, or that they are, secured under proper guards taken from the Pennsylvania Militia, by application to the commanding officer thereof.[9]

Washington's generals had devised the plan on how best to move the army out of Whitemarsh. The plan was that the Baggage Stores and Park of Artillery were to cross at the Swedes Ford at least two hours before the main army marched. Swedes Ford was one of two fords—low points that allowed people to walk across the river—in the immediate Whitemarsh area, the other being the Matson's Ford. The Swedes Ford was at the end of a road that was laid out from Whiteland Township, about 18 miles away in Chester County, through Easttown Township, Tredyffrin Township, and Upper Merion Township, in what was then Philadelphia County, through present-day King of Prussia to the western banks of the Schuylkill River in Upper Merion Township, present day Bridgeport.

Swedes Ford was a major transportation route that was once part of the Welsh Tract, a large area of land that John Penington purchased from William Penn, but was purchased in 1712 by Swedish settlers Mats Holstein, Gunnar Rambo, Peter Rambo, Peter Yocum, and John Matson. The Swedish land included such towns as Swedesburg and Swedeland, and such locations as Old Swede's (Christ) Church and the Matson's Ford—another crossing about 3 miles down the Schuylkill in the direction of the city of Philadelphia, at what is now West Conshohocken, Upper Merion Township, on the west side and Conshohocken, Plymouth Whitemarsh Township, on the east side of the Schuylkill River.[10]

The original settlers of the Welsh Tract gave the land the name Merioneth in 1696 and Merion after the shire where they came from in England. The land was divided in 1734 into townships called Upper Merion and Lower Merion. The Swedish bought land in Upper Merion Township.[11]

The baggage was to come over in this order: 1st Quartermaster's Stores, Commissary's Stores, the Baggage of the respective brigades in the same order as the troops marched. The baggage was to be preceded by the Artillery Park and attended to by the Artificers of the army. One brigade was to cross before the army and pass down for some miles towards the enemy on "the other side of the Schuylkill," which was right across the river to Swedesburg and Gulph Mills, "and take post on the Road leading from the middle Ferry," which was a bridge crossing the Schuylkill River from High Street, present-day Market Street, to Lancaster Avenue in West Philadelphia, to post between the enemy and the main army. Two "covering Parties of five hundred Men each to pass down the Ridge Road & German Town Roads to watch the Motions of the Enemy. One Regiment of Horse to go with each of these Parties. The other two Regiments to march in front of the main Army."[12]

Major General Sullivan signed the Order of March from Whitemarsh on December 10 as "Jno. Sullivan in behalf of the whole." Brigadier General Potter would lead first with part of the Pennsylvania Militia. Then, following in order, the 1st Maryland Brigade, 2nd (Maryland), the 1st Pennsylvania, the 2nd Pennsylvania, and then the troops led by Brigadier Generals Poor, Maxwell, Conway, Woodford, Scott, Huntington, Varnum, Glover, Learned, Patterson, Weedon, Muhlenberg, and then, the Maryland Militia Rifle Corps.[13] Major General Nathanael Greene further elaborated on moving the thousands of soldiers on to new grounds, but his writings showed that just where those new grounds would be was not yet wholly finalized or, at least, broadcast. "A party of one hundred men under the command of a Major to precede the Army *after the rout is fixt* [emphasis added], and repair the little foot bridges—and cover the wet places."[14] Presumably, Greene meant that these were the wooden foot bridges that the army was going to build to lay across the fords to make them easier for soldiers, wagons, etc. to cross.

One brigade was being sent into the Jerseys[15] "to serve as a covering party on this side of the Schuylkill"[16] to protect the main army should the British decide to move out. Greene instructed them to stay in Jersey if there was no intelligence that made it necessary for them to cross the Schuylkill and join the main army.

The uncertainty of where the army was going is evident in this passage from that part of the General Order that is attributed to Greene. "The first days march the head of the Column to reach the Lancaster road—the Engineers and Major General of the Day to examine the ground to encamp upon. To set off tomorrow morning if the Army marches tomorrow."[17]

Washington appointed a Major General of the Day to assume many of his duties, to communicate Washington's orders to the troops, and to assess the condition of the troops, the encampments, and the field of battle. This allowed Washington to focus on higher-level, more strategic matters.[18]

The language, "The first days march the head of the Column to reach the Lancaster road" certainly meant that the head of the line was to march to the Lancaster Road. But where on the Lancaster Road? The Lancaster Road, now called Lancaster Avenue, was a main transportation route that ran out of West Philadelphia, and still does, essentially straight on to the town of Lancaster, Pennsylvania. The road is 73 miles long and goes from Philadelphia through a number of major towns, from what is now called the Main Line area of Pennsylvania, through Montgomery, Delaware and Chester counties, to the town of Lancaster. If that first column crossed at Matson's Ford and headed straight for the Lancaster Road, they would probably end up in Radnor, Delaware County.

What was the meaning of the language "the Engineers and Major General of the Day to examine the ground to encamp upon"? Did they mean that the Engineers and Major General of the Day were to follow or march with the first group to cross the Schuylkill and to examine ground at "the Lancaster Road"? Or, is that language an entirely separate sentence with separate meaning? If so, the language could be interpreted as: the Engineers, led by General Duportail, and the Major General of the Day, who was likely Lord Sterling based on the orderly rotation of Major Generals of the Day,[19] were to examine the land where they crossed, which would be directly into the Upper Merion Township towns of Swedesburg and Gulph Mills to arrange the encampment there? Or, did that mean that they were going to examine the ground somewhere else in their eventual winter quarters camp ground?

The Order of March for the day goes on to clarify that "Potters militia to cross with the Army over the Schuylkill, but to recross it again when the Brigade of Continental troops leaves the ground to go into the Jerseys—the whole of the [Pennsylvania Militia] to act collectively between the Delaware and the Schuylkill. Head Quarters to be near or at the cross Roads—Guards to be established to cut off Provision going into the City."[20]

Washington planned to use General Potter's Pennsylvania Militia to lead the Continental troops across the Schuylkill, but to return to the east side of the river when the brigade of Continental Army troops under another general left the main army and headed to the Jerseys to protect that area. From that east side of the Schuylkill, the entire Pennsylvania Militia was to act as the fleas on the dog to protect the some 20 miles of land between the Schuylkill

River around Whitemarsh and the Delaware River, the two rivers that were the lifeblood and main transportation arteries in the Philadelphia area, to harass and engage, if necessary, the British Army, which was set to establish Philadelphia as its winter quarters. The Schuylkill River joins the Delaware River at the site of the former Philadelphia Navy Yard in South Philadelphia.

The Pennsylvania Militia men were to also stop provisions from going into the city of Philadelphia, typically from loyalists who wanted to support the British and from desperate farmers and craftspeople who needed to sell their crops and wares to the British. Many local people preferred to sell their food and goods to the British for the British Pound Stirling currency because the people had more faith in the British pound rather than the Continental dollar, whose current and future value was uncertain. This was the genesis of the degrading phrase that something "wasn't worth a Continental." The British also sought to devalue the Continental money by counterfeiting it.[21]

The rest of the main army was to disperse throughout the other contiguous states. Boats that were fitted for carriages were to be taken to Wilmington, Delaware, on those carriages, and the rest were to be hauled to Easton, Pennsylvania. The troops that were going into the Jerseys were to post at Mount Holly. One troop of the Light Horse was also to go to the Jerseys, while the remainder were to be with the main army on "the other side of the Schuylkill." The quartermaster was to get the baggage across the Schuylkill "at the most convenient fords to keep the back roads in the rear of the Army." One undetermined part of the army was to establish a "rope ferry" like the ones that existed at Bethlehem, Pennsylvania, at a distance of about 20 or 30 miles above the city.[22]

Describing the Battle of Whitemarsh in a letter to Brigadier General Thomas Nelson, Jr., then a member of the Virginia House of Delegates and a former member of the Continental Congress, Washington wrote:

> General Howe had been for several days making great preparations for a move which they did not scruple to say was intended against this Army, threatening to drive us beyond the Mountains. On Thursday Evening last they marched out and took post in the Morning upon Chestnut Hill, three Miles in our Front. In the Evening they shifted their Ground to our left, from which I thought they meant an attack upon that quarter. But after manuevering about us for some days, they suddenly decamped on Monday Afternoon and marched back to Philada in the most hasty manner. I detached light parties after them, but they were not able to come up with them.

In the middle of writing his account of the Battle of Whitemarsh, Washington took a moment to relay some of his considerable concerns about the state of the army and issued a reminder of the responsibilities of the House of

Assembly to support and supply the Virginia forces, which, as his home state troops, stayed on his mind:

> Unless we can fill our Regiments against the next Campaign, I very much fear that our past labours will have been in vain, for unless a War with France should divert the attention of Great Britain, I am convinced she will strain every Nerve to make up for the disappointments and losses of this Campaign and altho from many of our late accounts it should seem as if a War was inevitable, we ought not to count upon that score, but make our preparations as if we were to depend solely upon our own Bottoms.[23]

Nelson had asked Washington in correspondence that he was responding to here about the strength of the Continental Army. Washington stated that he did not want to tell Nelson the true number in a letter because "altho I have the fullest confidence in you I dare not trust the particulars to paper, for fear of accidents." He went on to say that "I can assure you that our numbers have been always much exaggerated, and that the Enemy has constantly exceeded our continental Force. The Battalions of the other States are in point of deficiency much upon a footing with yours and you may judge from thence, how much we stand in need of recruits." Commenting on the recent losses at Red Bank, also known as the Battle of Fort Mercer, and at Fort Mifflin in November, Washington noted:

> The Officers who commanded at Red Bank and Fort Mifflin were Colo. Green of Rhode Island and Lt. Colo. Smith of Maryland. They did all that brave Men could do, but the posts at length fell, being overpowered by dint of superior force. They however confess that the long and expected opposition which they received broke in upon their plans for the remainder of the Campaign.[24]

At the same time that Washington planned to move his army by necessity, he felt the need to report such a movement to Henry Laurens, President of the Continental Congress. To Laurens, he described the events of the Battle of Whitemarsh. When trying to calculate the damage to the British Army, Washington could only use accounts from the city that "five hundred wounded had been sent in" and that "eighty two Waggons had gone in with Men in this situation," but he was careful to note that he felt these numbers were exaggerated. He informed Laurens that 27 men in Morgan's Corps had been killed or wounded, plus 16 or 17 in the Maryland militia, but that firm numbers were yet to be tallied. He ended his letter by expressing a wish that Howe had pressed the attack, because Washington felt that the Americans had been in a strong enough position at that moment that the outcome might have favored them. He was careful, in light of recent accusations, to remind Laurens that "reason, prudence, and every principle of policy forbad us from quitting our post to attack them. Nothing but success would have justified the measure, and this could not be expected from their position."[25]

Washington apologized for the delay in writing to Laurens about the Whitemarsh battle and noted, "I have reason to think your Committee, who were in Camp most of the time, & who are now here, transmitted an Account of such Occurrences as they deemed important in any degree."[26]

While Washington wrote to Laurens, the Continental Congress devised its own suggestions about how to remedy the problem of lack of food and clothing—to take it from the local inhabitants. On December 10, Congress noted that up to that point in the war, supplies had been drawn, at great expense, from "distant quarters," while "large quantities of stock, provision, and forage, are still remaining in the counties of Philadelphia, Bucks and Chester." They warned Washington that if the American army did not take the supplies, the British would. Further, they insinuated that Washington hesitated to forage in the local countryside because he was reluctant to exert his full military authority, "a delicacy, which though highly laudable in general, may, on critical exigencies, prove destructive to the army." From that point on, Washington should forage from whatever communities the army was in at any given time, especially if they were in areas where the British could do the same. He would be permitted to leave households with only what they needed to survive. Whatever the army did not take, and the family did not need, was to be destroyed so that it did not fall into British hands.[27]

While the Continental Army ended the day prepared to march in the morning, unbeknownst to them, the British were already on the march. British Lieutenant General Archibald Robertson, Royal Engineers, wrote on December 10, "At 12 at night Lord Cornwallis with a detachment of about 5000 men cross'd the Schuylkill towards Derby [Darby] to cover a Foraging Party of Waggons."[28]

CHAPTER 3

The Battle of Matson's Ford, December 11

"History forgets far more than it remembers, for the remembrance of great events submerges the recollection of those countless lesser occurrences that add up to much of human history. Thus, the events of December 11, 1777 along Old Gulph Road in Lower and Upper Merion Townships are wholly overshadowed by the nearby glory of Valley Forge," wrote John Reed in an essay titled "The Fight on Old Gulph Road," to the Montgomery County, Pennsylvania Historical Society in 1966.[1]

Then editor of the Bulletin of the Montgomery County Historical Society and author of the book *Campaign to Valley Forge*, Reed observed:

> Today on Old Gulph Road modern man, whipped along by his automotive invention, unknowingly passes and repasses those nearly forgotten spots where the eyes of more than one Revolutionary Patriot closed forever on skies that still look down on American freedom; for no marker tells that here, patriots fought and fell a sacrifice to liberty. Indeed, who can tell whether or not that somewhere along the less than four mile route between Bryn Mawr and the Gulph still sleep the dusts of those Pennsylvania militiamen of Brigadier-General James Potter's little command who surrendered their lives in defense of that freedom? No records tell us where they might lie; no headstones mark their resting places. But fortunately, the past can still tell us what they did; and from its written words we can deduce nearly precisely the sites—the object of this essay—that knew their sacrifice.[2]

Pennsylvania Militia Brigadier General James Potter started the day tired. He opened up about his fatigue and a desire to be given a furlough in a letter to Thomas Wharton, President of the Pennsylvania legislature:

> I received your Excellency's letter of the first instant, I was then on the other side of the Schuylkill, and we drove from place to place, that I had not time to Answer it, I this day returned to this County again, and hope there will be Troops sufficient here in a day or two to keep all the Tories in this County in fear, if not in order, I expect the Army to march to-morrow if it did not today…"

Potter assumed that Wharton already heard about the outcome of the Battle of Whitemarsh. Howe's boast that, after Whitemarsh, he would drive Washington's army "across the Susquehanna" and out of the Philadelphia area was just "a sudden blast of wind," Potter concluded. Nevertheless, Potter added that at Whitemarsh, "our principal loss was our Worthy General Irvine," whom the British captured after they shot off three of Irvine's fingers and he fell off his horse.

Even though he believed that the army should undertake a winter campaign, Potter did not want to be a part of it. He hoped that the Pennsylvania Council would appoint a few more brigadier generals so that he could be relieved and return home. He explained, "in the last years I have been but three weeks at home, it is time I should go to see my family, my affairs call loudly for it, I believe fighting is over for some time." He concluded, "I am willing to do anything in my power to serve my Country, but it is necessary that I should have a little rest."[3]

Little did Potter know that the fighting, at least for him, was not over, and that he was not to have "a little rest" that day. Quite the opposite.

General George Washington was ready at 4 a.m. to begin moving his troops, according to the Order of March from their encampment at Whitemarsh, over the Matson's Ford, and on to an encampment in Gulph Mills. The baggage was to have been moved over two hours earlier. Whether Washington thought that he would establish winter quarters at Gulph Mills is unknown. But it is certain that Washington knew he had to move his army to the other side of the Schuylkill River, farther away from the center of Philadelphia and the British Army.

The entire army could not concentrate on moving across the Matson's Ford. Some parts had to be moved out first to surrounding areas to protect the rest of the army from every angle from a possible British advance. Moving almost the whole Continental Army at once made it extremely vulnerable to destruction if the British chose to move their entire army out of Philadelphia to engage in a major battle.

Washington ordered Brigadier General Potter to lead the men of the Pennsylvania Militia in establishing three advance pickets on the west side of the Schuylkill to warn the main army if the British moved towards them.[4] Those three pickets were to cover the distance from the location of the American army at the Matson's Ford crossing down to the three other major crossings between the Continental Army and the British. The farthest location of the pickets was at Middle Ferry, which was located at High Street (now Market Street) in the center of the city of Philadelphia, and reached across the Schuylkill to the Lancaster Road in West Philadelphia. The Continental Army built what was essentially a floating bridge at Middle Ferry in 1776 so that it "would have an easy way to escape the city if the British invaded."[5] The troops took the bridge down so the British could not use it in summer 1777 when they left Philadelphia for Wilmington, Delaware, but the British built a new floating bridge there in fall 1777 when they occupied Philadelphia.

The second picket was at the Black Horse Inn at City Line and Lancaster Road, further west towards Matson's Ford. Colonel John Lacey, from Buckingham Township, Bucks County, a member of its local militia unit that was incorporated into the Pennsylvania Line of the Continental Army, had charge of the second picket. This location was the dividing line between the city of Philadelphia and Lower Merion Township. The third picket was at Harriton House, then a 700-acre property with about 40 acres of tobacco plantation that was the home of Charles Thomson, Secretary of the Continental Congress, on Old Gulph Road in Lower Merion Township. Thomson was away in Lancaster with the Continental Congress. Potter was stationed at Harriton House.[6]

At the same time, British Lieutenant General Charles Cornwallis was in the area of the three pickets with about 3,000 soldiers on a brutal foraging operation just south of Matson's Ford, in and around Gulph Mills, in Upper and Lower Merion townships. British Major John Andre, who was also an aide-de-camp to General Charles Grey, wrote in his journal, "At 3 in the morning Lord Cornwallis passed the Schuylkill with the Light Infantry, Grenadiers, Guards, 23rd, 28th, 49th, 27th, and 33rd—100 Chasseurs and Lengerke's Battalion and the 16th and 17th Light Dragoons."[7]

The foraging expedition was by all accounts horrendous. Major Andre wrote, "It was said that great depredation had been committed by the soldiers on the March."[8]

John Johnston, who identified himself as being located in "Upper Merion near the Gulph Mill," stated in a letter to Washington, "That on the Eleventh of [December] last your Petitioner was Plundered by the British Army of almost everything I had, to a Considerable amount."[9]

"Plunder and devastation marked the enemy's progress through the Merions, but especially the section from the Gulph Road along the Ridge to the Schuylkill, had suffered and every inhabitant."[10] Those who "felt the devastating blow" filed claims that came to over 300 pounds sterling, including Philip Crickbaum, Jonathan Brookes, David Thomas, the Colfleshs, the Crawford properties, and Peter, Isaac, and Jacob Matson.[11]

John Roberts, a local Quaker flour mill owner from Radnor, who refused to join the Continental Army because of his faith, served as Cornwallis's guide on this foraging expedition. As earlier mentioned, in October 1777, Potter seized a good deal of cattle, sheep, and other provisions from Roberts, whom area patriots widely thought of as a Tory, or "an American upholding the cause of the British Crown against the supporters of colonial independence during the American Revolution," also known as a "loyalist."[12] Army and government officials charged Roberts with treason in July 1778, convicted him, and hung him in August 1778, despite Roberts's protests that Cornwallis's troops forced him to be their guide.[13]

Cornwallis had crossed Middle Ferry when a surprised, much smaller group of militia soldiers, in the picket there, fired upon the British forces.[14] The militiamen withdrew and fell back further west towards the other pickets.

The British then continued their march up the Lancaster Road towards the Matson's Ford for the foraging operation. The pickets at the Black Horse Inn at City Line and Lancaster Road fought the British as best as they could with their smaller numbers. But, outnumbered, outflanked, and generally confused in battle, the militia soldiers retreated back towards Harriton House in defeat.

Other soldiers had already ridden to Potter at Harriton House to warn him that Cornwallis and his troops were "advancing in force" up Gulph Road towards them. "Potter stationed five regiments of militia between the British forces and Harriton House," and although there was some fierce combat, "the militia were quickly overrun, and they hastily retreated back through Gulph Mills to Swedes Ford."[15] The militia ran back to the other side of the Schuylkill in any way that they could, with some even throwing away their weapons to run faster. After Cornwallis's forces chased Potter's, the British forces moved up into the high Conshohocken Hills, where they could have a clear view of the Matson's Ford and hide themselves in the deeply forested woods to spy on the Continental Army and possibly engage them in battle or defend themselves if the Continental Army attacked them.

While Potter and the Pennsylvania Militia battled the British, Brigadier General John Sullivan, who had command of two Continental Army divisions, one of which was under General Anthony Wayne, had built a temporary bridge over the Matson's Ford, by attaching wooden wagons together. Almost all the men in both divisions, some 800, had crossed over the bridge when they suddenly saw Cornwallis's soldiers lurking on the Conshohocken Hills. Sullivan, not sure of the size of the British force, hastily ordered the troops to cross back over the bridge and to destroy it behind them. "The retreat was so chaotic that militiamen literally threw away their muskets and ammunition as

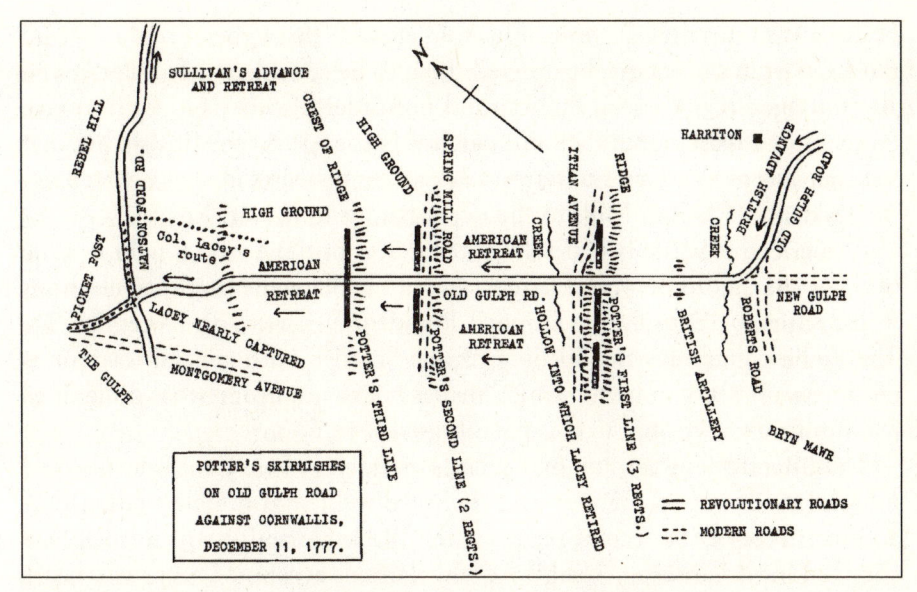

Map, "Potter's Skirmishes on Old Gulph Road Against Cornwallis, December 11, 1777." (From article, "The Fight on Gulph Road," *Bulletin of the Historical Society of Montgomery County XV*, no. 1 and 2 [1966]; 32–36; courtesy of the Historical Society of Montgomery County)

they ran. With the militia in retreat, Cornwallis discontinued pursuit and took up a strong position on the heights overlooking Matson's Ford."[16] Sullivan's troops did not provide any assistance or cover to Potter's militia men, some of whom had just made it back to Gulph Mills in retreat and ran back across the Schuylkill themselves.

Neither Potter nor Sullivan were sure of the size of the British party, whether it was hundreds, or thousands, or the bulk of the British forces looking for another fight. The men called General Washington out to survey the situation. He determined that it looked like a large party out for foraging and not the bulk of the main army out to battle the Continental forces one last time before both went into winter quarters.

Washington then ordered the Continental Army to move westward on the east side of the Schuylkill, a few miles down to Swedes Ford. Reconnaissance parties continued to try to ascertain what the British were doing and where they were going. After savagely foraging in Gulph Mills for the rest of the day, the British forces moved their foraging party on, further to the west of the Schuylkill, back down closer to Philadelphia.

In his General Orders on the 12th, Washington congratulated Potter and his militia for their bravery on the 11th in the Battle of Matson's Ford.

Potter was so incensed at some of his soldiers who threw their arms away and ran away from the enemy, he ordered them to be court-martialed. Potter was also outraged that General Sullivan did not order his troops to fight to give Potter's force assistance in their outmatched battle against the British, but that Sullivan ordered his forces to retreat back across the Matson's Ford, which left the residents of Gulph Mills to the depredations of the British.

As usual, this battle is best told in the voices of those who fought it. One of the most important voices is represented by General Potter's recollections in his letter to Pennsylvania Council President Wharton on December 15. The English grammar and spelling of this Scottish-born general was not as great as his bravery in battle, which makes his account somewhat difficult to read in his own writing, so it is paraphrased here.[17]

The other thrilling account of the Battle of Matson's Ford came from Colonel John Lacey. Lacey, who Potter said "behaved well," was initially stationed at and in charge of the second picket at the Black Horse Inn at Philadelphia's City Line and Lancaster Road.[18] As with Potter's account, Lacey's words are paraphrased below.

Potter began his letter to Wharton noting that on the previous Thursday, the British marched out of the city with a desire to forage, but that they had to drive Potter and his troops out of the way first. As soon as the sun came up, Potter's first picket was surprised and stunned to see thousands of redcoats leaving the city of Philadelphia, marching across the Schuylkill at a bridge at Middle Ferry. Several hundred soldiers at the advance picket fired on the British. Overwhelmed by sheer numbers, the Continental forces retreated. Colonel Edward Heston, an officer in the 6th Company, 7th Battalion of the Pennsylvania Militia, jumped on his horse and hightailed it to the second picket. Heston alerted the troops at the second picket that "the British were advancing up the Gulf Road."[19] Lacey and his roughly 100 men fired on the British and then retreated further up the Gulph Road towards the third picket at Harriton.

Potter was stationed at Harriton with several hundred more troops. He stationed two regiments at Harriton, and those soldiers vigorously attacked the British. On the next hill, Potter stationed three regiments, one of which was Lacey's. Lacey's regiment was posted with its right to the main road, presumed to be the Gulph Road, on a high hill with one other regiment on his left and one other regiment on the right. Potter told the regiments to form in lines. He told the first line of soldiers that when they were overpowered, they must retreat and form a line behind the second line of soldiers. Potter jumped on his horse and rode to the next hill, down the Gulph Road, to warn the Continental Army where they were crossing at the Matson's Ford. The militia men formed and retreated for four miles and, stated Potter, "on every [h]ill we disputed the matter with them."

A shocked and surprised General Sullivan, who was leading the Continental Army over their makeshift bridge at Matson's Ford, received word from one of Potter's horsemen that Potter and his forces were fighting off thousands of redcoats that were headed in his direction. Sullivan's first thought was not to help Potter in this fight. Sullivan stopped the army's march over the river and ordered the 800 men who had already crossed over to turn around and march back over the bridge to the other side of the Schuylkill where the rest of the main army stood, wondering what was going on. Once the 800 retreated back across the river, Sullivan ordered them to destroy the makeshift bridge.[20]

Meanwhile, when the British appeared about 200 yards in front of them, Lacey ordered his men to begin firing, which they continued doing for three rounds. Then the British opened a battery of cannon with a discharge of small arms. Lacey's forces stood their ground, and the men did not give way until Lacey saw the enemy advancing on their flanks. Then, both the regiments on his left and his right gave way and retreated at the first fire. That left Lacey's forces exposed on both flanks. Lacey, who was on horseback, ordered a retreat. Three or four men were shot by the enemy, and the other soldiers had to leave their bodies where they fell. Lacey and his forces retreated into a hollow, while the British cannon balls passed over their heads, cut down the tops of the trees, and struck the ground in front of them where they had first formed. Lacey ordered the men to halt for a few moments because the enemy had stopped firing.

Then they continued their retreat. Lacey's forces passed the line of soldiers that Potter had formed in their rear, and they took post a few hundred yards in the rear of those soldiers to cover their retreat. The British soon ran up to the second line, which withstood only one round of fire before they broke and fell back to Lacey's line.

Lacey, Potter, and other officers tried to rally the rank-and-file soldiers in vain. With the British advancing, they continued firing, but then a general rout ensued. Everyone began making their way out of there the best way they could. Many men threw away their guns so that they were less encumbered in running. Lacey was among those in the rear, and having tried to rally the men, he got some distance from the road. Lacey came to a fence, which he got over with his horse without much difficulty, but he then came to a second fence after he passed through a field. This was on one side of a lane that led from the Schuylkill to the Gulph Road area.

Lacey called to the men who were passing over that lane to "throw off a rider" to get on Lacey's horse and ride it over the fence, but the men were in such a hurry and thought of nothing but self-preservation that they did not pay attention to Lacey but left him to get over that fence as best as he could. Twice, Lacey ran his horse against the fence to no avail. The third time, the fence gave way, and then Lacey found himself in a lane and rode full speed ahead to the main road. About 200 yards in, he discovered a column of the enemy's Light Horse on top of the hill about 50 yards from him. The British called out to Lacey to surrender.

Lacey stopped, but as he looked down the road, he saw the patriots' Flying Horse, which was a "Flying" rapid response unit that was on horseback, about 200 yards below. By "mere mechanical movement without time to think," he clapped his spurs to his horse and went full speed after them. The British fired at him with their carbines and pistols. He heard the bullets whizzing by.

Two Dragoons rode after him in hot pursuit. Finding the Dragoons gaining on him as he came up to the rear of the patriot troops, Lacey ordered the patriots to turn around and fire at the British. Several soldiers did just that as they continued to run in retreat. But, by them firing straight off their shoulders at the troops behind Lacey without stopping or turning around, Lacey thought they were going to shoot him. Figuring that he was in more danger by friendly fire than by the enemy, he called on the patriots to cease firing "or they would shoot me."

Once he reached the rear of the Continental troops, one of his soldiers took Lacey's horse because the other soldier's horse, being "of too much mettle," refused to yield to the rider. The rider and his horse dashed among the men, and both were shot down together.

The battle was so sudden and instantaneous, Lacey explained, that it was impossible to save either man or horse, because more than 20 guns were being discharged at them at the same time. Yet, Lacey and his men, minus one officer and 17 privates that the British either killed or captured, passed the Matson's Ford and Gulph Mills and made it to Swedes Ford, where they found Washington and the rest of the Continental Army waiting for them At the end of all of this, Lacey wrote, they were again ordered to take post on the west side of the Schuylkill.

In his letter to Wharton, Potter stated that his troops behaved well, especially the three regiments that were commanded by Colonels Chambers, Murray, and Lacey. Even General Washington thanked Potter and his men in his General Orders.

Yet, Potter was perturbed. He wrote that the number of soldiers who fought the British that day would have been more substantial if General Sullivan covered the militia's retreat with the two divisions of the Continental Army that he had about half a mile in the rear of his militia, towards the Matson's Ford. Potter wrote that, instead, Sullivan ordered his forces to retreat and join the main army that were still on the other side of the Schuylkill, about a mile and a half away from Potter. Sullivan's failure to engage the British gave the British leave to plunder the country, which Potter said they did, without partiality or favor to any, leaving none of the necessities of life behind them that they could not conveniently carry or destroy.

Potter stated that he did not know the exact number of men he lost in this action, but it was not as many as one might expect. Those killed did not exceed five or six, taken prisoner about 20, and wounded about 20. The enemy got the worst in the action, he wrote, especially its Light Horse, which charged at Potter's men.

Potter added a postscript to his letter that Washington was not with the army when this happened. The army was on the march, and Washington had not yet come from his headquarters at Whitemarsh. Potter noted that he was writing from Chester County, which was the county that was contiguous to Upper Merion Township, which was in Philadelphia County, where Gulph Mills was located. Potter did not give his exact location. He was either confused as to what county he was in, or, at the time of writing, he might have been in Chester County in the area of Valley Forge, as an advance party for the Valley Forge Encampment.

John Laurens, an aide-de-camp to George Washington, wrote a letter to his father, Continental Congress President Henry Laurens, on December 23, about the battle.

"When we march'd from Whitemarsh Camp, and were in the act of crossing the Schuylkill, we received intelligence that the enemy were advancing on this side of the river; in fact a ravaging party of four thousand under the command of Lord Cornwallis had pass'd the river and were driving Potter's Milita before them. Two regiments of this corps, however, are said to have conducted themselves extremely well and to have given the enemy no small annoyance as they advanced. General Sullivan was Major Gen of the day and consequently conducted the march" of the whole army, leading them across the makeshift bridge at Matson's Ford.

Sullivan's division and part of General Wayne's had crossed the river. Sullivan was uncertain about the number of the enemy and feared that they had come out "in force." With part of the army on one side of the river and part on the other, Sullivan ordered the troops to recross and render the bridge impassible so that the British could not cross to attack the Continental forces.

Laurens recounted that several soldiers then rushed to the back of the lines to notify Washington that the British troops were out and what happened at the bridge. Washington rode up and "when he arrived, parties of the enemy were seen on the commanding heights on this side of the river. There was a pause for some time and consultation of what was to be done." Parties of horse were sent to "gain certain intelligence of the enemy's number and designs." Because of the particulars of its geographic location, the Continental Army was essentially hemmed in, located in a difficult position that could have turned catastrophic. Laurens explained that the "army was near a river to which it had marched by a narrow road on each side" and surrounded by "thick woods" all around. If General Howe kept up his show of force on the opposite side of the Schuylkill "and at the same time marched in force from Philadelphia upon us, we must in these circumstances inevitably be ruined." The army would have been hemmed in on at least three sides.

Some members of the Continental Army "pronounced hastily that the enemy had received intelligence of our march," and "that they were prepared to oppose our passage." Laurens did not think so because the decision to march that day had only been made in Washington's council the night before. Washington had an assessment similar to Laurens'. "Gen Washington who never since I have been in his family has pass'd a false judgment on such points, gave it his opinion that the party in view were foragers; that the meeting was accidental, but, however, the enemy might avail themselves of this unexpected discovery and might draw as much advantage from it as if the reconnoiter had been premeditated."

The parties that had been sent off to gather intelligence returned with word that "the enemy were retiring in great haste." But that was not satisfactory for Washington to keep the army where it was, so "the army was ordered to march to the Swedes Ford three or four miles higher up the river and encamp the night to the Schuylkill. The next morning the want of provisions—I could weep tears of blood when I say it—the want of provisions render'd it impossible to march. We did not march till the evening of that day."

Once Washington released the army to march, "our ancient bridge, an infamous construction which in many parts obliged the men to march by Indian file, was restored, and a bridge of Waggons made over the Swedes Ford." The bridge, out of necessity, was built with fence-rails, not wood planks, which resulted in "a very unstable footing" that allowed only "a trifling number of troops to cross."

Laurens thought that General Sullivan's retreat at the first sign of the British was "unspeakably unlucky" because Laurens believed that the Continental Army could have scored a win over the British. "If we had persevered in crossing in the first instance, or if we had even crossed in the evening of the first day, the flower of the British Army must have fallen a sacrifice to superior numbers" since the whole Continental Army of some 11,000 soldiers was out, compared with only a few thousand British soldiers. As an example of his army's superior skill, Laurens closed with, "Among the parties of horse that were out upon this occasion a small detachment of Bland's Regiment composed of trumpeter, farmer, and whatever could be collected for the moment, their Colonel at their head, charged a sergeant and guard of Hessians and took them all prisoners."[21]

Samuel Armstrong, a lieutenant with the 8th Massachusetts Regiment, wrote of the day that the whole army marched for review by its officers by 4 a.m. for the march across the Schuylkill. The march over the bridge the army built at Matson's Ford did not start until sunrise. When the army reached the bridge, they saw British soldiers. The advance guards of General Potter's forces "met and skirmished some" with the redcoats until the redcoats drove the Continental solders back into a retreat. The Continental soldiers cut down the bridge, and then "we sent our Scouting parties, which brought in some prisoners and about two OClock we Retreated back two Miles, and about four O'Clock took another Road & marched two Miles, and there Encamped."[22]

Albigence Waldo, a surgeon in Colonel Jedidiah Huntington's 1st Connecticut Regiment, wrote about his miserable day. He began by recounting that the whole army, with their baggage, was on the march at sunrise, to the Schuylkill River. Then came the surprise. "The enemy had

December 11, 1777 entry; Journal of Lt. Samuel Armstrong, 8th Massachusetts Regiment.

marched up the West side of the Schuylkill, but General Potter's Brigade of Pennsylvania Militia were already there, & had several skirmishes with them with some loss on his side and considerable on the Enemies." An English sergeant deserted to the Continental camp and informed them that men from Colonel Charles Webb's 2nd Connecticut Regiment had killed many British soldiers on December 7 during the Battle of Whitemarsh. The sergeant said that he himself took prisoner the sergeant major in the regiment, a man who had formerly deserted from the British Army. He added that the British were going to hang the poor soldier that day.

As for Waldo himself, he continued to be very sick. "I am prodigious Sick & cannot get anything—what in the name of Providence am I to do with a fit of Sickness in this place where nothing appears pleasing to the Sicken'd Eye & nausiating Stomach. But I doubt not Providence will find out a way for my relief. But I cannot eat Beef if I starve for my stomach positively refuses to entertain such Company, and how can I help that?"[23]

Waldo wrote that after the Battle of Matson's Ford, at around 4 p.m., "the whole army were Ordered to March to Swedes Ford on the River Schuylkill, about 9 miles NW of Chestnut Hill and 6 from White Marsh, our present Encampment." The army then "encamped in a semicircle" near the Swedes Ford for the night.

Lieutenant Colonel Henry Dearborn, of the 1st and 3rd New Hampshire Regiments, who was at the Battle of Saratoga and whose unit had just joined the main army at Whitemarsh on November 22, wrote of the 11th: that the whole army were ordered to strike tents and parade, ready to march when ordered. At 6 a.m., they marched, and at 9 a.m., "began to cross the Schuylkill on a Bridge about 14 miles from Philadelphia, and when General Wayne's Division had crossed we found the Enemy had got possession of the heights" near the bridge and were "so strongly Posted that it was thought best for General Wayne to retreat back over the bridge." Dearborn wrote that the "whole Army formed in Lines of Battle & Remained so until Near Night." Then the army marched "about five miles up the river to a place called Swedes Ford" and encamped."[24]

Lieutenant John Marshall was then a member of the 11th Virginia Regiment. He went on, in 1801, to become Chief Justice of the U.S. Supreme Court for 34 years, the longest-sitting Supreme Court Justice. He helmed the legendary "Marshall Court" which, through a series of important decisions, mostly unanimous, cemented the importance of the Supreme Court as the third branch of government, established that federal law was supreme over state law, and made it clear that the Supreme Court was the ultimate arbiter of the U.S. Constitution.[25]

Of the chaos of December 11, Marshall wrote that the meeting of the two armies in Gulph Mills was just by chance, not by any design of the British to confront the Continental Army one more time before going into winter quarters. He confirmed that in the confusion of that morning, the first intelligence that reached Washington was "that General Howe had taken the field in full force" with his whole army. Hearing that, Washington recalled the troops already on the west side "and moved rather higher up the river, for the purpose of understanding the real situation, force, and designs of the enemy."[26]

Colonel Israel Angell of the 2nd Rhode Island Regiment wrote that around 6 a.m., the army marched towards the Schuylkill to cross a bridge about four miles below the Swedes Ford, "but before we got there the enemy had gotten possession of the right on the other side of the river and had a smart skirmish with Gen. Potter who commanded the militia." Potter "lost a few men but how many I cannot say." The army then marched three or four miles back towards Whitemarsh. They then received orders to halt and "lay still" until 4 p.m., when they were commanded to march to the Swedes Ford. "We marched within a mile of the ford, there took up our quarters in the woods, where we Rested peaceable that Night."[27]

Lieutenant James McMichael of the Pennsylvania Line wrote, "At 3 A.M. we struck tents, passed White Marsh Church, and on to the upper bridge over the Schuylkill, when the enemy having crossed at Middle Ferry, attacked a party of Militia under Gen. Potter. The loss was inconsiderable on both sides. We then turned W.N.W. and proceeded thro' Hickorytown and encamped near Swedes Ford."[28]

Captain Paul Brigham described the day this way: "was up at 3 o'Clock and a Cold morning it was the whole army was on ye move this morning and part of our army crossed [the Schuylkill River] and found ye Enemy there and we Could not Pass Some of ye Miletia that had Got acrost were [made] Prisoners our Brigade Lodged in a wood about 15 miles from ye City I and my Company had nothing But ye heavens for our Covering this Cold freezing night."[29]

Sergeant John Smith of the 1st Rhode Island Regiment described his experience of the day this way. His troops marched forward around daybreak towards the Schuylkill, "where the King's Troops" had engaged a brigade of militia commanded by General Potter, whose men "took or killed" many redcoats. His forces turned back "a little way and halted a while when an Express came and ordered us to march" onward. Then they turned about and took another road that led towards the Schuylkill. They lodged "in the woods on the ground without covering."

Smith wrote that his fellow soldiers in Colonel Christopher Green's 1st Rhode Island Regiment "had nothing to eat as there were no provisions" left for them after other soldiers had gotten theirs. So, "after we halted we killed two beavers and drew something for ourselves to eat." He concluded that "this was a Very Cold Day but clear and pleasant for the season." With the good weather and a beaver dinner, he ended, "this night slept something comfortable."[30]

Lieutenant Ebenezer Wild, of the 1st Massachusetts Regiment, described his experience:

> We struck our tents at 5 o'ck this morning and loaded our baggage About daylight we marched. We went within about a mile of the Schuylkill. We found the enemy had possession of a hill that commanded the bridge, so we went no further [on] that road, but countermarched back into the woods and lay there till about 4 o'clk in the afternoon; and then we marched about 4 or 5 miles up [Lancaster] road and lay in the woods this night without our tents.[31]

The British Army regulars and officers also recorded their reflections and experiences of the Battle of Matson's Ford. British soldier Archibald Robertson, a Lieutenant General with the Royal Engineers, started his diary entry with the British activity on the 10th:

> At 12 at night Lord Cornwallis with a detachment of about 5000 men cross'd the Schuylkill towards Derby to cover a Foraging Party of Waggons. They fell in with Potter's Militia and Part of Washington's Army that had crossed the Schuylkill on their New bridge, and drove them back over the Schuylkill. The Light Horse kill'd and Wounded a good many of them and took 13 Horses of the Rebel Dragoons. This was the 11th in the Forenoon. This night all the Waggons that could be collected were sent over and the whole Detachment return'd by Greys Ferry (where a Bridge of Pontoons had been Thrown over the 10th at night) the 12th at 11 at Night without any Mollestation. Washington is said to be across the Schuylkill.

Robertson also noted that on the 11th, the British troops began their winter quarters in Philadelphia.[32]

Hessian officer Johann Ewald was among the 30,000 soldiers from the German state of Hesse-Cassel whom the British hired to fight for them during the Revolutionary War.[33] Their military skill, discipline, and often savage nature made them sought-after mercenaries and hated occupiers. Ewald wrote that "at about four o'clock in the morning of the 11th, Lord Cornwallis crossed the Schuykill bridge with a Jager attachment, the light infantry, the English and Hessian grenadiers, six six-pound cannons, two troops of dragoons, and an English brigade." He explained that they marched to Darby, in southeast Pennsylvania, about 10 miles from Philadelphia, where they found General Potter with an American corps which "was covered by a strong defile." He said that Cornwallis attacked the enemy, beat him after a stubborn resistance, and captured about 160 men. He stated that the entire area was foraged for around six to eight hours, several plantations of "disaffected persons" were burned, and all the cattle collected for the army on the evening of the 12th before the foraging party rejoined the main army.[34]

Another Hessian officer, Carl Leopold Baurmeister, wrote:

> His Excellency General Howe was exceedingly satisfied with General Cornwallis's conduct but not with those who did the foraging and drove in the cattle. They all thought first of themselves and not of the commonweal. In fact, many deserve being openly accused and punished without consideration. In this, as well as in several other things, we have been going too far and have done infinitely more to maintain the rebellion than to smother it. These excesses, though we gain but little by them, may have very serious consequences.[35]

British Army Captain James Parker was a loyalist from Norfolk, Virginia, who joined the Royal Army as British Master of Works and Engineer Extraordinary. Parker received his commission from Lord Dunmore, the Crown's governor of Virginia, in November 1775. Parker wrote on the 11th to Charles Stewart,

Journal entries, December 11 and 12, 1777, from James Parker, loyalist soldier for the British Army, describing the Battle of Matson's Ford. (Courtesy of the Liverpool Record Office, Archives, Liverpool Central Library, Liverpool, England)

an attorney acquaintance, in Liverpool, England: "A large detachment [marched] earlier this morning over the Schuylkill under the Command of Lord Cornwallis. We are informed that this evening a party of Rebels commanded by General Potter were flying before Lord Cornwallis. Also that Washington has left his post at Whitemarsh Church and that he had crossed the Schuylkill."

Many soldiers and their families mentioned the Battle of Matson's Ford in their applications for military pensions and bounty land warrants based on service in the Revolutionary War. A sample of some of those applications follows. Most of the following applications and others can be found in the Revolutionary War pension applications records in the Pennsylvania Archives[36] and the Revolutionary War Pension and Bounty-Land Warrant Application Files in the National Archives.[37]

The petition for Thomas Blair, Lt. 5th Battalion of Cumberland County (Pennsylvania) Militia, 2nd Lt. of a Company of Foot in 5th Battalion of Cumberland County Militia, stated, "On December 11, 1777, in a skirmish with British troops near Gulph Mills he was wounded in shoulder by a musket ball."[38]

The petition of Cathrine Alexander, the widow of Alexander Alexander, a private in Captain William McCalla's Company of Militia, stated that he was wounded and captured by the British at an engagement in 1777 at Gulph Mills, of which he languished and died on or about December 13, 1777.[39]

Timothy Lennington (also spelled Lemington) of Tyrone Township was a sergeant in the 4th Battalion of Militia of Northumberland County, Pennsylvania. He was wounded 16 times in his head, body, and arms in the Battle of Gulf Mills, December 11, 1777 at age 38. Pension granted.[40]

Jennet Wilson, widow of John Wilson, a private in Cumberland County Militia, stated that John Wilson was wounded and captured by the British in an engagement at "Gulph Miles" on December 11, 1777, and that shortly after he died in captivity in Philadelphia. Pension granted.[41]

Charles Clark was commissioned as a First Lieutenant in Captain Arthur Taggart's Company of Northumberland County Militia in a regiment commanded by James Morrow, Esq., then called the 2nd Battalion of Northumberland County Militia. He marched with a detachment commanded by James Morrow, Esq., and served as first lieutenant of said detachment. The application for his pension, which appeared to have been written by someone else on Clark's behalf, stated, "In the attac[k] made by the British at The Gulph Mills, he was wounded in three different places, in his left arm, his skull was fractured, and he was made prisoner and remained in captivity three years and one month." He was 38 years old. Pension granted.[42]

Robert McWilliams of Northumberland County in 1777 enlisted in Captain Robert Taggart's Company of Northumberland Militia, commanded by Colonel James Murray, Esq. The application read, "On December 12, he was mortally wounded by a musket ball at the attack made by the British upon the Americans under the command of General James Potter, Esq. At Gulf Mills in Philadelphia County, and in the evening of the same day was cut to pieces by the Light Horse in the British Service. He was 28 years of age. His widow, Elizabeth McWilliams, is in need of a pension by reason of bodily infirmities and the care of three small children." Pension granted.[43]

The pension application of Manassah (Manasseh) Coyle,[44] transcribed by Will Graves, states that about October 1777 he entered service under Colonel Chambers in Capt. Samuel Patton's Company in Cumberland County, and marched to Little York, from there to Lancaster, from there to White Marsh Hills, where he joined the army under George Washington. It notes that soon after the Battle of Whitemarsh, "we (the militia) were sent to the Gulf Mills, where we had a small skirmish with the British, but were obliged to retreat with some loss &c."

George Ament's [also referred to as Blos as last name] application explained that he enlisted for two months in his second tour of duty in 1777. The "skirmish near Gulf Mills" was what he put in under the column titled "battles engaged in." In his pension application, he wrote, "the whole Army crossed the Schuylkill, and Encamped near the Gulf Mills, we had a small affair with the British, Genl Potter commanded us, we recrossed the Schuylkill & encamped near the Plymouth Meeting house." At the time of his enlistment, he lived in York County. Application was made on January 8, 1833, and the claim was allowed.[45]

Henrich Herring (also referred to as Henry Hering) was born October 12, 1753, in Haycock Township, Bucks County. His pension and bounty land warrant records noted that he was with Captain Lacey at the battle at Gulph Mills.[46]

Samuel Quigley's pension application noted that he was in the battles of Brandywine, Iron Hill, Whitehorse [probably meaning Whitemarsh], and the Gulph Mills.[47] Quigley, who lived in Shippensburg, Pennsylvania in 1777, was a member of the Ohio Line of the Continental Army, but he was commanded by Colonel James Dunlap in the Pennsylvania Line for eight months in 1777.

Samuel Shaw, who enlisted in the Continental Army from Cumberland County, was also in the battles of Gulph Mills and Whitemarsh. He survived and died in Illinois, where he moved, on July 1, 1853.[48]

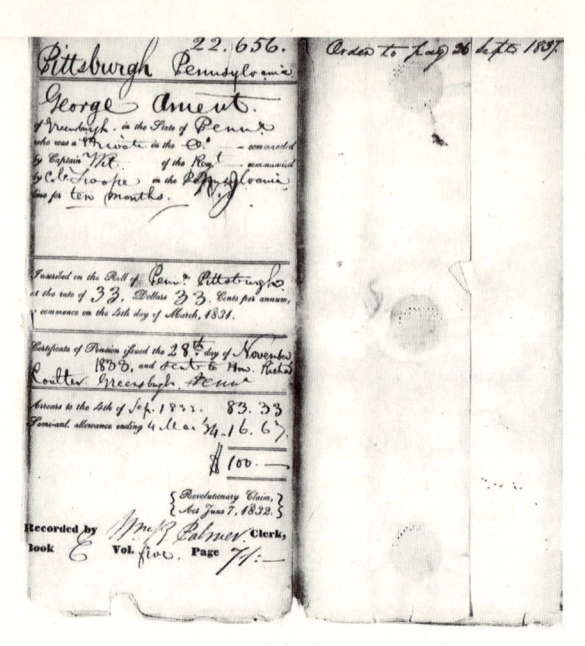

Excerpt from pension application of soldier George Ament, describing the Battle of Matson's Ford and crossing at Swedes Ford. (National Archives)

Catherine Samsell petitioned the Bucks County, Pennsylvania, Orphan's Court on June 26, 1792, for a pension from the State of Pennsylvania as a widow with eight minor children of Peter Samsell. She presented an affidavit from John Lacey, who was then Commandant of the Bucks County Militia, that read:

> I do certify to the best of my recollection, that Peter Samsell was a Sergeant in Captain Stiven Company of Bucks County Militia under my command in the month of November in the year 1777, in actual service was wounded and taken prisoner near the Gulf Mills on the west side of Schuylkill River, by the British Army and was taken into [Philadelphia] and there died of his wounds as I was afterwards informed by a person who sent me a list of the prisoners taken into the City at that time.[49]

Some of the other soldiers who were captured at the Battle of Matson's Ford were sent to prison on Long Island, New York. William Dempsey, an ensign in the Pennsylvania Militia, appeared on a return of the Officers and Prisoners on Long Island dated August 1778. It noted that he was taken at Gulph Mills, Pennsylvania, on December 11, 1777. The same information was found for Charles Clark, First Lieutenant of the Pennsylvania Militia, previously mentioned, and Samuel Fischer, from the Light Horse Militia, Pennsylvania.[50]

Other soldiers who were injured in the Battle of Matson's Ford included Captain Jonas Ingram, who "was in the fight and narrowly escaped capture by the Light Horse"; George Gelwich, an ensign in the York County (Pennsylvania) Militia, who was "present at the fight"; William Demsey, a private in Colone Harmer's Regiment, who was captured,[51] and Robert McQuillan, who "was badly cut up by the light-horse, taken prisoner, and kept in captivity for three years."[52]

While not directly involved in the Battle of Matson's Ford, it impacted Reverend Henry Melchior Muhlenberg, a Lutheran minister who has been called the father of the Lutheran Church in Pennsylvania. Muhlenberg lived in Trappe, Pennsylvania, about 17 miles from Gulph Mills. The battle touched just about every inhabitant in the area that day. Muhlenberg's son, Peter, who was also a clergyman, was a brigadier general in the Continental Army, first in charge of the 8th Virginia Regiment and then the Virginia Line.

Reverend Henry Muhlenberg wrote about the disorder and depravation of Lord Cornwallis's foraging expedition in his journal for December 11. Muhlenberg lived near the site of the Whitemarsh Encampment, near where the Continental Army had stored hundreds of its baggage wagons. Washington's Orders of December 10 called for the baggage and wagons to move out first on December 11 and to cross the Schuylkill at least two hours before the main army, which was ordered to be ready to march at 4 a.m.

Muhlenberg's journal attested to the movement of the baggage wagons in the wee hours of the morning and the calamity that ensued at about 11 a.m. when the Continental Army discovered thousands of redcoats up in the Conshohocken Hills in Gulph Mills, which forced them to retreat back to their Whitemarsh camp. Muhlenberg wrote:

> At one o'clock this morning an express came from the American camp with an order that the baggage wagons and the men in charge of them should move back in the direction of the camp. An hour later the noise and tumult began, and such hay, straw, chickens, etc. [as] the rapacious beasts could still lay hand on were taken among. The movement of wagons, and the noise, etc. [c]onnected therewith, are still proceeding. What a difference there is between peacetime and wartime, especially when hospitals are pushed to extreme!

Just when Muhlenberg thought that he was going to have some peace in the neighborhood, calamity arose. "About eleven o'clock some of the wagons and carts returned at full gallop and a terrible clamor arose: The British, the English are only two miles from here and intend to take the baggage wagons, etc. The confusion defies description. Between three and six o'clock in the afternoon all of the several hundred wagons returned…and encamped hereabouts."

Later that evening, he learned what had caused all of that uproar. "In the evening my two sons, Friedrich and Henrich, came to our house with Pastor Buskerk; they have been in Germantown and have seen the destruction. The poor inhabitants are wandering about naked and hungry, bewailing their condition." They explained to a distressed and befuddled Muhlenberg that the Continental Army "broke camp before dawn today and marched as far as [Matson's] Ford, where there is a new bridge" over the Schuylkill and where some Continental troops were posted on watch. "Unexpectedly, however, the British army broke camp in Philadelphia even earlier in the night and took a position" in Gulph Mills. He continued, "The British killed some of the militiamen and put the rest to flight. So the American army, with nothing accomplished, pulled back to its former camp. This is the reason—because the British were so near—why the baggage wagons were ordered to return."

On top of all that bedlam, Muhlenberg learned that the British and their Hessian hired gun soldiers were out to get him. "I am told on all sides that the English and Hessian officers have singled me out for revenge and that they will have me captured by their dragoons at the first opportunity. I do not know what offense I have committed against their cause, nor do I understand what they will find to devour on such an old carcass as mine." Muhlenberg opined that there were some angry, false accusers who, for whatever reason, "take of this situation in which partisan insinuations are accepted and acted upon without investigation. Everyone advises me to get out of the way. But where should I go? I have a sick wife, am myself old and feeble, and other families are at a loss to know how to meet their own needs in this time of scarcity." Leaning on his faith at such a time as this, Muhlenberg wrote, "Show me thy ways, O Lord."[53]

It appears that Washington did not attach any text to his General Orders for December 11, except to state that he was at Headquarters—Swedes Ford—that the password for Parole was *Maryland*, and that the password for countersign was *Annapolis, Baltimore*.[54] Just about every one of Washington's General Orders lists the countersign and the parole for the day. The countersign was a password to be used by someone who wanted to pass a military sentry or guard. The parole was the password that officers gave to the sentries, so the sentries knew whom to take orders from. So, the sentries had to know and ask for both the countersign and parole. The parole was the more secretive password, and those who knew it were even more limited. Washington explained the system of parole and countersign and its order of distribution in his General Orders of October 18, 1775.[55]

While at Swedes Ford, his army having just been attacked and beaten back and his plans for the army's march for the day delayed, Washington wrote to William Livingston, Brigadier General of the New Jersey Milita who, in 1776, was elected as the first governor of New Jersey. Ever the gentleman, Washington first wrote that he did receive Livingston's letter of December 1, "but the Situation which the Army has been in, must apologize for my not answering it sooner." Washington explained the reason for the delay. "Genl Howe after making great preparations, and threatening to drive us beyond the Mountains, came out with his whole force last thursday Evening, and after maneuvering round us till the Monday following, decamped very hastily and marched back" to Philadelphia.

Livingston had asked Washington about the propriety of conducting a trial for high treason for some residents of the United States who were captured fighting for the British. Brigadier General Philemon Dickinson, of the New Jersey Militia, and his forces captured about 25 members of the New Jersey Volunteers, a group of loyalists who fought for the British Army during the Battle of Staten Island on August 22, 1777.

Washington wrote back that such a trial would be imprudent. Even though the prisoners had left the New Jersey Militia and joined the British after such conduct was declared to be treason, since the persons had not taken the Oath of Allegiance to the United States nor entered into Continental Army service, it could be said that these people had a right to choose sides.

"Again, by the same rule that we try them, may not the Enemy try any natural born subject of Great Britain taken in Arms in our Service. We have a great number of them, and I therefore think we had better submit to the Necessity of treating a few individuals, who may really deserve a severe fate, as prisoners of War, than run the risk of giving an opening for retaliation upon the Europeans in our Service."

In closing, Washington stated that he was glad that the New Jersey Assembly was "in so good a disposition to regulate the price of necessaries for the Army. I could wish that they would not forget to regulate the prices of country produce, which the Commissaries tell me has risen to so exorbitant a Rate that there is no purchasing a Single Article from the Farmer."[56]

Colonel Theodorick Bland, Commander of the 1st Continental Light Dragoons, referred to as Bland's Virginia Horse, sent Washington a note by express rider, informing Washington exactly what Bland and his forces were doing in real time. Bland's letter showed his location as Jonathan Robertson's Smith Shop near the road that "leads down to Bedwin's Ford," which would be somewhere not far from Gulph Mills.

Bland's men still were on the tails of the British. Bland had detached Lieutenant Colonel Benjamin Temple with a small party from Matson's Ford to the Lancaster Road, "with orders to fall in at the seventeen milestone," which is present-day Daylesford, between Paoli and Berwyn, in Chester County, Pennsylvania. Those forces had instructions to "proceed down the road on the front of the enemy," and if the enemy was retreating, to join Bland at the Merion Meeting House, near the second picket that General Potter's forces had first set up.

Bland also detached Major John Jameson, with another party, to two or three miles in the rear to fall in on the right side of the enemy, suspecting that the enemy would head towards Lancaster Road. Bland proceeded down towards Merion and the ferries, such as the Middle Ferry. "I have just heard a firing which continued pretty smart about two minutes and ceased. It was in the direction of the Buck Tavern," in Haverford, near the Lancaster Road. He added, "the Country people say almost exactly where it began yesterday with the Militia."

Bland closed that unless he could get good intelligence on the number, reinforcements, and destination of the British, he would not send any more expresses, but that Washington could conclude that the British "are incamped as a foraging Party, at or near the Buck, which is their situation from all the Intelligence I have yet been able to get."

In a postscript, Bland wrote, "at—½ past eleven Some intelligence says that they are returned to Phil. others that they are gone up the Lancaster Road in No. 9,000 but neither to be depended on as yet. Capt. Call one of the party sent off towards the firing says that he is informd the Enemy (the main body that was out) are gone towards Darby & that there is a small party of Hessians only left where the firing was but this intelligence is not yet certain in my opinion."[57]

Apparently, also on December 11, Washington wrote a letter to his cousin, Lund Washington, who served as his caretaker at Washington's home and plantation, Mt. Vernon, in Virginia.[58] While the letter has not been found, Lund Washington's December 24 letter in response to George Washington's December 11 letter has been published.[59] George Washington was in regular communication with Lund about many and detailed matters related to the business of Mt. Vernon. The letters between the two often concerned how much money the plantation generated, how much and what type of produce the farms produced, how much corn meal and flour was generated from the mills or whiskey from the distillery, the state of the tobacco fields, and the conditions of Washington's enslaved persons, including who was bought, sold, gave birth, or ran away to claim their own freedom. While Washington ran the Continental Army, he was still a businessman involved in running his plantation.

⚜

Meanwhile, in France, the American Commissioners continued their work to persuade France to officially and diplomatically recognize the United States. Franklin wrote to his friend Thomas Walpole, a Member of Parliament and banker in Paris:

> I ought long since to have acknowledg'd the Receipt of the Bills you sent me, in full Discharge of the Balance of your Account, For which I thank you. I am sorry Lord Chatham's Motion for a Cessation of Arms, was not agreed to. Every thing seems to be rejected by your mad Politicians that would lead to Healing the Breach; and everything done that can tend to make it everlasting. Not being sure that we remember perfectly Mr. Wharton's Direction, we beg leave to send some American Newspapers to him under your Cover. From a Sketch Dr. B. had which was drawn by your ingenious and valuable Son, they have made here Medallions in *terre cuit* [terra cotta]. A Dozen have been presented to me, and I think he has a Right to one of them. Please to deliver it to him with my Compliments.[60]

Italian sculptor Jean Baptiste Nini created a clay or terra cotta medallion with the likeness of the internationally popular Ben Franklin, with the large fur cap he frequently wore. Franklin obtained the cap, made of the fur of a marten (a mink-like weasel), in Canada when he traveled there in 1776 to seek the support of the Canadian government and its people for the American Revolution and to spur Canada, unsuccessfully, to its own independence from England. The clay medallions were very popular in France, as was Franklin. The drawing was done by Thomas Walpole's son. "The intention of the first Nini medallion was to present a popular figure in a simple, popular way."[61]

The American Commissioners gave instructions to John Thornton, from Culpeper County, Virginia, who was a major in Colonel Charles Thruston's Additional Continental Regiment, about his upcoming visit to United States prisoners. The Commissioners constantly lamented that the British treated the American prisoners inhumanely, with little food, medical care, and ravaging exposure to deadly diseases like typhus and smallpox, as opposed to the way the Americans treated the British prisoners. Now that General Burgoyne and 5,000 of his soldiers were imprisoned in the United States, the Commissioners thought that the British might be more interested in treating the American prisoners humanely or even doing a prisoner swap.

The Commissioners advised Thornton that he would receive a letter to Lord Frederick North, England's Prime Minister, and another to Sir Grey Cooper, Secretary of the Treasury, and that he was to try to get an answer from them. The purpose of the letter was "to obtain permission to visit and examine into the situation of our people in their Gaols [defined as confinement to jails], and administer to their Relief, we hope a Request so consonant to Humanity will not be refused."

But, if he could not get permission, they would like him to see the American prisoners, take an account of their name, their rank and unit, the states they belonged to, "in what Vessel, and by whom they were taken and such other particulars as may tend to give us perfect Information of their Circumstances." The British regularly held prisoners on ships where there was, again, insufficient food and galloping disease.[62] The Commissioners told Thornton that he would receive "Fifty Guineas for travelling Expenses," to which they would require an account, to which they closed the letter, "We wish you a good Journey, being Sir, Your most humble Servants."[63]

So, December 11 ended with the Continental Army still on the eastern banks of the Schuylkill, most of the soldiers finding shelter only under the cold, night sky, preparing to try again in the wee hours of December 12 to march to the other side of the Schuylkill.

CHAPTER 4

The Army is on the Move Again, December 12

The Continental Army awoke that morning to a sunny day, but still on the east side of the Schuylkill River, in Norristown, near the Swedes Ford, some 15 miles from Philadelphia. Norristown is land that Isaac Norris, a Quaker merchant and former mayor of Philadelphia, purchased from William Penn in the early 1700s.[1] Swedes Ford was one of three fords that could be used to cross the Schuylkill River into Upper Merion Township. The soldiers likely appreciated the day's rest, as the generals tried to make sense of what happened the day before.

The weather grew cloudy and colder, and the rain that first fell turned into snow as the army waited around all day. Finally, in the evening of the 12th, the Continental Army crossed the Swedes Ford on two bridges, one an existing old wooden bridge, and one that the soldiers just built.

Washington's detailed order from December 10 on how the army should move out of their almost six-week encampment at Whitemarsh and the precise Order of March that the generals developed on the 10th fell by the wayside. Instead of one bridge over the Matson's Ford, there were now two rickety makeshift bridges—at Matson's Ford and at Swedes Ford—to get them across the Schuylkill. John Laurens wrote that one was "an ancient bridge, an infamous construction, which in many parts obliged the men to march by Indian file," one right behind the other, and the other was a "a bridge of wagons" which resulted in "very unstable footing" and only a "trifling number of troops" crossing there.[2] The soldiers were scattered in their impromptu and disordered camp by the Swedes Ford. The baggage wagons were back about 17 miles, further away from the river crossings than they were the day before. There was also a general unease because of the army's battle with the British at Matson's Ford and questions about whether the British might come back out again with intentions for a larger battle.

Colonel Angell wrote that his troops received orders to march at around 6 p.m. He noted that the troops expected to cross the Schuylkill at Swedes Ford because other soldiers had built a bridge of wagons, "laying a length of Rails from one [wagon] to another." But, when it was time to march, their particular wagons were ordered to cross at Swedes Ford and the troops were ordered to cross at "the ford below where we attempted to Cross the day before the troops arrived," which would have been Matson's Ford. Then, by seven o'clock in the evening, all the troops were on the move to cross over, but they did not all cross over until about 6:30 a.m. the next day because there was only one "poor bridge to Cross upon being built with logs and plank rails from one [pair] of logs to another which [floated] on the water" and their wagons and horses kept falling through the unstable bridge. "We Suffered much this night as it was a Cold Stormy Night with snow and rain."[3]

December 12, 1777 entry in Orderly Book of Major Richard Platt, Headquarters of General George Washington. (Library of Congress)

Lieutenant Ebenezer Wild recorded in his journal that the soldiers drew two days' worth of rations, and around daylight they packed their belongings in preparation for marching off. Before they could do so, more orders came down to stay where they were, so they cooked their provisions, crafted huts with brush and leaves to protect themselves from the continuing snowstorm, and got themselves settled in for the night. After they got themselves as comfortable as they could, and after the sun started to set, another set of orders came down that threw them back into confusion—pack up and get ready to march. Through the snow and rain, they marched around five miles, crossed the Schuylkill, and marched another three miles before they were able to stop on a very high hill. They finally were able to rest there for the evening, without tents, or even axes to cut wood and make fires.[4]

Lieutenant Samuel Armstrong wrote on the 12th that the army formed around 4 p.m. and began to march around 5 p.m. They marched three miles, crossed the Schuylkill, then marched another mile, and finally encamped.[5]

Captain Brigham wrote, "Pleasant morning But Clouded up and Looked Likely for a Storm." One of his fellow soldiers, whom he referred to as Ensign Tilden, had gotten permission to leave his army service, whether for a furlough or for good is not certain. "Toward night it began to Storm with Snow and Continued Snowing all night." The army crossed the river and his division "Lay out in ye Storm all night and Crossed about Break of Day."[6]

The soldiers recounted waiting at Swedes Ford for most of the day before they went on the move. Colonel Henry Dearborn wrote that in the morning, the army built a brigade of wagons across the Swedes Ford for the army to cross on but that near nightfall the enemy had moved from the ground that they occupied and the whole army marched down to the Swedes Ford bridge where they crossed over, took possession of "some Heights," and encamped. He noted that 11 Hessian soldiers were taken prisoner that day.[7]

A sick and hungry Dr. Waldo recalled the misery of that day:

> A Bridge of Waggons made across the Schuylkill last night consisting of 36 waggons, with a bridge of Rails between each. Some skirmishing over the River. Militia and dragoons brought into Camp several prisoners. Sun Set—we were order'd to march over the River—It snows—I'm sick—eat nothing—No whiskey—No Forage—Lord-Lord-Lord. The Army were 'till Sun Rise crossing the River—some at the Waggon Bridge & some at the Raft Bridge below. Cold & uncomfortable.[8]

Lieutenant McMichael recorded, "At 6 P.M. we marched to the bridge [made of wagons], which we crossed in Indian file, and at 3 A.M. encamped near the Gulph [Mill], where we remained without tents or blankets in the midst of a severe snow storm."[9] Since the baggage wagons with supplies had to hurriedly retreat back to Trappe, some 17 miles away, on December 11 to protect their provisions from Cornwallis's foraging troops, the soldiers were without many of their critical supplies.

France's Major General Johann de Kalb, who was assigned to a division of Maryland and Delaware troops, was with the Maryland troops commanded by General Sullivan at the Battle of Matson's Ford. He reflected on the army's crossing the Swedes Ford and the previous day's battle at Matson's Ford in a letter he wrote on December 17.

Ruins of Old Grist Mill at Gulph Mills. (Courtesy of Radnor Historical Society)

That letter was to Charles Francois de Broglie, Marquis of Ruffec, a former French military officer and diplomat. De Broglie was an ardent Revolutionary War supporter, who procured arms, supplies, and funds for the American cause and who surreptitiously worked to secure French and Spanish support for the American Revolution. On August 8, 1775, the Marquis de Lafayette attended the Diner de Metz, which de Broglie hosted in honor of King George III's brother, the Duke of Gloucester. The Duke apparently spoke a bit too freely at the dinner about the deteriorating relationship between England and the American colonies, which convinced the Marquis de Lafayette that there was justification to the revolution in the colonies.[10] Unfortunately, de Broglie's zeal got the best of him in 1776 when he suggested to de Kalb and the American Commissioners in France that he, an experienced military officer, should replace Washington as Commander in Chief of the Continental Army. This surreptitious and unsuccessful plot was called the Broglie Intrigue.

De Kalb wrote:

> On the 11th of December we broke camp, to take up a position on the right bank of the Schuylkill, six miles in advance. Two visions of the right wing had already passed our pontoon bridge at Matson's Ford, when suddenly an intrenched camp was seen there, from which the enemy had assailed and cannoned the militia marching in the front. The great distance made it impossible that General Howe should have been informed of our movements in time to have thrown his main body in our way. It was clear that this was only a strong detachment, which had ventured out in search of provisions.

De Kalb continued with serious criticism of General Sullivan's unwillingness to take the fight to the British to support General Potter's militia.

> Instead, however, of falling upon the enemy and engaging him, or making a detour, General Sullivan, who commanded our right wing, retreated across the bridge, and ordered it to be

taken down, abandoning the militia to their fate. Thus we remained on the left bank, at Swedes Ford, three miles above, where we constructed a new bridge, no better than the old one. Before the day was over we learned that the hostile corps numbered but two thousand men, and made off in the utmost haste.[11]

The British seemed satisfied with what occurred on the 11th, except that General Howe was angry that some of the soldiers took the forage directly to their camp instead of delivering such to the Commissary of Foraging. Howe's After Orders for December 11, given at 10 p.m., read:

> It is the Commander in Chief's Positive Orders that all forage brought in this Evening, be sent to the Magazine tomorrow Morning by Day Break, being to his Great Astonishment, informed that the Waggons, of some Corps have been sent with it to Camp. The Commanding Officers of Corps, to be Answerable this Order is Comply'd with and the Commissary of Forage is to take an account of the Quantity delivered to him by Each Corps.[12]

The British wrote favorably about their foraging operations. Major Andre wrote:

> The wagons of the Army were escorted to the other side of the Schuylkill by the 42nd Regiment, and were employed in bringing in forage. It was said that great depredations had been committed by the soldiers on the march. The whole of the cattle which the Troops had procured was stopped at the bridge and delivered to the Commissary, to the great disappointment of many people. In the evening General Grey crossed the bridge at Middle Ferry in order to secure the retreat of the wagons, but it being very soon after, reported that Lord Cornwallis was returned and had brought in the forage. General Grey received Orders to retire to Camp again.[13]

Archibald Robertson wrote of the 12th that the whole detachment returned by Greys Ferry, where a pontoon had been thrown across the Schuylkill on the 10th at night. He said the army returned on the evening of the 12th "without any [m]olestation" by the Continental Army and that Washington was said to be "across the Schuylkill." Once the British troops returned, he noted that the troops began to be quartered in Philadelphia for the winter.

Washington reflected on the Battle of Matson's Ford in his General Orders for the day from his headquarters at Swedes Ford. "The Commander in Chief, with great pleasure, expresses his approbation, of the behaviour of the Pennsylvania Militia yesterday, under Genl Potter, in the vigorous opposition they made to a body of the enemy on the other side of the Schuylkill."[14]

Washington turned his attention to the sick who were left behind at the camp in Whitemarsh. "A careful subaltern[15] from each brigade is to repair this day to the last encampment of the army, to collect and take care of the sick and conduct them to Reading—These officers are to apply to the regimental Surgeons for information where to find the sick of their—brigades—Every motive of duty and humanity requires the most exact attention to this order."[16]

Reading is some 45 miles from Swedes Ford, in Berks County, Pennsylvania. By the time of the American Revolution, Reading's total production of iron exceeded England's. The town became a depot for military supply and provided the Continental Army with cannons, rifles, ammunition, and other weapons.[17]

Philadelphia's William Shippen, Jr., Director of Hospitals for the Continental Army, had written to Washington about where to locate the sick, hospitalized Continental Army soldiers who were, at the time, in Princeton, New Jersey. Washington wrote back to Shippen that leaving the sick in Princeton could lead to their capture, but also acknowledged that moving some of them in their precarious conditions might cause further injury. For those sick and injured who could be moved, it was safest to keep them at the rear of the army where the other soldiers could protect them. For those sick in hospitals in Princeton, or in Easton or Bethlehem in Pennsylvania, Washington wrote that Colonel Lewis Nicola's Invalid Brigade could be assigned to the hospitals to protect them.[18]

The so-called Invalid Brigade was headed by Philadelphia's compassionate Colonel Lewis Nicola, who was appointed mayor of the city of Philadelphia in 1776. Nicola also created the General Circulating Library of over 1,000 books in Philadelphia and was a member of the American Society for Promoting Useful Knowledge, with his colleague Ben Franklin, which eventually merged into the American Philosophical Society.[19]

The Invalid Brigade was a collection of sick and injured soldiers who were unfit for duty on the battlefield but who could do other things that were not very physically demanding, such as serving as stationary guards at hospitals and garrisons or training young recruits. By establishing an Invalid Brigade, those soldiers could remain part of the army, be paid, and reserve much-needed battle-ready soldiers for the field. The brigade had about 1,000 soldiers and eight companies. It was originally stationed in Philadelphia until the British invaded. The brigade was then moved to Trenton, New Jersey and Allentown, Pennsylvania, before the it moved to Easton and Bethlehem, Pennsylvania.[20]

Washington's General Order for the day went on to note that "Daniel Clymer Esqr: is appointed Deputy Commissary of prisoners, to act in the absence of the Commissary General of prisoners." As Deputy Commissary of Prisoners, Clymer was responsible for assisting the Commissary General in ensuring that, to the extent that they could, American prisoners were treated as humanely as possible by their British captors as far as being provided with food, clothing, and other necessaries of life.[21] The Continental Army Commissaries could only hope that any provisions that they delivered to the British prisons to support the American prisoners were actually used as intended.

While Washington worried about how he would finally get his army across the Schuylkill, Continental Congress President Henry Laurens, who was sick with gout, sent Washington a series of resolutions that Congress passed that were "calculated for availing your Excellency's Troops & for depriving those of the Enemy, of the benefit of provisions adjacent to Philadelphia."[22] The letter was sent to William Jones at Whitemarsh, Laurens apparently not yet caught up as to where Washington was located.

Several of the enclosed resolutions were those recommended by the Continental Congressional Camp Committee (CCCC), which reported to Congress on December 10. The Congress agreed with the Committee's recommendations and observations. One of the charges to the Commission was "to take into consideration the state of those counties in the states of Pennsylvania, Jersey, and Delaware, which border on the enemy, or are in the neighbourhood of General Washington's army, and report the most effectual and vigorous measures for subsisting the army under the command of General Washington, and distressing that of the enemy."[23]

Before it left camp on December 10, the CCCC had left with Washington its resolution regarding Washington's need to increase the Continental Army's foraging. Part of the resolution that Laurens enclosed in his correspondence that day called on the Pennsylvania legislature to enact a law that required its citizens to provide a certain amount of their grain to the army since "many inhabitants, through motives of avarice or dissatisfaction, refuse to thresh out their grain."

That part of the resolution read:

> That it be earnestly recommended to the legislature of the commonwealth of Pennsylvania, forthwith to enact a law, requiring all persons within their State, at the distance of seventy miles and upwards, from General Washington's head quarters, and below the Blue Mountains, to thresh out their wheat and other grain, within as short a period of time as the said legislature shall deem sufficient for that purpose; and, in case of failure, to subject the same to seizure by the commissaries and quarter masters of the American army, to be paid for at the price of straw only.

It excused from compliance and penalty "such families only, who, from the absence of the master, sons or servants, in the service of their country, can give good proof that their compliance with the said law was not practicable."[24] No doubt, the proposed Pennsylvania law would help Washington feed his troops. Yet, he strongly believed that his army was doing the best it could about foraging. Congress's resolution and instructions did not sit well with him, and Washington told Congress so in a letter a few days later.

At the same time, the Pennsylvania General Assembly criticized its own son, General Anthony Wayne, for using his personal funds to buy clothes

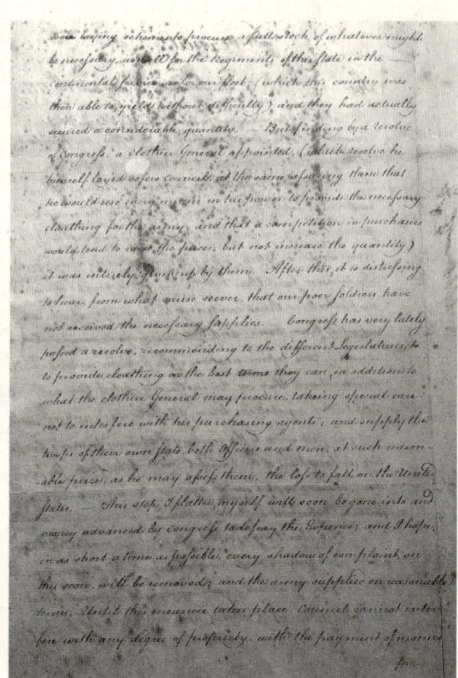

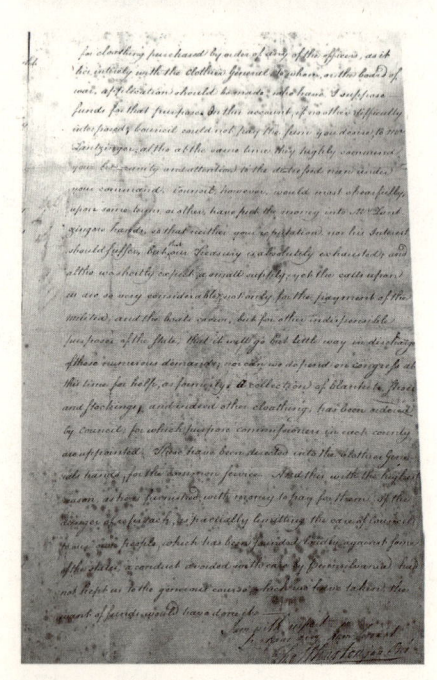

December 12, 1777 letter from His Excellency Thomas Wharton, Jr., Esquire, President of the Supreme Executive Council of the Commonwealth of Pennsylvania, Captain General and Commander in Chief in and over the same, to General Anthony Wayne regarding the clothing, recruitment, and status of the Pennsylvania troops. (Courtesy of the Historical Society of Pennsylvania, Anthony Wayne Papers)

for his troops and then to ask for reimbursement. The Pennsylvania General Assembly told Wayne that they would not reimburse him for the clothes that he purchased or pay Wayne's pending debt to the private clothier that he used, no matter how much the men needed them, because, first, the General Assembly did not authorize him to do that, and second, clothing the troops was the Continental Army's and the Continental Congress's responsibility.

Wayne became angry at the Supreme Executive Council's response, which he attributed to a lack of care for the soldiers or an understanding of their dire needs. He went ahead anyway and continued to clothe his troops. It helped that he was on his own home turf of Pennsylvania, only about 11 miles from his plantation, Waynesborough, in Paoli, Easttown Township, where he had resources of all types.

President Wharton wrote to Wayne on behalf of the Supreme Executive Council, from its location in Lancaster, Pennsylvania. First, Wharton explained—or complained—about how the state's militia law had drained the Pennsylvania treasury. Too many men, instead of fulfilling their service when the state drafted them, appointed a substitute whom the state paid. Many farmers and tradesmen signed up as substitutes "without rendering that service which was expected of them."

Now that the Supreme Executive Council was convened, Wharton predicted that it would change the militia law. Instead of drafting men for the Pennsylvania Militia, he predicted that the council would focus on drafting men for the Pennsylvania Line of the Continental Army, "for from them we must expect success against our Enemies and the full establishment of Independence."

Wharton admitted that the "Cloathing of our Troops is a matter of the most serious consequence, and demands our greatest attention." In fact, he explained that, for the past year, the Council of Safety had "actually secured a considerable quantity" of whatever might be necessary, as well, for the Pennsylvania regiments in the Continental Service and for their fleet.

When the Pennsylvania Council learned that the Continental Congress appointed a Clothier General, who assured the council "that he would use every means in his Power to provide the necessary Cloathing for the Army, and that a competition in purchases would tend to raise the prices," the council gave up the business of procuring clothing for its Continental Army troops. "It is distressing to hear, from what cause so ever, that our poor soldiers have not received the necessary supplies." On top of that, Congress recently asked different state legislatures to provide clothes, "in addition to what the Cloathier General may procure, taking special care not to interfere with his purchasing

Agents, and supply the troops of their own state." Pennsylvania would soon advance funds to Congress for this purpose and "I hope, in as short a time as possible, every shadow of complaint on this score will be removed, and the Army supplied on reasonable terms."

Standing on some sort of misplaced intergovernmental propriety against a man who went into his own pocket to clothe the state's troops, Wharton wrote that until Pennsylvania sent the money to Congress to clothe the Pennsylvania troops, "Council cannot interfere, with any degree of propriety, with the Payment of Monies for Cloathing purchased by order of any of the officers, as it lies entirely with the Cloathier General." Therefore, the Pennsylvania Council's position was that if Wayne wanted to get reimbursed, he should apply to the Clothier General or the Board of War.

Nevertheless, Wharton told Wayne that the council "highly commend your humanity and attention to the Distressed men under your Command." He wrote that normally the council would "most cheerful, upon some terms or other" have paid Wayne's clothier directly, "so that neither your reputation nor his interest should suffer, but our Treasury is absolutely exhausted."

While the council expected some small funds to come in, "the calls upon us are so very considerable" for payment of the militia, the boat crews, and "other indispensable purposes" of the State. Council also could not depend on the Continental Congress as they used to. Council had already ordered a "collection of Blankets, Shoes, and Stockings, and indeed other Cloathing through Commissioners in each county." This clothing would go to the Clothier General "for the common service," not just for the Pennsylvania troops, "as he is furnished with money to pay for them."[25]

At the same time that the Pennsylvania Council criticized Wayne for caring for his troops by clothing them, Council President Wharton wrote to Major General Armstrong again criticizing the Pennsylvania Militia. Wharton's letter was in response to Armstrong's letters to Wharton of December 4 and 7, in which Armstrong relayed the details of the Battle of Whitemarsh. Wharton wrote:

> The precipitate retreat of the enemy, after so much Gasconading [boasting], is a convincing proof that their army is not so formidable as they would wish us to believe, or that they put great dependence in our want of bravery, and therefore expected our army would retreat from hill to hill as soon as they approached, they have however been disappointed, and I trust we shall benefit by this last movement of theirs.

Turning to the militia, Wharton continued, "The Conduct of our militia gives me real pain. Council is informed from various hands that they have behaved very infamously." Wharton explained that he was informed that the British

Army's capture of the Pennsylvania Militia's General Irvine was "owing entirely" to the militia's "base behavior." He expressed hope that the Pennsylvania legislation would "fill the battalions in the Continental Service, so as the necessity of calling out the militia may in a great measure be dispensed with."[26]

⚜

Meanwhile, in France, the American Commissioners wrote to the Right Honorable Lord North, First Lord of The Treasury, Chancellor of the Exchequer, and Principal Minister of the King of Great Britain, to reiterate their letter of nearly a year ago, to which they had not received a reply. In that letter and the current one, the Commissioners asked for an exchange of prisoners in Europe and complained about the treatment of American prisoners by the British compared to the more humane manner in which the Americans treated British prisoners. In the fashion of Benjamin Franklin's *Poor Richard's Almanac*'s down-home wisdom, the letter began with the declaration "that moderation is a mark of wisdom, and humanity an ornament to the highest station." The United States had exercised this wisdom, as documented by Congressional records "filled with proofs of tender care and attention, not only the wants, but the comfort and accommodation of their prisoners."

All that the Americans saw from the British government in this regard was "the public declaration of the governors and general who was chosen to commence this war, that the American officers and soldiers should be treated with equal indignity, and all devoted, without distinction, to the most ignominious fate, in terms too low for us to repeat. We have never heard of this proceeding having been censured by the government from which he derived his authority."[27] They continued that for "these cruelties," the United States could "make ample retaliation upon the numerous prisoners of all ranks in their possession." However, that was not the American way. "Upwards of 500 British seamen have been generously treated, set at liberty by our cruisers in these seas, and sent at the public expense to their country." The Commissioners told Lord North that they hoped that he would feel "bound to dismiss an equal number of seamen, taken in the service of the United States."

The letter concluded, "We also desire, that a person appointed by us, may have permission to furnish the subjects of the United States, who are in your prisons, with the necessaries they may want from time to time; and that a general cartel may be immediately settled, by which the unfortunate on both sides may be relieved as soon as possible from the miseries of imprisonment." The letter was signed by Benjamin Franklin, Silas Deane, and Arthur Lee.[28]

The American Commissioners' efforts to garner support from other countries in Europe was working. Charles Frederick Dumas, the American agent at The Hague, Netherlands, and a tireless advocate of the American cause, wrote from The Hague in response to Arthur Lee's letter of December 4 about the Continental Army's victory at Saratoga. "The news caused the greatest possible sensation in this country. A deep consternation among those who have all their property in England; a marked joy in those who hate your enemies: this is the only thing to be seen; and the latter make up the great number." It continued that in Dumas's conversations with the Grand Pensionnaire d'Amsterdam, the leader of the Dutch Republic who essentially functioned as the prime minister, it had escaped the Pensionnaire:

> that it was time for *Holland to take advantage of the conjuncture, so as not to be the last in Europe to seek the friendship and commerce of America* [emphasis in the original]. I replied to him, that I was ready to send you, gentlemen, in the greatest secrecy, all the overtures, in this respect, with which he thought he could begin; and I proposed that he should feel the pulse of the Grand Pensionary. He told me that he would do so, without pressing anything, however, and after having first ascertained the true disposition and inclinations of this Minister.[29]

As the evening of the 12th ended, one by one, thousands of campfires, built by tired and hungry soldiers, began to dot the landscape on the Conshohocken Hills.

CHAPTER 5

The March into Gulph Mills, December 13

On the morning of December 13, the father of six-year-old Matthias Holstein grabbed him from his bed at their home in Swedesburg, also called Matsunk, a Swedish settlement in Upper Merion Township that was contiguous to Gulph Mills, and they hurried down their main road, by the river, to the banks of the Schuylkill.[1] Matthias's father wanted his son to see the astonishing event that was unfolding right in front of them—at least 11,000 soldiers of the Continental Army were crossing the Schuylkill at Swedes Ford and marching down the road, into Swedesburg and Gulph Mills.[2] The war had come to their backyard.

Drawing of the Swedes Ford crossing of the Schuylkill River, 1828. (Courtesy of King of Prussia Historical Society)

The Holsteins were no doubt joined that day by many of their neighbors in that Swedish settlement—the Rambos, Griffiths, DeHavens, and Yokums. Many of the Swedish settlers in the area were out preparing for the Feast of St. Lucia, which they would celebrate at their church, Christ Church, or Old Swede's Church, located on the road that was now filling up with Continental Army soldiers. Little did they know that the most important soldier in that army would soon be joining them.

The Feast of St. Lucia, also called the Festival of Lights, is celebrated in Sweden and Swiss communities annually on December 13. It honors St. Lucia, an early Christian whom the Romans killed in AD 304 due to her religious beliefs. One aspect of the celebration is that families traditionally dress their eldest daughter in white and serve coffee and baked goods to family members and guests throughout the day.

The festival is "meant to bring hope and light during the darkest time of the year," and it marks the start of the Christmas season and a return to light. The community aspect of the celebration features one girl designated as St. Lucia who leads a procession that includes other "young girls dressed in white and wearing lighted wreaths on their heads and boys dressed in white pajama-like costumes singing traditional songs."[3]

What do you do when the war comes to your backyard? Life goes on with some sense of normalcy.

As the soldiers continued to march in, the members of Old Swede's Church gathered their food and supplies and headed to church. Matthias and other parishioners were in the church, re-enacting the feast, watching the tired soldiers continue to march.

Church members tell this story: Suddenly, there was a commotion at the door. They had a visitor. In fact, they had several. General Washington along with General Lafayette and General John Paul Jones were at the door. Washington told the parishioners that he and his men saw the lights burning inside the church and decided to stop in. Imagine the settlers' surprise as Washington and his generals joined them for the service. The parishioners gave Washington an opportunity to speak, which he did, explaining and pleading the new nation's cause. Eight members of the church volunteered to join the army that night. After the service was over, Washington and his generals continued on their way down the river road, towards Gulph Mills.[4]

So now 11,000 soldiers had marched into a small village of farms and mills. The Major General for the Day was General Greene, and the other officers for the day were Brigadier General Weedon, Field Officers Colonel Febiger and Major Miller, and Brigadier Major M. Cluer.[5]

Washington immediately sought to get his army settled. In his first General Orders with the Gulph as his headquarters, he ordered the officers to examine the arms of the men and ensure that they drew their allotted provisions, which should be cooked in preparation for the next two days. Included in those provisions was a gill of whiskey. Washington ordered that no tents be pitched, but that axes be distributed for the cutting of wood for fires. The soldiers were to be ready to march precisely at 4:00 a.m. He also ordered each regiment to send an officer back to the "encampment on the other side of the Schuylkill" to search local houses for stragglers and grounds for any wagons that were left and bring them back to the army as soon as possible.[6]

The soldiers tried to settle themselves by cutting trees to build a fire or to build rough-hewn huts from branches, trunks, and leaves. Detailing the chaos of no doubt thousands of trees being cut down and gathered, Lt. Samuel

Armstrong wrote, "This day one man was kill'd and One wounded so bad his life is dispared of, which is happened by the falling of trees."[7]

Dr. Waldo described the march into Gulph Mills, where he thought the army was going to establish its winter quarters.

> The Army march'd three miles from the West side the River and encamp'd near a place Called the Gulph and not an improper name either, for this Gulph seems well adapted by its situation to keep us from the pleasures & enjoyments of this World, or being conversant with anybody in it. It is an excellent place to raise the Ideas of a Philosopher beyond the glutted thoughts and Reflexions of an Epicurian. His Reflexions will be as different from the Common Reflexions of Mankind as if he were unconnected with the world, and only conversant with immaterial beings. It cannot be that our Superiors are about to hold consultations with Spirits infinitely beneath their Order, by bringing us into these utmost regions of the Terraqueous Sphere. No, it is, upon consideration for many good purposes since we are to Winter here.

Waldo listed five reasons why he thought that Gulph Mills would be a good place to spend the winter. First, there was plenty of wood and water. Second, "There are but few families for the soldiery to Steal from—tho' far be it from a Soldier to Steal." Third, "There are warm sides of Hills to erect Huts on." Then he added, sarcastically, his last two reasons. Fourth, such an awful environment would keep the men "heavenly minded like Jonah when in the Belly of a Great Fish." Fifth, the men would not become homesick because conditions would be so bad, they would be thinking about going on "to another Home"—their heavenly one.[8]

Like Waldo, many other soldiers probably thought they would spend the winter in Gulph Mills, because they knew that the army would likely move into winter quarters soon.

Lieutenant Colonel Dearborn wrote of that day, "We Lay still to-Day—the Enemy have Retreated in to Philadelphia."[9]

Colonel Angell wrote about how the day was fairly comfortable for him:

> Marched this Morning from Swedes Ford about five or six miles. There turned into a peace of woods, between Eight and nine oClock in the morning and got our Breakfasts. There tarried that day and the night following where we built our Huts of bushes and leaves and lodged Comfortable that night in peace as the Enemy had Retreated into Philadelphia. It cleared off this afternoon and was fine weather.[10]

Lieutenant Wild wrote, "It was a very bad snow when we stopped. We lay here in the woods this forenoon. We drew one day's provision, and had orders to cook it and be ready to march; but did not march then, but drew one day's more of provision, and had orders to cook it & make ourselves as comfortable as we could for the ensuing night, and be ready to march at 4 o'clk in the morning."[11]

Captain Brigham wrote, "It cleared off Pleasant. We Incamped in ye woods about 2 miles from ye River. Sergeant Merrifield came into Camp this Day and Brought a man to Take his Place."[12]

It was a relatively quiet day for the British Army, too. Captain Ewald, a Hessian soldier, stated that "on the 13th, I took one hundred Jagers to protect the army's woodcutter in the woodland on the other side of Middle Ferry. I returned at ten in the evening."[13]

General Reed, who noted his location as Norriton, which was the city at the Swedes Ford on the eastern bank of the Schuylkill River, wrote to Pennsylvania Council President Wharton with a report about the march out of the Whitemarsh Encampment and the Battle of Matson's Ford. He also relayed his concerns about the current condition and location of the Continental Army. Usually one of Washington's chief confidants and supporters, Reed even expressed concerns about Washington himself.

Reed wrote that on the 11th, when he and some of the other general officers saw Cornwallis and his troops, they thought "this a favourable opportunity to attack the enemy." He continued, "very unhappily, in my judgment, a contrary opinion prevailed." While the British "made a grand forage, burnt many houses and plundered the inhabitants," the Continental Army basically stood by and did nothing. "It was somewhat mortifying that this should be done in the face of our whole army; but the danger of crossing while the enemy was in the neighbourhood, occasioned some gentlemen pressing earnestly to avoid an offensive measure. I believe they will very soon see things in a different point of view, for in love and war, opportunities are everything."

General Washington made the wrong decision, Reed wrote. "The General has suffered his own better judgment to be controlled by others, as that would have led to an attack, which I am well satisfied would have proved great and glorious to America, as well as signally serviceable to this State."

General Potter, however, deserved praise. "General Potter, being on the west side of the Schuylkill when the enemy came out, they fell upon and routed him. His people, particularly three regiments, behaved exceedingly well, but were obliged to give way to superior numbers. I believe they have not suffered much. The most of them are come in, and have crossed again with the General and army."

Reed had previously assured Wharton that the Pennsylvania Council's plan of cantoning the army, which was that "a brigade of Continental troops was to be left with the militia on this side of the Schuylkill, and which, when I wrote, I thought was approved by his Excellency (Washington), has upon advise been totally changed." He continued:

General Green, Cadwalader and myself had fixed upon this plan the most eligible to quiet the minds of the people, and cover the country. Instead of this, the remains of Potter's brigade are taken over the river, though I earnestly requested they might be left as a protection from small parties. The Jerseys, who have all their own militia, will not be satisfied without a cover of Continental troops, and I trust my zeal in the cause will vindicate me from all suspicion of whimsical caprice and dissatisfaction when I say that the situation of the country from Delaware to Schuylkill is very distressing, and calls loudly for attention and help from some quarter.

Reed feared that the loyal Whig inhabitants near Philadelphia would have to leave because there would be no Continental troops nearby to protect them, except "General Armstrong with about one thousand militia, many without arms and without a single troop of horse." And even Armstrong had to move back 25 or 30 miles from the city of Philadelphia, giving the British free rein in that area.

Yet, all was not lost. "If the State will raise a few troops for the winter for the salutary purpose of covering the country, I should think it a happy measure." Reed even offered himself for any "post or office" where he could be useful. He stated that he had "given over thoughts of proceeding farther in the military life" but that more should be done to protect Pennsylvania residents in and near Philadelphia. He concluded, "I shudder at the distress of the inhabitants, who must either submit or suffer much hardship. I am of opinion that a bounty for this purpose could be well applied. I have only given the hint. Wiser heads may improve or respect it."[14]

With a few days' reflection, also on December 13, British Army Commander in Chief General Howe wrote about the Battle of Matson's Ford and the Battle of Whitemarsh in a letter to Lord George Germain, "one of his Majesty's principal Secretaries of State."[15] Howe sent his letter by way of Lord Cornwallis, who, that day, began the process of leaving the United States to sail back to England

Entry, British Army General William Howe Orderly Book, December 13, 1777. (Courtesy of William L. Clements Library, University of Michigan)

for a long-sought and long-delayed respite from the war. Howe wrote, "My Lord, Lord Cornwallis having applied for Leave of Absence to attend his private Business in Europe, I take this Opportunity of sending my Dispatches by his Lordship in the Brillant armed Ship."

After he described the Battle of Whitemarsh, Howe analyzed the Battle of Matson's Ford, as follows:

> On the 11th at Day-break Lord Cornwallis, with Major-General Grant under his Command passed the Schuylkill with a Strong Corps, and the Waggons of the Army, to collect Forage, for the Winter Supply, which his Lordship accomplished and returned Yesterday Evening. The Enemy having quitted their Camp at White Marsh some hours before Lord Cornwallis marched from hence, his Lordship met the Head of their Army at a Bridge they had thrown over the Schuylkill near to Matson's Ford, about Three Miles below Swedes Ford, and Fifteen Miles distant from hence. Over this Bridge the Enemy had passed 800 Men, who were immediately dispersed by his Lordship's advanced Troops, obliging Part of them to recross it, which occasioned such an Alarm to their Army, that they broke the Bridge; and his Lordship proceeded to forage without meeting any Interruption.

Howe, who assumed that his intelligence was correct, wrote, "The Enemy's Intention seems to be, to take their Winter Quarters at Carlisle, York, and Lancaster, and probably they may have a Corps at Reading, and another at Burlington in Jersey." Somehow, Gulph Mills, Valley Forge, or anywhere else closer to Philadelphia was nowhere on Howe's radar. Howe went on to explain that he proposed "to put the Army immediately into Winter Quarters in this Town, where there is sufficient Room."[16] He also noted that "for the Defense of that Post," he was immediately sending two of his regiments, the 71st Regiment and the Regiment of Mirbach, to New York "to reinforce Henry Clinton," one of his generals.

Then Howe included a "Return of the Killed, Wounded, and Missing, in the different Skirmishes, from the 4th to the 8th of Dec 1777," listing the various regiments and battalions. These included the Light Infantry, Guards; 4th, 7th, 15th, 17th, 26th, 28th, 33rd, 37th, 46th, and 49th Regiments; the Queen's American Rangers, Hessian Jagers, Royal Artillery; noting one lieutenant, two sergeants, and 16 rank-and-file killed; three lieutenants, four sergeants, and 53 rank-and-file wounded; and 13 rank-and-file missing.[17]

In his Orders for the day, Howe included a Memorandum from General Hutchinson, Deputy Adjutant General, about reimbursing the soldiers for the forage from Gulph Mills that they had impermissibly purchased off other soldiers, which Howe required them to return to the Commissary of Forage.[18]

Similar to General Reed, the Pennsylvania Council continued to be concerned. President Wharton wrote to Elias Boudinot, then Commissary

General for Prisoners and named delegate to the Second Continental Congress on behalf of the New Jersey legislature, from the Pennsylvania legislature's location in Lancaster, in response to Boudinot's December 9 letter to him. Wharton again stated that he hoped that whatever winter quarters Washington selected would not leave the state "open to the ravages and insults of the enemy." Wharton also relayed his thoughts about the Battle of Whitemarsh, his concerns about the poor state of the militia, and the British capture of the Pennsylvania Militia's General Irvine.

The British Army's failure to engage in a full attack on the Continental Army at Whitemarsh and "their precipitate retreat disgraces them much." He concluded that the British Army is "not so strong as many believed them, or they wrongly expected our army would" retreat upon their approach. However, he added that the "base conduct of our militia gives me much pain, the loss of General Irvine to this State is very considerable, and he was a brave vigilant Officer. I hope the Legislature of this Commonwealth will adopt some mode that will effectually fill the battalions of this State in the Continental Service, so that there may be little or no necessity to call out the militia. I hope our troops may not retire to winter quarters and leave our country open to the ravages and insults of the enemy, possibly some opportunity may turn up in the course of the winter for our army, if they should be near the enemy to attack them, with a good prospect of success, which, if scattered, or at a great distance, cannot be put in execution."[19]

Wharton also wrote to General Potter with similar sentiments and concerns from the Pennsylvania Council. Wharton explained, "Council being very anxious to know what is passing in your quarter, as they understand you are on the West side of the Schuylkill, have ordered" an express rider to call on Potter on the rider's way to Washington's headquarters. Potter should then give the rider "any intelligence" that he "may think worth communicating."

Again, Wharton opined that the British Army's last movements have "disgraced them much." After so much bragging and boasting about their superior military abilities, "they should have attacked you—it convinces me that they are not so formidable as they have given out, or that they expected our army would retreat immediately on their approach."

Wharton closed the letter both warmly and with the realities of war, "I have several times order'd some News Papers to be sent to you for the perusal of yourself & officers, I hope they got safe to hand—some goes by this Express."[20]

While the army was in Gulph Mills, the residents and the soldiers intermingled by necessity and affinity. While the rank-and-file soldiers built huts, many local residents opened their homes to the officers. For several soldiers,

Gulph Mills was their home already, so when the army came to Gulph Mills, the soldiers had the joy of coming back home.

One of the most prominent residents of Gulph Mills was Isaac Hughes. In July 1777, he was appointed Lieutenant Colonel of the Philadelphia Flying Camp Battalion, having been a captain and a major. He was said to have been wounded twice during the war. Hughes was a prominent businessman who, in 1777, owned 81 acres of land from the back side of Rebel Hill to the river road in Swedesburg. Hughes had a working plantation on his land, called Poplar Lane, which included crops and enslaved persons. He was also a member of the Committee of Correspondence, a two-time member of the Pennsylvania Assembly, and one of the assessors of the Board of Commissioners of Philadelphia County, where his land was located. Hughes's home was about half a mile away from Walnut Grove Farm, also a working plantation in every way, that was formerly the home of Hughes's late father, John Hughes. John was one of the area's Swedish settlers, a prominent attorney, a businessman, and an active participant in the early days of the Revolution.[21]

Isaac inherited Walnut Grove, a long, rambling, two-story stone building, when John died in 1772. John Hughes[22] was a friend and correspondent of Benjamin Franklin and also a member of Pennsylvania's colonial assembly. Franklin used his influence to have John appointed as the stamp officer of the Province of Pennsylvania in October 1765, about seven months after England passed the Stamp Act, which required that persons purchase a stamp for every document to be used in trade in the American colonies. The colonists objected to the Stamp Act and its expense. The rebel group, Sons of Liberty, was organized to oppose the Stamp Act and for the general defense of the rights of the colonies. The act generated protests all over the colonies, and England repealed it in 1766. The mobs in Philadelphia threatened John Hughes if he did not resign as stamp officer. He resigned, and became more of a patriot, yet went on to become Collector of Customs in New Hampshire in 1769 and in Charleston, South Carolina in 1771.[23]

No one knows for sure where Washington stayed during the Gulph Mills Encampment, but it certainly was in someone's home. Washington had a canvas tent that he used as his headquarters and sleeping quarters while he was in the field when there were no suitable homes in the area that he could use as headquarters.[24]

In Gulph Mills, the Hughes family and local residents maintained that Washington headquartered at Isaac Hughes's properties, Walnut Grove, or Poplar Lane. Washington and Isaac were friends, as were many of the key figures in the Revolutionary War. The Hughes homes were on large plots of land that were off the main roads in the area and could be protected.

Anna Holstein, "family historian" and sister of John Hughes's wife,[25] noted in her diary that Washington stayed at Hughes's home of Poplar Lane "because the house was on a knoll across the lane from the Walnut Grove and was nearer to the Continental campgrounds on 'Rebel Hill.'"[26] The family also reported that, "After the close of the war, Washington visited his friend, Isaac Hughes, at this place, where he remained over night, and did so at various times."[27]

Others speculated that Washington's headquarters could have been "in the immediate vicinity of" the Gulph Mill, on Gulph Road, at the Gulph Creek, just yards away from the Hanging Rock. One writer noted lore that Washington stood on the rock as an observation stand to review his troops as they paraded by.[28] Because General Muhlenberg's Orderly Book included the language "The Guards to Parade at the Gulph Mill at 3 o'clock" on the afternoon of December 13, one historian opined that "if such is the case, the house which stands on the opposite side of the road may be entitled to distinction."[29] This house at the time was the residence of John Sturgis, who owned 63 acres in Upper Merion, mostly on Rebel Hill, and another 200 contiguous acres on the other side of the Matson's Ford Road in Lower Merion Township. He lived in a house across the street from the mill with his family and "a few hired hands who lived and ate and slept in the massive fireplace in the stone-bound basement of the house." There is no doubt that Sturgis's home was used as a picket post during the Gulph Mills Encampment.[30] It later became the site of a restaurant called the Picket Post.[31]

Other Gulph Mills families welcomed their soldier family members back home during the encampment and supported them and the other soldiers. One returning soldier, Jesse Roberts, was the son of Joseph and Sarah (Eastburn) Roberts of Upper Merion. He was also a relative of the DeHaven family of Gulph Mills. Family lore told how Roberts, who went on to Valley Forge with Washington, was back in Gulph Mills on a furlough with friends when he took then-child Matthias Holstein, son of Samuel Holstein, out for a walk with them, with Matthias on Roberts's shoulder. It began to rain, and Roberts turned his jacket inside out, exposing a red cloth lining. Roberts noted that an American picket soldier, who happened to see him in this now red coat, would have shot him if Roberts had not had young Matthias on his shoulder.[32]

The Gulph Mills DeHaven family was quite involved in Revolutionary War activities. Samuel DeHaven was a soldier in the Pennsylvania Line, Philadelphia County Militia, 1st Battalion, 5th Company, 7th Class. Samuel's eldest son, John, was in the 3rd Pennsylvania Regiment.[33] Both were presumed to be at the Gulph Mills Encampment.

This building, at South Gulph Road and New Gulph Road at the bottom of Rebel Hill in Gulph Mills, was the home of Jonathan Sturgis in 1777 and the site of the Gulph Mills picket during the Valley Forge Encampment in 1778. Either this building or the home of Lt. Isaac Hughes, Walnut Grove, is the probable site of George Washington's Headquarters during the Gulph Mills Encampment. (Author's photo)

Samuel's brother, Jacob, who lived in Gulph Mills during the encampment, was a staunch supporter of the American Revolution before, during, and after the encampment. One of Jacob's sons died at the Battle of Brandywine while another died in infancy. The DeHaven family asserts that Jacob lent the new United States government some $450,000 "in specie from cash realized from securities on his land, and the residue consisted of supplies furnished the Army" in 1777 at four percent interest, "through Robert Morris, the financier of the Revolution, at the head of the government's finances at the time," when the new nation was in dire need.[34] Despite various government acknowledgments of some or all of the debt, Jacob was never repaid. Part of the failure of repayment was due to Jacob's refusal to accept Continental currency from the new government because of its depleted value. Jacob was financially destitute when he died in 1812.[35] Jacob's other descendants filed a lawsuit against the federal government in 1894 to have the money returned, but it, and subsequent family lawsuits, was unsuccessful.[36]

Jacob and Samuel DeHaven's other brother, Peter, who lived in Philadelphia, supported the troops at Gulph Mills in other ways. Peter had a business with the Pennsylvania government to manufacture gun powder and manage a gun-lock factory to support the American army at his facility in the city of Philadelphia, which was later moved to French Creek, Chester County, Pennsylvania. DeHaven's factory stored arms that were sent on order of the "Council of Safety" to the Continental Army. DeHaven received $60,000 from the government from November 16, 1776 to January 20, 1778, according to the Colonial Records and Pennsylvania Archives, 2nd Series. "It is not stated for what purpose this sum was applied, though it is probable a portion of it was for the expense of [gun] powder manufacturing." Support for the rebels was a family affair. Peter's son, Hugh, "was appointed to assist his father while arms and stores were at French creek, by order of the 'Board of War.'"[37]

Gulph Mills residents Hance and Magdalene Supplee welcomed home their son Peter, who had enlisted in the Continental Army in September 1777.[38] Their time in Gulph Mills might have been the last time they saw Peter because he died at the Valley Forge Encampment.

When the Continental Army arrived at Gulph Mills, the rank-and-file soldier had to build his shelter from sticks, branches, and leaves into tent-like structures called wigwams. The tents that the army had been using were not at Gulph Mills; the majority of the tents were taken to the Skippack Road, about 20 miles from Gulph Mills, sometime during the Whitemarsh Encampment. So, the soldiers had to shelter themselves as best as they could until they could get back their tents.

The generals, however, usually were housed in the homes of area residents. An advance party usually scouted out the area for homes where the generals could stay when they arrived. So, where did the other officers stay during the Gulph Mills Encampment?

M. Regina Stiteler Supplee, a longtime resident of Rebel Hill, wrote in 1947 that Lafayette had his headquarters at an old house on the site where Mary McFarland Cutler's house "now stands."[39] This house was on the back side of Rebel Hill, where Gulph Road and the Gulph Creek wind down towards what is now Ballygomingo Road. The house was torn down to make way for the Gulph Mills exit of the Schuylkill Expressway in the 1950s.[40]

Many of those who have studied the Gulph Mills Encampment, including this author, have written that General Alexander Lord Stirling stayed at the home of John Rees at the top of Rebel Hill during the encampment,[41] based on recounts of local residents at that time. One of Stirling's biographers wrote that as Washington "moved his army the week before Christmas, he ordered

Stirling's division to Radnor Meeting House, about five miles from Gulph Mills, to shield the Continental soldiery from enemy assault, to patrol the roads in that area, and to forage." Stirling remained in Gulph Mills at least until early January, when the Continental Army was safely ensconced at Valley Forge. Stirling then joined the main army there, where he stayed at the home of local resident William Currie, referred to as Homestead Farm.[42]

Gulph Mills resident M. Regina Stiteler Supplee also wrote that "General Alexander, Lord Stirling who had charge of the outpost at Gulph Mills, spent the winter at the home of John Rees on Rebel Hill. Lt. James Monroe, later President of the United States, was an aide on General Stirling's staff" also with him at the Rees home.[43] "Monroe, who had served in the 3rd Virginia Regiment under Stirling in the retreat across New Jersey in 1776, had been one of four Americans wounded at Trenton while leading a charge against German cannon and had joined Stirling's staff as aide-de-camp in November 1777."[44]

Henry Woodman, whose immediate family hosted some of the generals in their homes during the Valley Forge Encampment, included in his 1850 book, *History of Valley Forge*, an interview with Elizabeth Rees, John Rees's daughter, who was then age 82. She remembered, as a nine-year-old, Lord Stirling living in her home, which was the home in which she still lived at the time of the interview. He always dined at the same table as the family and frequently gave them some of his own supplies, especially things that were difficult to acquire due to disruptions in trade or destruction by the British. She recalled that Lord Stirling was particularly fond of her, and when about to leave the house, he took from his breast a ribbon, to which was fastened a star, which he always wore as a badge of his nobility. He presented it to her, telling her to keep it as a remembrance of him. Rees recalled foolishly giving it away to a playmate, and she never saw it again, much to her regret.[45]

Even though it was sparsely populated, there were a significant number of other property owners in Gulph Mills at this time. The University of Pennsylvania Archives project, Mapping West Philadelphia, is a wonderful resource to see the names, and often the professions, of the landowners and the locations of their land in 1777, overlayed with the land today.[46]

Some of those property owners were Charles Jolly, Esq., whose 51 acres included the area of the Hanging Rock and the Gulph Mill; Margaret Jones, whose 24.25 acres included the area on the top of Rebel Hill where a townhouse development called "Rebel Hill" was built, starting in the 1980s;[47] Peter Matson, Samuel Colick, Amos Wilits, Joseph Williams, Andrew Supplee, Moses Yocum, Jonathan Rambo, Ezekiel Rambo, Peter Rambo,

William Crawford, John Rambo, Peter Holstein, Jeremiah Rambo, Lindsay Coates, Abraham Nanna, David Potts, William Dewees, Phillip Reese, Jonas Yocum, and John Inglis.

Meanwhile, about 86 miles up the road, in York, Washington's foes in the Continental Congress managed to pass a resolution that appointed Brigadier General Conway as the first Inspector General of the Continental Army. This appointment, which was a call to action by Washington's critics or a shot across Washington's bow, was another chapter in what was called the Conway Cabal.[48]

Conway was a French colonel. He thought that he could receive more rapid promotion in the French Army if he gave meritorious service on France's behalf in the American Revolutionary War. In 1776, he met with Silas Dean, one of the American Commissioners. He left France around December 14, 1776, with a letter of introduction from Dean to the Continental Congress "that presumed him an appointment of high rank in the Continental Army."[49]

Just as Washington needed the support of his troops and his government at this critical time in the new nation's development, the Continental Congress put an officer who had been critical and largely disloyal to Washington into a new, critically important position. This was even though Washington suggested the creation of the position.[50] This position was common in the disciplined European armies that Washington and his officers so admired, such as that of Frederick William II, King of Prussia, widely admired for his prowess on the battlefield against all odds that made Prussia "the foremost military power in Europe."[51]

However, one could say that Congress intruded on and questioned Washington's authority and leadership. Congress charged the new inspector general with the development of a training manual and the assembling of a guide to military maneuvers.

Naturally, one would suppose that there was tension between Washington and Conway in camp. It was reported that Washington tried to keep his physical distance from Conway as best as he could.

The Conway Cabal began in October 1777 when Brig. Gen. Conway wrote a letter to General Horatio Gates, fresh off the brilliant military victory at Saratoga for the Continental Army. That letter contained a paragraph that many viewed as critical of Washington. "Heaven has been determined to save your Country; or a weak General and bad Councellors would have ruined it."

The letter came to light when General James Wilkerson, an aide to Gates, visited the headquarters of General Lord Stirling, in Reading, Pennsylvania, on October 27 on Wilkerson's way to inform Congress about Gates's victory at Saratoga. After drinking too much at dinner, Wilkerson told one of Stirling's aides, Major William McWilliams, about the letter. McWilliams told Stirling, who reported the letter to Washington.[52]

On November 5, Washington wrote Conway to let him know that he had received a letter the night before that told Washington that Conway had written to Gates, "Heaven has been determined to save your Country; or a weak General and bad Counsellors would have ruined it."[53] Washington let Conway's own words land back on him.

That same night, Conway, still in camp with Washington, denied that he called Washington a weak general. He wrote that even though he thought that Washington was a good man, he believed that Washington was "influenced by men who were not equal to him in point of experience, knowledge or judgment."[54]

Conway, who thought that he already should have been promoted to General, wrote an eight-page letter to the Continental Congress on November 14 and tendered his resignation. Washington had objected to Conway's promotion to general over other American-born officers who were more senior in rank. Washington had previously said that Conway was someone "without capricious merit" and whose promotion would "strike a fatal blow to the existence of the army."[55]

Conway also wrote to Washington on November 16,[56] notifying him that he tendered his resignation to Congress on November 14. Conway said that he hoped that Washington would let him leave the main army and return to France, where he had lived since age six, was raised, and educated, as soon as possible, as there "were rumors of an impending war between France and Great Britian due to a French ship capturing 52 British ships out of Jamaica."[57] Conway implored Washington:

> I Believe; can attest that the expression weak General has not slopped from my pen, however if it has, this weakness by my very Letter can not be explain'd otherwise by the most malicious people than an excess of Modesty on your side and a confidence in Men who are Much inferior to you in point of judgment and knowledge, I defy the most Keen and [irascible] Detractors to make it appear that; levell'd at your Bravery, honest, honour, patriotism or judgment of which I have the highest sense.[58]

Conway's letter of resignation was read in Congress and referred to the Board of War on November 24. On December 13, Congress passed a resolution that stated, "The Board of War, to whom were referred the letter from Brigadier General Conway, brought in a report, which was taken into consideration; whereupon, Resolved, as the opinion of this Congress, that it is essential to the promotion of discipline in the American Army, and to the reformation of the various abuses which prevail in the different departments, that an appointment be made of inspector general, agreeable to the practice of the best disciplined European armies."[59]

The resolution went on to list the inspector general's duties, including detailing the various returns that he should order prepared and forwarded to Congress regarding clothing, arms, and accoutrements; money for recruits; the troops that were wounded, fit for the Invalid Corps, or totally unfit for service; losses sustained from troop deaths, desertions, or otherwise; and the officers, with observations about their behavior and capacity. It called for these returns to be made in the beginning and later end of every campaign or whenever the Commander in Chief or the inspector general or Board of War deemed proper. Further, the inspector general was ordered to attend to the complaints and representations of soldiers and officers and transmit their worthy petitions and grievances to Congress, and that the inspector general should not just depend on what the officers told him about the regiments but shall examine the officers in person. It also noted that the inspector general should examine the regiment's pay books to make sure they were uniform and that there was no mismanagement or malfeasance in them. Further, the inspector general was to let Congress know if he thought additional rules or measures should be put in place.

Estimate of Damages done by the British in 1778 and 1777 in Upper Merion Township as filed in the Philadelphia Office of the Board of Revision of Taxes (1868). (Courtesy of the Sol Feinstone Collection of the American Revolution, American Philosophical Society)

Finally, the resolution called for the appointment of two inspector generals. Brigadier General Conway was elected as one of them, and the other was to be elected the next week.⁶⁰

⚜

Across the Atlantic Ocean in France, the American Commissioners continued their work to build foreign support for the patriots and to manage what support they received. Commissioner Arthur Lee, who was then in the town of Challiot, wrote to his fellow Commissioners, Franklin and Silas Deane, who were then in the town of Passy.

Lee wrote that 10,000 blankets that he brought as well as "a very great quantity of Saqil and tent cloth, Anchors, Cables, Cordage and Dreggs" were ready to be shipped. Lee asked Franklin and Deane if he could order a French supporter, M. Gardoqui, to secretly purchase the ships to transport those goods. Stealth was required, because goods headed for the United States had to be secreted on ships so the British would not seize the ship. "Mr. Gardoqui has hitherto done his business with so much secrecy and expedition, that no suspicion has arisen of him nor any vessel been taken."⁶¹

While Franklin played such a role in managing the war, he also attended to the scientific pursuits that made him so internationally famous and in demand related to them. Joseph Priestly, renowned British scientist and supporter of the American Revolution, was in regular correspondence with Franklin. They shared a common interest in chemistry, air, and electricity. Priestly was most renowned for "discovering" oxygen and nine other gases, inventing carbonated water, and, like Franklin, experimenting with and writing about electricity.⁶²

Priestly told Franklin that he would continue to keep him updated on his scientific work. He also wrote, "The late news from America has contributed very much to give me this hope, as it must, I think, convince the most sanguine, that the war cannot be continued without disgrace and ruin. Still, however, I feel deeply for what your poor country has suffered, and now suffers; and I have passed many an anxious and melancholy hour since this unnatural war began."⁶³

As the Continental Army's first full day in Gulph Mills drew to a close, the night sky, no doubt, was lit up even brighter than the night before with hundreds, if not thousands, of fires made by the soldiers as they struggled to stay warm.

CHAPTER 6

Hardships at the Gulph, December 14

In the first full day where almost all of the Continental Army woke up at the Gulph Mills Encampment, the army focused on trying to settle themselves. With a day of rest behind them, the soldiers tried to ease their deprivations. Washington was now situated in his Gulph Mills headquarters, the precise location of which no one is absolutely certain. With his army successfully moved to "the other side of the Schuylkill," Washington wrote a number of letters that addressed the most urgent needs of his troops and his country.

1908 photo of ruins of buildings thought to be the headquarters of "Washington's men" during the Gulph Mills Encampment. (Courtesy of King of Prussia Historical Society)

Dr. Waldo, still ill and "with a Melanchollic Gloom, which makes everything about you appear gloomy," wrote of an active camp where "Prisoners & Deserters are continually coming in. The Army which has been surprisingly healthy hitherto, now begins to grow sickly from the continued fatigues they have suffered this Campaign. Yet they still show a spirit of Alacrity & Contentment not to be expected from so young Troops." He, on the other hand, was sick, discontented, and humorless because of the bad food, hard lodging, cold weather, and fatigue. He described them all wearing nasty clothes and eating nasty food, "full of burnt leaves and dirt" that made him vomit half the time. The smoke from the campfires to keep the soldiers warm, dry, and fed, made a bad situation worse. He wondered, "Why are we sent here to starve and Freeze—What sweet Felicities have I left at home; A charming

Wife—pretty Children—Good Beds—good food—good Cookery—all agreeable—all harmonious. Here all Confusion—smoke & Cold—hunger & filthy mess—A pox on my bad luck."

Yet, he praised the stamina of his fellow soldiers. "See the poor Soldier, when in health—with what cheerfulness he meets his foes and encounters every hardship—if barefoot, he labors thro' the Mud & Cold with a Song in his mouth extolling War & Washington—if his food be bad, he eats it notwithstanding with seeming content—blesses God for a good Stomach and Whistles it into digestion."

Even so, Waldo could not help but describe the forlorn state of the soldiers:

> There comes a Soldierr, his bare feet are seen thro' his warn out Shoes, his legs nearly naked from the tatter'd remains of an only pair of stockings, his Breeches not sufficient to cover his nakedness, his Shirt hanging in Strings, his hair dishevell'd, his face meagre; his whole appearance pictures a person forsaken & discouraged. He comes, and cry's with an air of wretchedness & despair, I am Sick, my feet lame, my legs are sore, my body cover's with this tormenting Itch—my Cloaths are worn out, my Constitution is broken, my former Activity is exhausted by fatigue, hunger & Cold, I fail fast I shall soon be no more! ...and all the reward I shall get will be—"Poor Will is dead."

The contrast between the deprivations of those in service of their country on those hillsides and those ensconced in civilian lives with their families must have been especially stark that day. Waldo wrote:

> People who live at home in Luxury and Ease, quietly possessing their habitations, Enjoying their Wives & families in peace, have but a very faint Idea of the unpleasant sensations, and continual Anxiety the Man endures who is in a Camp, and is the husband and parent of an agreeable family. These same People are willing we should suffer every thing for their Benefit & advantage, and yet are the first to Condemn us for not doing more!![1]

Colonel Clement Biddle also weighed in on the depleted and dangerous state of the troops. In a letter from Camp, Gulph Mill, to Pennsylvania Council President Wharton, Biddle warned Wharton that Pennsylvania must do more to support the troops, especially since the Pennsylvania legislature repealed an ordinance that regulated the price of goods. Biddle wrote, "the most dangerous Consequences will ensue unless some mode is adopted to secure a constant supply for the Army, which is now the greatest part on the West side of the Schuylkill." Biddle asked Wharton to get the legislature to form "some Plan to secure a constant supply, and for forming the necessary magazines in our rear, to answer this necessary purpose. The removing of all Forage between us & the Enemy is constantly attended to, but our chief Dependance must be from the Country back of us, as the Enemy have ravaged the Country below."[2]

HARDSHIPS AT THE GULPH, DECEMBER 14 • 83

Colonel Dearborn wrote, "this fournoon we are all Quiet—this afternoon a Party of the Enemys Light Horse & some Light Horse Troops came within 3 or 4 miles of us & Carried off some Liquers from a Tavern."[3]

Lieutenant Armstrong wrote similarly, yet he commented on the undoubtedly thousands of fires at the encampment, keeping the soldiers warm and cooking the little food they could find or were provisioned. But, he recorded one cheery note—the soldiers received their gill of whiskey. "Sunday 14th. Nothing more troublesome than the Smoke, & Nothg more Extraordinary than our receiving a gill of Whiskey pr. Man, Which we have been deprived of for a week or more!!" He also wrote a margin entry for the 13th and 14th: "Encamp'd at this time in Uper M[err]y," meaning Upper Merion.[4]

Part of the promised daily rations for soldiers, at least on paper, included a gill of whiskey, which amounted to about four ounces. Orders called for enlisted personnel to receive a gill of rum, brandy, or whiskey per day, along with enough salt for a pound of meat, so much flour, and a quart of vinegar to a hundred rations. The vinegar was used to staunch the flow of blood and as a preventative to ward off the disease of scurvy.[5]

Extract of a letter describing a December 14, 1777 encounter with the British near Philadelphia after taking post on a road to protect the army that had crossed at Swedes Ford, written by a captain of Light Horse in the Southern Department, to his Friend in Connecticut. (*The Continental Journal and Weekly Advertiser*, January 29, 1778; courtesy of Historical Society of Pennsylvania)

Captain Brigham wrote, "Expected to march Early But Did not march."[6]

Lieutenant Wild wrote, "We did not march this morning agreeable to the orders we received last night. Drew two days provision this day."[7]

General Armstrong, who was with his brigade at a camp on the North Wales Road near the Spring Tavern in Ambler, about 10 miles from Gulph Mills, also wrote to President Wharton asking that the Commonwealth appoint a few more brigadier generals to help the already tired and depleted army with the hard task of roaming and protecting the Pennsylvania countryside from the British. He opened his letter by thanking Wharton and the legislature for sending various newspapers for the troops, which they truly enjoyed.

Armstrong was concerned about the depleted state of the Pennsylvania troops and the demands put upon them. He wrote that while Washington and the Continental Army had "moved over the Schuylkill," he was left on the other side of the Schuylkill "to attempt covering a large country with about one thousand of our Militia; a task perhaps impossible fully to effect" because not even the whole army was able to do it.

Armstrong doubted that Howe would come out in full force to attack the Continental Army since it was winter, but that Howe would come out to "Forrage & plunder." Unless Washington split the army to have more forces on the east side of the Schuylkill, which Armstrong did not think he would, Howe could not be stopped from terrorizing that part of the country. Armstrong also asked that the Pennsylvania Council appoint one or two more brigadier generals for the Pennsylvania Militia since General Irvine was captured at the Battle of Whitemarsh, and General Potter had told

Extract of a letter from an unidentified soldier, dated Camp, west of Schuylkill, 14 miles from Philadelphia, December 14, 1777. (*The Continental Journal and Weekly Advertiser*, January 15, 1778; Boston; courtesy of Historical Society of Pennsylvania)

him several times that he could not stay on the field for the winter. He then suggested some names of colonels, lieutenant colonels, and even General Reed, to serve as brigadier generals, acknowledging "that there are but few men who can serve constantly in the Militia."[8]

In the evening on this day, a group of about 20 Continental Army Light Horse that Washington sent from Gulph Mills closer to Philadelphia to observe the movements of the British, engaged in a skirmish that resulted in the brutal death of a group of Continental Army soldiers. The Continental *Journal Weekly and Advertiser* newspaper out of Boston, on January 29, 1777, included an "Extract of a letter, written by a Captain of Light Horse in the Southern Department, to his Friend in Connecticut."[9] The encounter is described as follows:

The Continental Army detachment posted at Vandering's Mills, on the Ridge Road, which ran along the Schuylkill River. From the time that they were dispatched, this detachment changed their location late every evening so the British would not find them. This evening, their luck ran out. Someone alerted the enemy to their "strength and situation." An "internal tory" led the redcoats down a nearby road to within a mile of the rear of the patriots, which enabled the redcoats to avoid the patriot sentinels that posted on all of the main roads that led towards Philadelphia. Luckily, the detachment commander had also posted videttes about half a mile in the rear to guard the troops. At around 2 a.m., the videttes returned to the detachment and warned them that a body of the British Horse was moving down the road on the left, on their rear.

The captain ordered the men, who were already equipped for any emergency, to mount their horses, which were kept constantly saddled for just such an occasion. Before all the men could get on the road, about 100 redcoats fired upon them. The patriots fired a few shots, but "finding it impossible with about ten men to oppose a hundred," they rode off as soon as possible and took cover in a house and barn. Immediately, the redcoats surrounded them. Five men—Quartermaster Samuel Mills, Isaac Brown, John Cauncy, Ephraim Kirby, and Naboth Lewis—tried to escape, but they were quickly taken, disarmed, and stripped of their spurs and watches.

The British officers ordered the men killed, but, "notwithstanding the entreaties and prayers of the unfortunate prisoners for mercy, the soldiers fell upon them (the officers setting the example), and after cutting, hacking and slashing them till they supposed they were dead, they left them (Brown excepted, whom after most cruelly mangling, they shot) setting fire to the barn to consume any who might be in it." After they wounded Mills in several places, they spared his life, but took him prisoner. The redcoats also killed Cauncy. The patriots somehow rescued Kirby and Lewis and took them to safety.

The owner of the house did not fare so well. After cutting and wounding him badly, the redcoats shot him. "Thus, both the army and country have a [striking] example of what they have to expect from the savage cruelty and barbarity of the British troops."[10]

Also on this day, Washington seemed to have settled down a bit himself. He addressed a number of foreign and domestic matters, and he even wrote to British General Howe.

Surely, his first order of business for the day was to issue his General Orders, which he wrote from "Headquarters, the Gulph." It read, "The regiments of horse are to draw provisions of any issuing Commissary, lying most convenient to them, upon proper returns therefor. Such of the baggage as is not absolutely necessary for the troops, and all the Commissary's and others stores, are to remain on this side of the gulph."[11]

To establish better military order and discipline, Washington required, after January 1, 1776, that each regiment and company keep an Orderly Book in which his orders could be "regularly read, and carefully explained." Washington followed this process in issuing his daily General Orders. First, Washington dictated his General Orders to his aides-de-camp, who would write them down as daily entries in the headquarters' Orderly Book. Then, the aides-de-camp dictated Washington's General Orders to adjutants from each regiment, who wrote them down in the Orderly Books for their regiment. The adjutants would then take those Orderly Books back to their regiments and read them to the soldiers, giving them their daily directives from General Washington. Each company also had to keep an Orderly Book.[12]

Following this process, the Orderly Books should mirror

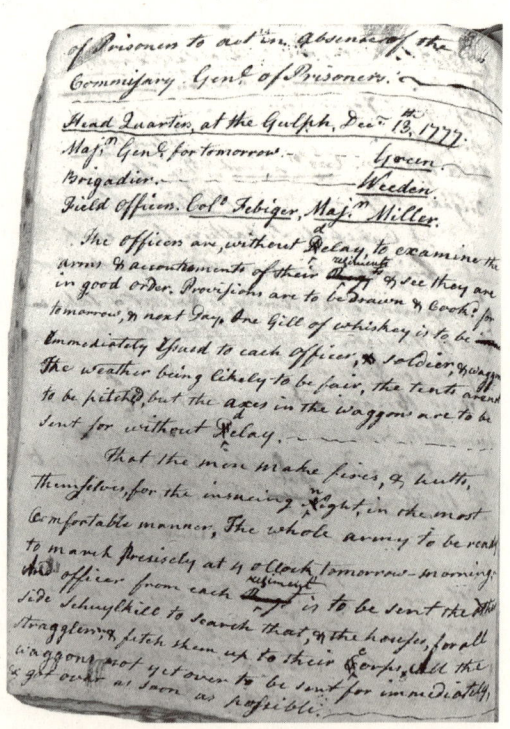

December 13, 1777 entry, Orderly Book of Brigadier General John Glover, from Headquarters at the Gulph. (Library of Congress)

each other, but some adjutants put additional information into the books, such as conditions in camp, supplies, names of and activities regarding soldiers in that regiment, and other material that the scribe of that particular orderly book thought was important, including goods other soldiers had for sale or had lost that day and posted a reward for. Some of the Orderly Books contained additional information under the category of "After Orders," which were directives given later in the day, after the first General Orders. Some adjutants' Orderly Books mirrored Washington's, but in some, the wording is paraphrased.

The language of the Orderly Books directly attributed to Washington can be found in a transcribed digital version in Founders Online[13] as well as the Library of Congress George Washington Papers.[14] Amazingly, many other individual and regimental Orderly Books have survived the Revolutionary War. These Orderly Books can also be found in the Library of Congress digital collections and some original versions in the Library of Congress Manuscript Room, whether the actual Orderly Book or in a microfiche version.

These additional Orderly Books often provide a more complete picture of what Washington's General Orders consisted of or additional information that the various regimental commanders and generals wanted to transmit to their troops. Some Orderly Books contained information that has been largely hidden from history, until now.

One of the most well-preserved, helpful, complete, and legible Orderly Books covering the Gulph Mills Encampment is that attributed to General George Washington's Headquarters, Pennsylvania, November 12–December 26, 1777. Major Richard Platt, an aide-de-camp to Major General Alexander McDougall, from New York, kept this book. He even signed it. An archivist has noted, "Because Richard Platt kept the McDougall orderly books before and after this period, it is probable that this too is an orderly book kept for McDougall's division."[15]

Major Platt's Orderly Book for every day of the Gulph Mills Encampment contains additional information. One listing is that of the "Major General of the day for tomorrow." As explained earlier, the Major General of the Day functioned as Washington's chief of staff and right hand for that day. The Orderly Book for December 14 listed the Major General of the Day for tomorrow as Lord Stirling. Platt's additional information is, "Col. Stewart is appointed Field Officer of the Day in the [place] of Col. Febiger['s absence]—Detail for Guards the same as yesterday only Gen. Weedon's, Learned's, Varnum's & Scott's Brigades give Captains in the [place] of those which furnished Captains yesterday. The Guards to parade at 3 O'Clock this afternoon."

So, the soldiers were getting back to their routines as Washington sought to maintain regular order. Platt's Orderly Book did not include General Orders for December 13, perhaps because that was the day that he was on the move into Gulph Mills, the same as Washington. However, Platt's Orderly Book noted on December 12 that he was at "Head Quarters at the Gulph," while the General Orders attributed to Washington noted that he was still at Head Quarters at Swedes Ford.[16]

Washington wrote to Richard Peters, a Philadelphia lawyer who was then a member and Secretary of the Board of War. Washington's chief concern focused on the need for clothing for his men and the need to recruit more soldiers. Washington explained that he had sent officers to surrounding communities "to make collections" and "impress what the holders would not willingly part with," essentially to forage for clothes. However, Washington gave the officers warrants to give to those private persons that they could later submit to the Clothier General for payment of what was taken. Yet, the Commonwealth of Pennsylvania was one step ahead of Washington. It had already begun collecting clothes from private citizens, so Washington recalled his officers.

Pennsylvania's legislature had already directed the commissioners of the Pennsylvania Council of Safety, who were appointed in October and November, to remind Washington that "a Collection of Cloathing" was now being made in the state. This is another example of the intricate and intertwined role of the Pennsylvania government and its citizens with the Continental Army.

Washington added, "I shall direct Genl Armstrong who remains upon the East Side of Schuylkill to endeavor to find out what Leather is tanned in & about Germantown and to have it removed. I am informed that it will be needless to remove what is half tanned, for if it freezes it will be spoiled."[17]

Again, Washington focused on removing provisions from between the main army and the British. He wrote that he had directed the Muster Master General to muster Colonel Nicola's Corps of Invalids for this purpose. "Docr Shippen has requested me to allot them to Guard the Hospitals, and if there is no other duty assigned to them I don't know how they can be better employed."[18]

In the rest of his letter to Peters, Washington addressed the continued, troubling shortage of soldiers and weapons. He explained that he gave a leave to Colonel William Richardson, of the 5th Maryland Regiment of the Maryland Line, to return to his plantation in Gilpin Point, Talbot County, on Maryland's Eastern Shore, to attend to his health.

However, Washington stated that he could not spare Richardson's battalion. One reason was because Washington had granted furloughs to the soldiers in the nine longest-serving Virginia regiments, whose enlistments would have expired in February. Washington thought that the rest the soldiers got during the furlough would prompt them to reenlist. Then there were the Connecticut and Massachusetts troops who were drafted for eight months and scheduled to leave at the end of December. "These will weaken us more than is proper considering the Resolution of taking a position for the winter near the Enemy for the more effectual covering of the Country."

Still, Washington was unsure exactly how many men he had and how long they were staying. He explained that he had ordered a strength return, which is a detailed report, of the exact number of soldiers in the eastern regiments whose time expired in 1777. This list would constitute men who had not enlisted in the Continental Army but who had been drafted by different townships to fulfill their quota of soldiers. Further, he promised to "send up a proper officer to train and take command of the Recruits at York," Pennsylvania.

Another person who had left camp was the Judge Advocate. Washington agreed to send Peters several court martials that the Judge Advocate left for forwarding. Apparently, Peters had asked for certain court martial records, including that of General Adam Stephens, who Washington assured him was in the packet. Stevens faced a court martial for charges of drunkenness and abandonment of his command during the Battle of Germantown in October 1777, where soldiers under his command engaged in "friendly fire" and shot other Continental Army soldiers. Stephens pushed for a court martial to clear his name. However, he was found guilty of "unofficerlike behavior, in the retreat from Germantown, owing to inattention, or want of judgment; and that he has been frequently intoxicated since in the service, to the prejudice of good order and military discipline."[19] Stephens's court martial was the only one that resulted in a "general grade officer's immediate discharge from the Continental Army."[20]

Washington explained to Peters that he knew "that vast quantities of public Arms and stores are carried off by the Militia." However, Peters's recommendation to appoint an inspector general "would not remedy it in the least." Washington wrote that the "Mischief is not done by those who are regularly discharged, but by those who desert before the Expiration of their time and carry away their Arms" and such. A much more effective solution, Washington proposed, was "for the States to pass laws, imposing a certain penalty upon an Man who shall have any Arms, Accouterments or other Stores with Continental Brand found in his House."[21]

Washington also wrote to Continental Congress President Henry Laurens. His letter first dealt with the question of a possible prisoner exchange between Baron St. Ouvry, an acquaintance of General Marquis de Lafayette, and several British prisoners. Washington advised Laurens that he would make the inquiries that Laurens directed in his November 30 letters to Washington about "the loss of the Forts in the Highlands & of Fort Mifflin." However, Washington, just out of the Battle of Matson's Ford and still not yet in winter quarters with his barely clothed and barely fed army, advised that the inquiry might take some time because of "the situation of our Affairs and inevitable necessity."

Having had a few days' reflection on what occurred, Washington reported to Laurens about the Battle of Matson's Ford. He recounted the battle this way: On Thursday, December 11, the army marched from their encampment at Whitemarsh with intent to cross the Schuylkill River at Matson's Ford. Advance troops had already laid a bridge across the river. The first division crossed. Then a part of the second division crossed. Suddenly, the troops saw a body of some 4,000 British soldiers under Lord Cornwallis posted high on the Conshohocken Hills and on both sides of the road that led from Matson's Ford to "the defile called the Gulph," with which Washington assumed that some members of the Continental Congress were very familiar. The Continental forces stopped crossing over.

The British did not have any special inside intelligence that the Continental Army would be crossing at Matson's Ford that morning. It was happenstance that the British were out at the Matson's Ford and the Gulph "to secure the pass while they were foraging in the Neighboring Country."

General Potter with the Pennsylvania Militia met the British advance parties. Potter and his men "behaved with bravery and gave them every possible opposition" until Potter's much smaller numbered forces had to retreat.

If the Continental forces had been at the Matson's Ford an hour sooner, or if they had some advance intelligence that the British would be there, Washington believed that they could have hit Cornwallis hard in a battle. At the very least, they could have "obliged him to have returned without effecting his purpose," or drawn out the entire British Army to support Cornwallis, which the American force's first intelligence reported was nearly out.

Cornwallis "collected a good deal of forage and returned to the City," and his foraging expedition was brutal. "No discrimination marked his proceedings—All property, whether Friends or Foe, that came in their way was seized & carried off."[22]

Additionally, Washington enclosed a letter from General Burgoyne. Burgoyne had requested that he and the 5,000 or so British soldiers who were captured when they lost the Battle of Saratoga and were then in jail in Boston, awaiting return to England, be allowed to go to Rhode Island or "some place on the Sound" and return to England from there. Or, if the Continental Congress did not agree that all of the redcoats could be moved, Burgoyne was fine with just he and his immediate party being moved. Burgoyne had made this request before. Washington thought it was impossible then and now. Yet, if Congress wanted to move Burgoyne and his immediate party, Washington would obey and inform Burgoyne.

Washington wrote that someone from Boston had told Washington that Burgoyne had a change of heart and mind as to the superiority of the Continental Army over the Royal Army. Burgoyne apparently now believed that "it would be next to impossible for Britian to succeed in his views," and that he would tell the British authorities just that when he returned to England. Consequently, Burgoyne believed that England should grant the colonies independence and recognize the United States as a nation under a Treaty of Commerce, which would define the conditions under which citizens of one country could do business in another, including the right to hold property, enforce claims, and establish tariff privileges. If true, "what a mighty change," wrote Washington.

Also, Washington advised Laurens that the Continental Congress should secure from England cash money, deposited in the bank, for the expenses the United States had incurred to feed and provide for the Saratoga prisoners before they were sent back to England. "Unless this is done, there will be little reason to suppose that it will ever be paid." Washington warned that the British had skipped out on their debts before. He proposed using the money that the United States would receive from this repayment of debts "to administer relief to our Unfortunate Officers and Men who are in Captivity."[23]

British General William Howe's assistance was needed to maintain Burgoyne and his troops. Washington wrote Howe this same day and asked him for passports to allow supply ships from the East Coast of the United States through to Boston because of "the exceeding difficulty of supplying them with wood and provisions" from the Boston area. Washington asked that the passports be blank because of uncertainty as to how many would be needed or who would command the ships. Then, thinking two steps ahead, Washington wrote, "to prevent any doubts of their being improperly used they may be countersigned by Genl Burgoyne." Along with his letter, Washington also enclosed several letters from Burgoyne, by his request,"[24] to Howe.

The Board of War wrote Washington on December 14.[25] The letter has not been found, but it likely concerned a prisoner exchange, judging by the contents of Washington's letter of December 22 to the Board of War, which he stated was a response to the Board's December 14 letter.[26]

That same day, Lt. Col. Isaac Sherman wrote Washington requesting a court martial inquiry into his conduct on December 7 during the Battle of Whitemarsh to clear his name and the reputation of Colonel C. Webb's Regiment. Sherman wrote that his men were not the problem. He charged General Reed, former Adjutant General to Washington, with confusing the soldiers in Webb's Regiment's by giving orders that contradicted the orders that Sherman had already given his men. Reed gave his orders so quickly that it was impossible for Sherman "to make a proper disposition of my Men, or [to] get to form so soon as one ought to do when fired upon by an enemy." Sherman told Reed at the time that he could not keep his own men in order under such a conflicting situation, but Reed "paid no attention to what I said." Worse yet, Sherman charged, Reed took Sherman's men into a tough battle situation, but when "the Enemy began to fire, [Reed] left the Regiment and Field" with hastiness.[27]

⚜

Across the seas in France, Franklin continued to receive a batch of correspondence from his fellow scientists. Jan Ingenhousz, a Dutch/Netherlands physician, biologist, and chemist who discovered photosynthesis,[28] wrote to Franklin from Delft. He conveyed warm greetings from Hendrik Hoogeveen, the scientist who worked on the Greek Particles,[29] and his "old acquaintances at Rotterdam."[30]

Ingenhousz wrote that what was occurring in America was "the most interesting" transaction for the whole of Europe and "the most allarming for Brittain." He remarked that Franklin was prescient when he told the British government to "let things remain in the same situation as they were before and not to force the Americans to insurrection against the mother country by measures which they could never consider as consistent with the British constitution itself." He continued, "Now Britain be convinced (but perhaps too late) that America was not to be overawed by threats nor overpowered by arms and that it lost a much braver Nation, than it did seem to consider it before." The Americans were smart enough to make a war against England an interest of all of Europe and not just England."[31]

The rest of Ingenhousz's letter was prophetic.

> The Americans will now not only become masters of that part of their continents, which is still feebly kept in their weakened hands but they will soon set up as conquerors of the new world. They will subject not only to their own empire the Neighbouring Empire of Mexico, the back settlements of the Spaniards, but they will soon look upon the sugar and

indigo islands as a necessary acquisition for their welfare and drain by a monopoly of those universally necessary commodities the most solid riches from the rest of the world. They will depopulate half of Europe from its [inhabitants] who will crowd to that happy shore where true liberty and a new wealth [unknown] in Europe will attend them. They will soon invade the British dominions in the east and take to them self the immense riches with [which] the English have derived from them. *In short America will soon become the most powerful nation which ever existed upon the face of the earth and will as a second Rome extend their dominion far out of their own country and become arbiters of Europe itself making it dependent of its will* [emphasis added].[32]

Ingenhousz also asked Franklin to reply with some charming tale or report that he could use to entertain his "Royal Mistress," a probable reference to Empress Maria Theresa of Austria, to whom he was the Court Physician and personal physician.[33] Political tales from the famous Dr. Benjamin Franklin would keep his royal mistress in good humor towards him and just might result in his being able to stay in France and visit with Franklin a little longer. And if Franklin told him something that Franklin thought was a secret, Ingenhousz reiterated that he would keep it to himself "according to your command."[34]

So ended the first full day of the Gulph Mills Encampment.

CHAPTER 7

The Army Settles Down, December 15

Brigadier General James Varnum walked through the encampment with his officers—Colonel Dunker, Colonel Green, Colonel Chandler, and Colonel Angell—surveying the condition of his troops. So did the other generals in charge of regiments. Today was the day that the weekly strength returns were due to show Washington the conditions of each regiment: the number of soldiers who were fit for active duty, the number who were sick, the number who were injured, and the number who had deserted from the last week's return.

Sadly, after much research, this author has only been able to locate one return from this date showing the true military presence in the Gulph Mills Encampment. Many archivists with whom this author has consulted, including at the National Archives, presumed that the December 15, 1777 returns from the other generals were among the many in the U.S. Department of War records that were destroyed in a fire in 1800 in Washington, DC or in the fires in Washington during the War of 1812.

The "Weekly Return of Brigadier General Varnum's Brigade" noted that he wrote it from "the Gulph." It showed the number of commissioned officers (colonels, lieutenant colonels, majors, captains, lieutenant, ensigns); the number of staff (chaplains, adjutants, quartermasters, paymasters, surgeons, sergeants, drums and fife); and the condition of the rank and file—present and fit for duty, sick present, sick absent, on command, and on furlough. The number of dead was recorded as five, deserted at two, discharged was unintelligible, and then some headings for sergeants, drum fifes, and rank and file were recorded as four. Varnum recorded 797 soldiers present for duty, 77 sick present, 372 sick absent, 210 on command, and eight on furlough for a total of 1,464 in the brigade, in the Gulph.[1]

Weekly Return of Brigadier General James Varnum's troops at Gulph Mills, December 15, 1777, with return of December 22, 1777, at Valley Forge. (Library of Congress)

Perhaps one reason the Gulph Mills Encampment has been so overlooked and dismissed is because the other strength returns from December 15 could not be found. Weekly returns for December 22 from Valley Forge and December 8 from Whitemarsh are freely available. Perhaps December 8 was deemed to be important because of the scope of the Battle of Whitemarsh, and the 22nd, of course, was the first weekly return that was filed from Valley Forge.[2]

Dr. Waldo continued to describe conditions in great and philosophical detail. He wrote that he had a meal at the home of a Gulph Mills resident, which showed how the army interacted with local residents.

> Eat Pessimmens, found myself better for their Lenient Operation. Went to a house, poor & small, but good food within—eat too much from being so long Abstemious, thro' want of palatable. Mankind are never truly thankful for the Benefits of life, until they have experience'd the want of them. The Man who has seen misery knows best how to enjoy good. He who is always at ease & has enough of the Blessings of common life is an Impotent Judge of the feelings of the unfortunate…[3]

Lieutenant Armstrong reported improvements, too. "Nothing extraordinary happened 'till [evening], for this Evening I supp'd on a Couple of good fowls & a Brothe made of the same."[4]

Colonel Dearborn wrote, "We have fine weather for the season."[5]

Washington's aide-de-camp, Laurens, wrote from the Gulph to his father, Continental Congress President Henry Laurens, on this day about the Gulph Mills Encampment and Washington's determination to "set the example of passing the winter in a hut himself." He wrote that the "army cross'd the Schuylkill on the 13th and has remained encamped on the heights on this side." He continued that "Our truly republican general has declared to his officers that he will set the example of passing the winter in a hut himself."[6]

As further evidence that Washington had not yet decided on the winter quarters location, or, if he had, he had not broadcasted it, young Laurens wrote, "The precise position is not as yet fixed upon in which our huts are to be constructed; it will probably be determined this day; it must be in such a situation as to admit of a bridge of communication over the Schuylkill for protection of the country we have just left; far enough from the enemy not to be reached in a day's march and properly interposed between the enemy and the most valuable part of this country on this side of the Schuylkill." Further underscoring the brutality of the British December 11 foraging expedition, Laurens closed his letter with, "The last plundering and foraging party of the enemy under Lord Cornwallis on this side of the Schuylkill have gone beyond themselves in barbarous treatment of the inhabitants."[7]

Colonel Angell wrote, "A fine pleasant Morning and Nothing Remarkable happened. The Baggage wagons was ordered out of Camp four or five miles and at Night we had orders for what wagons there was left to be Sent off in the morning by Seven oClock and the whole Army was to march by ten oClock to a place about Eight miles up the Schuylkill, when we was told that we was to take up our winter Quarters."[8]

Colonel Angell's writings from this day are the most remarkable and, perhaps, revealing. Did he reveal that the decision as to where to establish winter quarters had already been made? And that it was communicated to certain soldiers? Was his 2nd Rhode Island Regiment part of an advance party that was to go to Valley Forge before the rest of the main army? Angell does not mention Valley Forge directly, but his mention about the 8-mile distance between where he was then located, and Valley Forge, was about right.

Lieutenant Wild wrote, "Last night there were two huts burnt in our regt. This forenoon our regt. was mustered. Afterwards we were ordered to turn out at 4 o'clk."[9]

Captain Brigham wrote," Lay out and nothing to cover us But ye heavens for 4 nights Together I went out of Camp about 2 miles had orders to march at 1 o Clock."[10]

At the same time, the British Army stayed busy roaming the countryside. Colonel Andre wrote on the 15th that "Lord Cathcart, with forty Dragoons, surprised a troop of the Rebel Cavalry, and killed or took prisoners several of them."[11]

The loyalist Captain James Parker also wrote about Lord Cathcart's skirmish. "Last night Lord Cathcart with 14 horse surprised an equal number of the Rebels brought in half and killed the others. His Lordship was shot at by a Rebel close to him, who missed, and was instantly put to death."[12]

Parker continued to report back to England on the status of the Continental Congress and the Continental Army. He reported that the Congress ordered the sale of the estates of loyalists who ran to General Howe for protection. He added that the Congress moved from York, Pennsylvania, to Fredericktown, Maryland, which they did briefly when they heard that the British were on "the other side of the Schuylkill."

Parker reported that "debates are run high lately amongst them," as he heard that some Congressional delegates from the Northern states wanted Generals Nathanael Greene and General Gates at the head of the Continental Army. He reported on Pennsylvania delegate Robert Morris, who was born in Liverpool, England, which was where Parker's correspondent, Charles Stewart, Esq. resided. Morris lived in Liverpool until he was 13. Parker wrote that Morris "has left Congress." Morris actually resigned from the Continental Congress in 1778 to focus on his shipping businesses, which were extremely successful. Those businesses enabled Morris to use a great deal of his own money to fund the American Revolution, which earned him the name of "Financier of the American Revolution."[13]

The documented presence of General Varnum's Rhode Island Continental Army brigades, which included free African Americans like William and Ben Frank of the 2nd Rhode Island Regiment,[14] undoubtedly raised questions for Gulph Mills residents—that of the greatest hypocrisy and shame of the Revolutionary War, which was the fight for freedom for white colonists while African American colonists, including many in Gulph Mills, were still enslaved. In 1777, all of the states in the United States allowed slavery, and enslaved persons were present in all 13 states. "On March 1, 1780, Pennsylvania passed 'An Act for the Gradual Abolition of Slavery,' which stopped the importation of slaves into the State, required all slaves to be registered, and established that all children born in the State were free regardless of race or parentage.

While individuals who were slaves before 1780 remained in slavery, this Act was the first Act abolishing slavery in a democratic society. This Act became the model for abolition laws across the Northern states."[15]

A prominent local historian noted, "No doubt, before the Revolution, there was a considerable number of slaves in the county. Even the census of 1790, it should be remembered, gives to Montgomery County (the county that since 1784 included Gulph Mills) one hundred and fourteen slaves" and 440 free African Americans.[16]

Gulph Mills residents saw African American soldiers proudly serving as members of Varnum's Brigade. Some of those soldiers were free men, yet others were enslaved men who were forced to go to war by their enslavers and to fight for their enslaver's freedom but not their own. Others were forced to go to war as substitutes for their free, white, male enslavers who responded to their states' military drafts by sending their enslaved persons to fight instead of going to fight themselves.[17]

Massachusetts and Connecticut also had a number of free African Americans serving with their forces. One such soldier was Bristol Budd Sampson, who enlisted in the Continental Army and served in the 2nd Regiment of the Connecticut Line during the Gulph Mills Encampment and until the end of the war in 1783.[18] Another was Prince Perkins, also known as Prince, Negro, who also served with the Connecticut Line.[19]

Free African Americans fought with their various state militia units because the Continental Army did not allow African Americans to enlist until February 1778. Washington opposed the enlistment of African Americans in the Continental Army, as did many other enslavers. They strongly objected to arming enslaved African Americans for fear that enslaved persons would turn their guns on their enslavers to secure their own freedom.[20]

Yet, when the Continental Army desperately needed soldiers in early 1778, Washington relented and allowed African Americans to enlist in the Continental Army. Varnum vigorously argued for this when Rhode Island had to fill its quota of soldiers to send to the Continental Army ranks and could not do it based on free white men alone. The Rhode Island legislature agreed that enslaved persons could enlist, the state would purchase their freedom from their enslavers, and then the state would seek reimbursement from Congress for those costs.[21] In early 1778 discussions about the Revolutionary War and the new country, the Convention of Massachusetts Bay pleaded for whites and people of color to be treated equally. "God hath made of one blood all nations of men, whether black, white, or otherwise colored."[22]

Washington had his enslaved valet, William "Billy" Lee, with him, right by his side, throughout the Revolutionary War.[23] Pennsylvania's James Potter, who owned a number of enslaved persons throughout his lifetime, had an African American servant named Hero Wade with him throughout the Revolutionary War.[24] It is not known whether other Pennsylvanians who also owned enslaved persons, like General John Cadwalader,[25] had any of their enslaved persons with them.

General George Weedon, from Virginia, also had some of his enslaved people with him. "He had a number of private baggage wagons, conducted by his own slaves, and used for the purpose of conveying supplies for the use of the army."[26] Henry Woodman, whose family owned property, including enslaved persons, in the area of Valley Forge, and whose family housed and interacted with many of the soldiers and generals during the Valley Forge Encampment, wrote that Weedon "accumulated a large amount of Continental money, and fearing it would die on his hands, he sold his teams, collected his slaves, resigned his commission, and returned to his home, to invest his money in real estate."[27] Woodman wrote that Weedon treated his soldiers like he treated his slaves. He recalled Weedon as a man of "a very haughty and arrogant disposition" who "treated the soldiers under him with the utmost cruelty and tyranny, viewing them more in the capacity of his negro slaves." Woodman added about Weedon, "the milk of human kindness never warmed his breast."[28]

Gulph Mills had its share of slaveholders whose enslaved persons worked on their plantations and farms, including Lt. Col. Isaac Hughes, who was part of the Philadelphia Flying Camps Battalion and the Pennsylvania Militia, and who might have been allowing his home, Walnut Grove Farm, to be used as Washington's headquarters.[29]

Isaac Hughes had at least three enslaved persons at his plantation in December 1777. Isaac inherited three enslaved persons from his father, John, when he died in 1772. Hughes's relative, Anna Holstein, wrote about Isaac in her history of the Holstein Family. In the "Account of Sundries Left By John Hughes at his Plantation" for the use of his son, Isaac, "There is also two live Negro Men and Negro women & two Negro Children Left on the Place. Negro Man Jack and his wife Dinah He gives to his son Isaac."[30] The Inventory of the personal estate of John Hughes listed "one negro man—30 [pounds sterling value]" and "one negro woman 50 [pounds sterling value]." Endorsed on the back in John Hughes's handwriting, related to the estate of Catherine, his wife, listed under "Catherine's Effects" is "My Negro Man, Peter, his wife, and child 1 ½ years old called Harriott." Note that these enslaved persons, like most, were not given the dignity and personhood of a last name.

Jack and Dinah were still enslaved by Isaac Hughes when he died in 1783. The inscription on Hughes's tombstone gives him the oxymoron of "a humane master."[31] His will, which was probated on May 13, 1783, showed among the inventory, with old farm tables, paper, a couch, a number of bottles, bushels of wheat and rye, an old cart, 11 acres of grain in the ground, "Two Old Negroes Jack & Dinah—value 500 and a Negro Boy Pompey—value 4000." Hannah Hughes listed as expenses for the estate, for "my Negro Man Peter, his wife, and a child of 1 ½ year old called Harriott."[32]

One of the most notorious slaveholders in Gulph Mills, apparently, was Richard Bevan, whose great-grandfather, John, was one of the original settlers

"An account of Sundries," including five enslaved persons, left at his death by Gulph Mills resident John Hughes at his plantation, Walnut Grove, for the use of his son Isaac, who went on to become a lieutenant colonel in the Pennsylvania Militia. (John Hughes and Isaac Hughes papers, courtesy of the Historical Society of Pennsylvania)

in the Welsh Tract area of Gulph Mills, Upper Merion Township.[33] Bevan advertised "in the Pennsylvania Gazette of July 24, 1751, that he had for sale, 'near the Gulf Mill,' a likely negro-man, about thirty years of age, fit for town or country business. Also a negro-girl, about fifteen years of age.'"[34]

Some enslaved people in Gulph Mills took their own freedom. *The Pennsylvania Gazette*, the most widely read paper in the Commonwealth, included many ads for runway enslaved persons. At least one enslaved person ran away from Richard Bevan. The ad read:

> Runaway from Richard Bevan, of Upper Merion, in the county of Philadelphia, on the 23d of April last, a negroe man, named Frank, of short stature, can speak good English, and is mark'd with the small pox: Had on when he went away, a light coloured old homespun

cloth breeches, with mohair buttons, an old felt hat, neither shoes nor stockings; but as it is thought he has got money with him, he may get other apparel, change his name, or say he is free, as he is a lying, artful fellow, and has done the like before. He formerly belongs to William Macneell of Philadelphia. Whoever takes up the said negroe, and brings him to or secures him, so that his master shall have him again, shall have Twenty Shillings reward, paid by RICHARD BEVAN. N. B. As he may attempt to go to sea, all matters of vessels are desired not to take him.[35]

Enslaved persons in Gulph Mills likely saw more African American soldiers in December than at any other time in their lives. Yet, they lived an awful dichotomy every day, surrounded by freedom fighters who denied their own freedom. Certainly, they encountered free African Americans in their daily lives, too, because of the anti-slavery beliefs of many of the Pennsylvania Quakers. Pennsylvania had more free African Americans than any of the other colonies. However, to see so many African Americans in whatever uniforms they wore, fighting for freedom alongside the white soldiers, must have raised questions.

Some of the other African Americans who also encamped in Gulph Mills included Agrippa Hull, "orderly to General John Paterson of the Massachusetts Line. At Paterson's side, Hull witnessed the surrender of British General John Burgoyne at Saratoga, New York, endured the winter of 1777/78 at Valley Forge, Pennsylvania and was part of the battle at Monmouth Courthouse, New Jersey in June 1778."[36] It is not known for certain that Pennsylvania's own Ned Hector, a hero at the Battle of Brandywine,[37] was at the Gulph Mills Encampment. Hector, who was formerly enslaved by Isaac Potts, the owner of the Valley Forge and whose home Washington used as his headquarters during the Valley Forge Encampment, lived in the town of Conshohocken, directly at the base of the Matson's Ford, on the east side of the Schuylkill River. Hector was part of the Continental Army until 1780, and those who have studied his life believe that it is probable that Hector stayed at his Conshohocken home during the Gulph Mills Encampment but, since the home was only directly on the other side of the Schuylkill, occasionally interacted with and assisted the army when he could.[38]

Undoubtedly, many of the African American soldiers fought also for the freedom of enslaved African Americans, hoping that their military service for their country would convince their white enslavers that African Americans should be free. Yet, the country that these men fought for did not end slavery until the Emancipation Proclamation of 1863 and when the 13th Amendment to the U.S. Constitution was passed in 1865. There is no question that the nation owes a heavy debt of gratitude to these patriots of African American descent who fought in the Revolutionary War.[39]

At camp headquarters, Washington's General Orders for the troops related to baggage.

"A field officer from each brigade, is to inspect immediately, all of the men of his brigade, now with baggage, and take from thence, to their brigades, every man who is able to do duty in the line—Major Sneed is (till further orders) to take charge of the men remaining after this for the baggage guard, and report any who are left with the baggage contrary to this order."

(Major Platt's Orderly Book also includes this line right after the word "order,"—"First Officer to examine into the Situation of the men with the Baggage—Lt. Col. Mead.")

Washington's General Orders continued, "After Orders. The baggage of the army is to move at seven, and the whole army at ten o'clock, tomorrow morning, in such routes and order, as shall be previously directed."[40]

It is unclear to what the "After Orders" refer. Perhaps the whole army was to march around the Gulph Mills Encampment to stay ready? Or, was the army to march in various routes around the area to watch the British from various locations? Or, did it mean that Washington meant to march the whole army into winter quarters the next day, perhaps disguising his intentions to prevent spies from communicating his plans to the enemy?

Major Platt's Orderly Book showed that Lord Stirling was the Major General of the Day. It also contained additional information about the guards. "Detail of Guards to parade at 9 O'Clock tomorrow Morning, only the 1st Maryland, 2nd Pennsylvania, and General Maxwell's Brigades to furnish Captains instead of the Brigades which gave them yesterday."[41] So, the soldiers were certainly kept active and ready at the Gulph Mills Encampment.

Washington also issued "Orders to Commissaries and Quartermasters," directing them to follow the Continental Congress's December 10 resolution, which Washington enclosed, to increase foraging to support the army rather than looking towards the Continental Congress to provide provisions. He particularly directed the soldiers to forage in Bucks, Chester, and Philadelphia counties in Pennsylvania, the nearby counties in New Jersey, and in Delaware. If they could not bring in all of the forage, stock, provisions, grain, and supplies to the Continental Army, they were ordered to move them to a secure location elsewhere and keep good records of what was stored so that the Continental forces could pay "a reasonable and equitable compensation for the same" to the disaffected inhabitants.[42]

Ever the obedient and politic general, Washington directed his army to follow its governing body. However, Washington was not too happy with the Continental Congress's resolution. His starving army already put their best efforts into foraging, all the while as they tried to exercise some humanity for local residents. A perturbed Washington wrote to Continental Congress President Henry Laurens.

> Congress seems to have taken for granted a fact that is really not so. All the Forage for the Army has been constantly drawn from Bucks & Philadelphia Counties & those parts most contiguous to the City, insomuch that it was nearly exhausted, and entirely so in the Country below our Camp. From these too, were obtained All the Supplies of Flour that circumstances would admit of. The Millers in most instances were unwilling to grind either from their disaffection or from motives of fear. This made the Supplies less than they Otherwise might have been, and the quantity which are drawn from thence was little besides what the Guards, placed at the Mills compelled them to manufacture. As to Stock, I do not know that much was had from thence, nor do I know that any considerable Supply could have been had.

Nevertheless, and again, likely politic, Washington admitted that he did not exercise military power as strongly as he could have when it came to foraging, primarily due to sympathy for the hardship the citizenry had already experienced.

> I confess, I have felt myself greatly embarrassed with respect to a rigorous exercise of Military power. An Ill placed humanity perhaps and a reluctance to give distress may have restrained me too far. But these were not all. I have been well aware of the prevalent jealousy of Military power, and that this has been considered as an Evil much to be apprehended even by the best and most sensible among us. Under this idea, I have been cautious and wished to avoid, as much as possible, an Act that might improve it.

Ever the collegial general on such an important topic, Washington wrote, "Congress may be assured, that no exertions of mine, as far as circumstances will admit, shall be wanting to provide our own Troops with Supplies on the one hand, and to prevent the Enemy from [doing so] on the Other." He stated that, still, Congress should know "that many Obstacles have arisen" to make foraging "more precarious and difficult than they usually were" due to "a change in the Commissary department at a very critical & interesting period."

Washington continued that he would be pleased if state legislatures, on their "own mere will" or through "the recommendation of Congress" would see "the necessity of supporting the Army" and "adopt the most spirited measures, suited to the end." The citizens are accustomed to obeying the dictates of their local government. In contrast, he concluded, "on those of Military power, whether immediate or derived originally from another source, they have ever looked with a jealous & Suspicious Eye."[43]

Perhaps because the poorly clothed and poorly provisioned Continental Army was right in their backyard and they could not help but see their forlorn state, Pennsylvania realized the great need to exert all effort into clothing and providing provisions for the troops. The Council of Safety of the Pennsylvania General Assembly issued an order that:

> the Commissioners appointed by an Ordinance of the Council of Safety, of the 8th of November last, to collect Arms, Blankets and Clothing, be empowered to appoint assistants & to use Force where it may be [necessary]; and all officers [enlisted] & military, & others are requested & commanded to aid and assist them in the Execution of the premises, and the [said] Commissioners are empowered to allow reasonable wages to their Assistants during the time they shall be so employ'd.[44]

George Stevenson, a Commissioner from Cumberland County, Pennsylvania, wrote President Wharton about several personal estates that he had seized from the British-sympathizing Tories, the debts and families that those Tories had left behind, and the now troubled people who depended upon those Tories for their subsistence. Stevenson explained that he seized the personal estates of seven people, consisting of horses, cattle, wheat, rye, oats, hay, and household goods, after three Whig supporters of the American Revolution told him that these Tories "were in General Howe's camp at Philadelphia."

The neighbors of those Tories had varied opinions of what to do with the seized property. Some felt that it must be used to support the Tories' wives and children. Others felt that the local governments should just maintain the property.

Stevenson made it clear that he had no sympathy for the Tories or their families. He thought that "they ought to be sent to General Howe's camp, to their Husbands and Parents. Why should Whig Inhabitants support the families of the Enemies of their Country?" The Tories, with their support of the English Crown, were the ones who brought on and escalated the war, he continued. So, he reasoned, let General Howe support them because "they ought not to starve."[45]

He continued, "I have been of the Opinion, from the Beginning of this war, that the Estate of every man who showed himself to be his Countries' Foe, ought to have been immediately seized; but There should 1st be an inquiry where several of those whose property was seized objected to what and how it was seized. The owner should first have to answer about his allegiances, without too much power to determine this in one man's hands." He then asked for guidance from Wharton and the Supreme Executive Council on how to proceed.[46]

Perhaps the most momentous occurrence on the 15th for the new United States was that the first state legislative body passed the Articles of Confederation. The Continental Congress passed the Articles of Confederation on November 15, 1777. The Congress sent the Articles to the 13 state legislatures on November 17, and it asked them to review the Articles "under a sense of the difficulty of combining in one general system the various sentiments and interests of a Continent divided into so many sovereign and independent communities, under a conviction of the absolute necessity of [uniting] all our councils and all our strength, to maintain and defend our common liberties."[47]

On December 15, 1777, "the Virginia House of Delegates passed resolutions that authorized and directed the Virginia delegates to the Continental Congress to ratify the articles of confederation."[48] The next day, the Articles were taken up by the Virginia Senate.

⚜

Meanwhile, in France, Benjamin Franklin continued to be besieged with requests from people who wanted him to exert his influence in the United States or who just wanted to meet him. On this date a man with the last name of "Boudet" (no first name noted) wrote from Lyons, France, about how his fortunes had taken a turn for the worst since 1770 when his partner deceived him. "Since then my misfortunes have been irreparable. I am intelligent and thrifty but, like many others, have not the luck to succeed in business; I must look elsewhere. Could you get me work in the New World, or with you in any capacity? I am not a soldier, and soldiers may be what Congress needs in its service; but I have some small talents to offer any sensitive and honest patron to whom you may recommend me."[49]

So ended another day of the Gulph Mills Encampment, with so many questions still unresolved.

CHAPTER 8

Tents Arrive, Skirmishes with the British, and the Army Waits, December 16

One of the most significant days in the formation of the government of the new United States occurred today. Virginia became the first state to adopt the Articles of Confederation. The Articles of Confederation had 13 articles, just like the United States was composed of 13 states. The Virginia Senate adopted the Articles on December 16, after its House of Delegates adopted it on December 15.[1]

Virginia's Resolution read, in pertinent part:

> a speedy ratification of the Articles of Confederation between the United States of America will confound the devices of their foreign and frustrate the machinations of their domestic enemies, encourage their firm friends and fix the wavering, contribute much to the support of their public credit and the restoration of the value of their paper money, produce unanimity in their councils at home, and add weight to their negotiations abroad, and completing the independence of their country establish the best foundation for its prosperity.

The resolution continued that the Virginia delegates were "authorized and instructed to ratify the same, in the name and on the behalf of this commonwealth; and that they attend for that purpose on or before the 10th day of March next."[2]

In Gulph Mills, the army continued to skirmish with the British on the outskirts of the encampment. Those closest to Washington understood that he had made the decision to move to winter quarters, even if they did not know where the quarters would be. The soldiers continued to suffer, but, by nightfall, conditions improved.

On the British front, Lord Cornwallis sailed home to England on a personal and professional visit. His troops settled into their comfortable winter quarters in Philadelphia under General Howe's watchful eye.

All was not quiet in the Gulph Mills Encampment. *The Continental Journal and Weekly Advertiser* newspaper, out of Boston, on January 22, 1778, published an extract of a letter that a soldier at the encampment wrote on December 17.

It read, "We have been for several days past posted on the mountain near the gulph mill, and yesterday a party of the enemy, to the number of forty five, were surprised and made prisoners."[3]

Dr. Waldo described the ongoing travails, but also the good news that tents for the soldiers had arrived. "Cold Rainy Day, Baggage ordered over the Gulph of our Division, which were to march at Ten, but the baggage was ordered back and for the first time since we have been here the Tents were pitch'd, to keep the men more comfortable." With characteristic humor, Waldo added, "Good morning Brother Soldier (says one to another) how are you? All wet I thank'e, hope you are so (says the other)."

Turning to the skirmishes that went on, Waldo reported that the British were still at Chestnut Hill, in the upper northwest part of the city of Philadelphia. While the British "made some Ravages, kill'd two of our Horsemen, taken some prisoners. We have done the like by them."[4]

Private Elijah Fisher of the 4th Massachusetts Regiment made a diary entry on the 16th, but he appeared to be describing his experience of the march into Gulph Mills. He wrote that the whole army had orders to march at sunset and when it grew dark, the weather turned very stormy, snowy, and windy. The artillery had gone before the main army and "cut up the roads." Unfortunately, the rain worsened the condition of the roads, which were nothing but dirt anyway. He felt unwell and had a pain in his side that became excruciating. At midnight, they came upon a wooded area where they built a shelter to get comfortable, out of the storm. Just as they "got shelter built and got a good fire and Dried some of our Cloths and begun to have things a little Comfurteble though but poor at the best there Come orders to march and leaves all we had taken so much pains for so we marches to the Gulfemills and built us Camps till the baggage Come up."[5]

Lieutenant Armstrong recalled, "We heard the Enemies Light horse was within four Miles of our Encampmnt. and Rob'd a woman of [70 pounds sterling]—We had a great deal of rain upon which account we had our Baggage sent for."[6]

Colonel Dearborn stated, "the weather is Cold & wet which renders our Living in Tents very uncomfortable—11 Prisoners were Brought in to Day."[7]

Lieutenant Wild noted, "We had orders to march at 10 o'clk. We did not march this day, but stayed in our huts all day. It rained very steady all day."[8]

Captain Brigham recorded, "on Tuesday 16th morning Lay Cold Last [night] had a Rainy Day and Did not march had a uncomfortable Day and Lay on ye wet Ground had News that Part of Capt [Tallmadge's] Company was Taken by ye Enemy Light Hors."[9]

General Potter confirmed in a letter of this day to Pennsylvania President Wharton that he had "taken more prisoners than I had lost" during the Battle of Matson's Ford when Potter last wrote to Wharton on December 15. Today he wrote, "last night I sent 13 British and Hessian prisoners to the Provo Guard, and one this day."[10] Potter and his forces were stationed between the main army and the British, with orders to harass them while they also protected the main army, Potter, and his Pennsylvania Militia men; other soldiers in those advance parties fell into several skirmishes with the British in November, December, and other points during the fall of 1777 and over the course of the Gulph Mills Encampment.[11]

One of the other company of soldiers that skirmished with the British during the encampment was led by Major Benjamin Tallmadge of the 2nd Continental Light Dragoons, the paymaster and leader of the Culper Ring of Spies, who led one of the other company of soldiers that skirmished with the British during the encampment.[12] Tallmadge wrote to Washington from the Ridge Road which ran through the area of the Whitemarsh Encampment. Washington sent Tallmadge to the Ridge Road from the Gulph Mills Encampment to engage with the British. Tallmadge reported about a December 14 skirmish that he and his troops had fought in with the British.

One of Tallmadge's Dragoons alerted him that a British party of Horse was on the east side of the Schuylkill where Tallmadge's forces were posted. The informant conjectured that the British might be planning to cross the Schuylkill at some of the upper fords and come down on Tallmadge's rear. Tallmadge posted himself above the seven milestone near Levering's Tavern, guarding the two lower fords, and hopefully not being discovered that evening. Tallmadge remained near the five milestone until about 9 p.m. Then he moved up to Andrew Wood's plantation in Roxborough Township, near where the Ridge Road crosses present-day Roxborough Avenue, where he proposed to take post.

At this point, he received intelligence from a captain that some redcoats were to move that night on the Germantown or Ridge Road. Tallmadge immediately detached a party of Horse on Germantown Road, at Hunt's Hill, about a half mile away from Philadelphia to patrol near the enemy's line. Tallmadge also kept patrols constantly on Ridge Road.

Tallmadge thought that he was secure in the front and the rear where another party of Horse was posted. However, he advanced another vidette another half mile up the Ridge Road and kept a sentinel constantly by the door to communicate any alarm.

Good thing. Around 1 a.m., the vidette in the rear came in with a report that a large body of Horse were moving down the Ridge Road. "I immediately ordered the Men mounted" on the horses that were kept constantly saddled. By the time his troops got partly on the road, he "discovered their whole body close upon us."

Tallmadge ordered a noncommissioned officer to go back and hurry up the men to get on the road to join them, but before he could return, the redcoats fired on them. The armies exchanged a few shots, but it was impossible for 10 or 12 Continentals to oppose 90 to 100 redcoats. So, the Continentals took a road running directly at right angles to the Ridge Road and intended to fall into the Germantown Road, where Tallmadge thought they would find redcoats again. True enough, the redcoats chased them for a little while, but Tallmadge's forces made it back to their old quarters.

By this time those soldiers whom the British cut off from reconnoitering with Tallmadge pushed towards some woods in the direction of the Schuylkill and escaped, all except for three soldiers whom the redcoats pursued and captured in the field. The British took the soldiers' arms from them, and the British officers directed that that the soldiers be killed.

Those three soldiers entreated and prayed for mercy, but the redcoats "fell on them with their swords & after hacking cutting & stabbing them till they supposed they were dead, they thus left them (one excepted whom they shot), setting fire to the barn to consume any who might be in it." Tallmadge continued describing the horror. "They also coolly murdered an old Man of the house, first cutting & most inhumanely mangling him with their Swords & then shooting him."

The redcoats then marched up between the Ridge and Germantown roads. Tallmadge believed that his men had already captured and made prisoner the head of this group of redcoats because he had sent a party of his men to capture him some time before. Tallmadge reported that a group of redcoats passed not far from a picket of militia of about 40 men without being fired up or questioned.

Summing up, Tallmadge reported that the British's grand maneuver "from which they promised themselves the pleasure of murdering about 20 men has proved nearly abortive." That is because Tallmadge's casualties amounted to one man killed and two badly wounded. He reported that the quartermaster to his troops was missing, but because he was with him and began to move off with part of Tallmadge's party, Tallmadge hoped that he probably fell off his horse, but escaped. Tallmadge was certain that he had not been killed but hoped, if he was missing, that he had been taken prisoner.

Finally, Tallmadge told Washington that the last account he got from his informant was that the British were soon to move on Germantown or Frankfort roads. But, not to worry. "As there is no Guard on the Germantown Road, I shall keep a Piquett on this night."[13]

Major General Armstrong, from his current camp near Spring Tavern, Pennsylvania, again had time to write to Pennsylvania President Wharton at length about Washington's genius and the sub-par, yet unfairly maligned, battle skills of the Pennsylvania Militia, especially in its not preventing the capture of Brigadier General James Irvine at the Battle of Whitemarsh. Armstrong was beside himself.

He wrote that the British Army's unexpected retreat from Chestnut Hill was not because of their lack of strength, but it was a prudent choice. Washington's "well-chosen ground & respectable Army presented to them a formidable front, which, had they attacked, must to them have been fatal." The British did not dare risk a circuitous march to get around to the rear of the Continental forces and attack from there because the American army must have cut them off. The British boasted about their superiority, but their retreat took off "the glitter of their Arms." Nor were the British "disgraced by their low Cruelty & philandering spirits."

No one more than he "resented" the "infamous conduct of the militia" that were in reach of General Irvine when the British shot his horse out from under him, and he fell to the ground. Yet, Armstrong added, very few of the militia men said that they saw Irvine on the ground, and whether they did or not, they were all apologetic. While Armstrong wrote that too many militia were "a Scandal to the Military profession," a nuisance in service, and a deadweight on the public, he also noted that it was equally true that taken as a body, the militia gave the service that was indispensable to the states and to the Continental Army. Armstrong explained that the militia constantly mounted guards, formed pickets, performed much occasional labor, and patrolled the roads that led to the enemy day and night. If you looked at the militia's raw numbers compared to the Continental Army soldiers, he stated, the militia had "taken a number of prisoners, brought in deserters, suppressed Tories, prevented much intercourse betwixt the disaffected & the Enemy," and met and skirmished with the enemy as early and as often as others.

Except for the Battle of Brandywine where little went their way, the militia have had a "proportional share of success, hazard, & loss of blood." Armstrong hated to make comparisons but did so to show Wharton that he had only received "partial representation" of the Pennsylvania Militia. These people unfairly judged the militia from what happened in a single action, "and still worse, who braved the whole with the infamous conduct of only a part, when others of the same body & on the same occasion have fully evinced their bravery." Although some men acted cowardly at Whitemarsh, enough acted with such skill and bravery that the British Army had to use nine wagons to carry off their wounded, and there were at least two graves found at the site of that skirmish.

Those militia who fought with General Potter, even though they had to retreat, "must have done the Enemy some damage." Potter wrote Armstrong that he "had five men killed, Ten wounded & Ten made prisoners, but a greater number missing."

Moving on, Armstrong wrote that Washington and the whole army had already taken their "winter position" in Chester County. (This was not exactly true since Gulph Mills was in Philadelphia County.) However, with the whole army on the west side of the Schuylkill, Armstrong wrote that the British now had easy access to the resources of Philadelphia and Bucks County on the east side of the Schuylkill. The only detriment to the British were the few militia that Armstrong already had, plus Captain Craig's troops of about 20 Horse stationed near Germantown, and a few Light Horse from Bucks County, sent to Armstrong by Colonel Kirkbride. Armstrong anticipated that "Gen. Potter's Brigade may be sent to me in the space of a week, or perhaps longer, but can make no very essential difference in a County of such extent, so many leading as well by roads without any natural impediment, except such as may arise from the Season."

Due to the wide-open east side of the Schuylkill, "the Enemy may come when & where they please, and doubtless come in force." The British might even advance so far as to take a post at Germantown.

Many impediments prohibited him from posting any detachments of foot on the Old York Road, Newtown Road, and Bristol roads, but Armstrong wrote that he intended to do so the next day, weather permitting. He opined that his only choice for the winter was between "difficult or doubtful measures, to be varied occasionally." He added that it would be difficult to supply provisions to these smaller parties posted to nearby roads. It was hard enough to provide provisions for the men that he had.

Back to the militia, Armstrong thought it a good move for states to fill their quotas of soldiers to the Continental Army with Continental troops rather than their state militia men. Armstrong urged Wharton to push Congress on this point, otherwise it will "prove peculiarly severe to whatever state is infected by the Enemy."

Armstrong asked Wharton to share his letter with General Roberdeau, a brigadier general in the Pennsylvania Militia, from Philadelphia, who also served in the Continental Congress, because he had no had time to write him. He also thanked the Pennsylvania Council on behalf of his troops. "The troops with me are much obliged to Council or the Newspapers—they are amusing & acceptable."[14]

General Washington's General Orders for the day are recorded as being direct and to the point: "The tents are to be carried to the encampment of the troops, and pitched immediately."[15] For soldiers like Waldo, as he recorded, that was a great salve and step up from hutting themselves in roughhewn lean-tos made from tree trunks, leaves, branches, mud, or whatever else they could find.

Founders Online records that General Muhlenberg's Orderly Book for the day is different than that in Washington's Orders.[16] Likewise, this author has found at least two other Orderly Books for the day that contain Washington's General Order about the tents as well as additional information. They are those of Major Richard Platt, who was aide-de-camp to Washington, and whose Orderly Book is marked as one from Washington's Headquarters, and that of Lt. Col. Joseph Storer, of the York County, Massachusetts Regiment. The question is: why and how? Is the Orderly Book attributed to Washington missing a page?

Muhlenberg's Orderly Book for the day began with a discussion of the supply of clothes for the troops. It read:

> In aid of the supply's of cloathing imported by Congress they earnestly Recommended to the Several States to Exert their utmost Endeavour to procure all kinds of cloathing for the comfortable subsistence of the Officers & Soldiers of their Respective Battalions & to appoint one or more persons to Dispose of Articles to the Officers & soldiers at such reasonable

December 16, 1777 entry in Major General Platt's Orderly Book from General Washington's Headquarters, showing additional information that is not included in the Library of Congress's Varick Transcript Orderly Books that are recognized as Washington's official papers, yet is included in other significant Orderly Books, such as General Muhlenberg's. In 1781, Washington ordered Lt. Col. Richard Varick to compile and organize Washington's official papers from the Revolutionary War. The Varick Transcripts were donated to the U.S. State Department in 1833 and to the Library of Congress in 1904. The Varick Transcript only attributes this sentence to George Washington's General Orders for December 16: "The tents to be carried to the encampment of the troops." (Library of Congress) prices as shall be assessed by the Cloathier Genl or his Deputy & be in just proportion to the Wages of the Officers & Soldiers Charging the surplus of the Costs to the United States, Congress have also resolved that all the cloathing hereafter to be supplied to the offices & soldiers of the Continental Army out of the Public Stores of the United States beyond the bounty already Granted shall be Charged at the like Prices the surplus to be defrayed by the United States.

The Orderly Book ended in the same way as Washington's Orderly Book, with the language: "The tents are to be carried to the Encampment of the Troops and pitched immediately."[17]

Platt, writing from Washington's headquarters, started the December 16 page in his Orderly Book as he usually did, noting the Major General for tomorrow, which was DeKalb, and the designated Brigadier General (Varnum), Field Officers (Lt. Cols. Brooks and Major Gilman), and Brigade Major (McGowan). Then he wrote language similar to Muhlenberg's:

In Aid of the Supplies of Cloathing imported by the Continental Congress, they have earnestly recommended to the Several States, to exert their utmost endeavour to procure all Kind of Cloathing for the comfortable Subsistence of the Officers & Soldiers of their respective Battalions & to appoint one or more persons to dispose of such Articles to Officers & Soldiers at such reasonable Prices as shall be asked by the Clothier Genl. [o]r his Deputy & be in just proportions to the Wages of the Officers & Soldiers, charging the Surplus of the last to the United States—Congress have also resolved that all Cloathing hereafter to be Supplied to the Officers & Soldiers of the Continental Army out of the public stores of the United States, beyond the Bounties already granted, shall be charged at the like forces. The Surplus to be defrayed by the U. States.

The Tents are to be carried to the Encampments of the Troops and pitched immediately.[18]

The information in Platt's, Storer's, and Muhlenberg's Orderly Books showed that Washington wanted all the soldiers to know that they would soon have tents for shelter at the Gulph Mills Encampment. However, besides that, Washington also wanted to let his soldiers know that the Continental Congress was in fact responding to just about everyone's concerns about the ongoing and constant need for clothes for the soldiers.

Washington also wrote Major John Clark, Jr.[19] on this date about allowing only certain citizens to go to the British camps in Philadelphia to get reimbursement from the British for what they had taken from them. "Altho' I would not grant permission to all those who want to go into Philadelphia to get paid for what they were plundered of, you may allow it to those on whom you can depend and from whom you expect intelligence in return. I have directed that all passes granted by you shall be sufficient for the purposes you want them."[20] So who were these people who asked for passes to go into Philadelphia, presumably to British Army headquarters, to secure compensation for what the British took from them? Perhaps it was the Gulph Mills residents who had lost so much during the British foraging expeditions of December 11 and 12. Washington understood their need for compensation, but he also wanted to get something in the bargain—anyone who got a pass to go to the British in Philadelphia also had to bring back intelligence to the Continental Army.

Washington's letter to Clark continued, "We have not at present much more paper than the sheet I write upon and not a whole stick of Wax. When I get supply you shall have part. I have given an order upon Colo. Biddle for one hundred dollars, but I am not certain that he has any Money. If he has Mr. Fawkes will Cary it to you. The Paymaster Genl has not arrived in Camp since our late move."[21]

Following up on this letter, Founders Online, in a note, also included portions of a letter that Washington's aide-de-camp John Fitzgerald[22] wrote to Clark on this date. It read, "I have just received your Note & shall forward the Letters you mention as soon as possible—the Commodities you mention are very scarce here & should be glad to have it in my power to pay you a Visit. *Tomorrow we shall move 4 or 5 Miles higher up & build for Winter Quarters* [emphasis added]."[23]

Apparently, Washington had decided by December 16 to move to Valley Forge for winter quarters, but he had not announced it to everyone, even to all of his trusted aides-de-camp. John Laurens wrote on December 15 that the precise location for their huts for winter quarters had not yet been determined.[24]

General Lafayette discussed the move to winter quarters in part of his lengthy letter from "Camp Gulph, Pennsylvania" to the Duke D'Ayen in France, on December 16. He wrote, "We are destined to pass winter in huts, twenty miles from Philadelphia that we may protect the country, be enabled to take advantage of every favourable opportunity, and also have the power of instructing the troops by keeping them together. It would, perhaps, have been better to have entered quickly into real winter quarters; but political reasons induce General Washington to adopt this halfway measure."[25]

The rest of Lafayette's letter from "Camp Gulph" includes some useful insights into the state of the Revolutionary War and the Continental Army on this day. Of the coming winter quarters, Lafayette wrote, "Whilst remaining there, the American army will endeavour to clothe itself, because it is almost in a state of nudity,—to form itself, because it requires instruction,—and to recruit itself, because it is feeble; but the thirteen states are going to rouse themselves and send us some men, My division will, I trust, be one of the strongest, and I will exert myself to make it one of the best."

The British generals had it so much easier, Lafayette wrote. General Burgoyne and his troops, waiting in prison in New York for shipment back to England, were fed and, if they lost any men along the way, they would be replaced. British General "Clinton is quite at ease in New York, with a numerous garrison; General Howe is paying court to the belles of Philadelphia."[26]

Lafayette continued in defense and praise of Washington:

> The loss of Philadelphia is far from being so important as it is conceived to be in Europe. If the differences of circumstances, of countries, and of proportion between the two armies, were not duly considered, the success of General Gates would appear surprising when compared to the events that have occurred with us,—taking into account the superiority of General Washington over General Gates. Our General is a man formed, in truth, for this revolution, which could not have been accomplished without him.

He noted, "I admire each day more fully the excellence of his character, and the kindness of his heart. Some foreigners are displeased at not having been employed, (although it did not depend on him to employ them)—others, whose ambitious projects he would not serve,—and some intriguing, jealous men, have endeavoured to injure his reputation; but his name will be revered in every age, by all true lovers of liberty and humanity."[27]

Lieutenant Colonel Angell wrote about events in camp that day but also about something strange about some local residents. The morning was cold and stormy. Despite being told that they were going to march that day, the tents arrived around 3 p.m. Soldiers hurried to either pitch them or spread them over the huts and lean-tos that they had already built. They remained in their quarters as the storm continued into the evening. This Rhode Islander got a lesson that day on "what manner Some people live in this part of the Country." Paymasters Holden and Green went out of camp about three miles to a local farmer's house, where they saw a large number of turkey and other fowls.

> They Enquired if they were to be sold. They said they were and they bought one of the turkeys and would have it Roasted, and Desired the old woman of the house to dress it for them but she said that she never saw one roasted in her life. They then Enquired of her how she did dress them. She said they never Eat turkeys nor no other fouls; but always Sold them, as they would always fetch the Ready money. So great is their love for money.[28]

From the British side, Major Andre wrote, "Seven deserters came In. Quarter Majors were employed in distributing quarters to the Troops in Philadelphia. Deserters came in daily, sometimes to the number of fourteen or fifteen in a day."[29]

One significant event of this day was that British General Lord Cornwallis left the United States to return to England. Now that the British Army, fresh with food and supplies from the brutal foraging campaign in Gulph Mills that he led on December 11, went into winter quarters in Philadelphia and the Continental Army presumed to go into winter quarters any day now, General Howe granted the request that Cornwallis submitted to return to England. Cornwallis asked to return to England in late 1776, after the closing of the New York Campaign, to check on his wife and family. Cornwallis was in New York preparing to leave when Washington surprised the British and attacked Trenton, New Jersey, on December 26, 1776. Howe ordered Cornwallis back to New Jersey to attack Washington, and they battled in Trenton, Princeton, Short Hills, and elsewhere in the Jerseys. After those Jersey battles, Cornwallis's Light Infantry assumed major roles in the Philadelphia Campaign battles in Brandywine, Germantown, Ft. Mercer, Whitemarsh, and Matson's Ford. Finally, Howe thought that he could spare Cornwallis. Further, the British King George wanted Cornwallis back in England so that Cornwallis could give the King a first-hand account of the progression of the Revolutionary War.[30]

Hessian soldier Captain Johann Ewald wrote on the 16th, "Today Lord Cornwallis boarded ship to travel to England, whither he had been called by the King, presumably to learn from him the true account of the two campaigns. I was fortunate enough to receive from him the following letter." The letter read, "Philadelphia 16. Dec. 1777. Sir. I cannot leave this country without desiring you to accept my best thanks for your good services during the two Campaigns in which I have had the honour to command the Hessian Chasseurs. If the war should continue, I hope we shall again serve together. If we should be separated, I shall ever remember the distinguished merit and Ability's of Captain Ewald."[31]

Also on this day, the Continental Congress received the full report of the Continental Congress Camp Committee and read it into the record. It provided more detail than the letter that the Committee wrote to and left with Washington on December 10. It was quite instructive about the Committee's full concerns about the possible winter campaign, winter quarters, and the war in general. Because of that, it follows here in full:

> The committee appointed to repair to the camp, having returned, made a report, which was read:
> The Committee appointed to repair to the army and confer with General Washington on the best and most practicable means of carrying on a Winter's Campaign with vigor and success, and with his concurrence to direct every measure which circumstances might require for promoting the public service, have attended that business, and beg leave to report:
> That your committee arrived on the 3d instant at White Marsh, where the Army was then encamped, and communicated to the General the resolution of Congress respecting their appointment, and were informed by him that he would attend them on the Business

the next day, and at the same time received from him for their perusal sundry Letters containing the Opinions of his General Officers "Respecting the propriety of an attack upon the Enemy's lines;" and also other Letters declaring their sentiments on the "necessity of putting the Troops into Winter Quarters, and the properest place to canton them;" which several opinions of the Officers on the questions stated were formed and given in previous to the arrival of your Committee.

That your Committee suggested to the General the necessity of resuming the consideration of a Winter's Campaign, and of calling in large reinforcements of the Militia, to render it vigorous and successful; which induced the General again to require the Opinions of his General Officers on these points; and several of their opinions in writ-ing being given in before, and others during the Conference with the General on the 4th were likewise laid before your Committee.

That it appears to your Committee from a perusal of the said Letters, that the General Officers considered an attack upon the Enemy's Lines and Redoubts as an enterprize too dangerous, and not to be hazarded but in case of absolute necessity.

That the numbers of the Enemy nearly equaled that of the continental Army, which should be double to attempt to force lines defended by veteran Troops.

That an attack on the City over the Schuylkill, when frozen, supported by a large Body of Militia, was liable to the same objections, as it was probable the Enemy would be informed of the design, and form a line of redoubts round the City as soon as they knew such an attack was meditated.

That the season was too far advanced to call in large Bodies of Militia in time from the distant States to cooperate with the continental Army, and sufficient force could not be collected from the adjoining States. That if a sufficient aid of Militia could be collected in time, it was doubtful whether they could be furnished with provisions and Forage, and brought to act in concert with the regular Army.

That the Officers and Soldiers were badly cloathed, the former in general discontented with the service, and averse to a Winter's Campaign.

That it would be most advisable to retire to Winter Quarters, to afford time for reforming the army, refreshing and disciplining the Troops, that they might take the Field early in the spring in health and vigor, and thereby prove more essentially useful to the American cause than by being exposed to a Winter's Campaign at the risque of a certain evil for an uncertain good.

Your Committee after deliberating upon these Reasons, hearing the sentiments of the General upon the subject, and considering the want of necessary Cloathing and Blankets to enable the Troops to endure the hardships of a Winter's Campaign, the uneasiness that on many accounts prevailed among the Officers, their indifference to the Service, and universal aversion to continue in the Field during the Winter, the shortness of time for calling forth a Body of Militia properly equipped to aid the continental Army, the want of military apparatus to invest and make regular approaches to the city, and the evil consequences that would result from raising the expectations of the continent without accomplishing the purpose, the great expense that would be incurred and the certain prejudice to the recruiting Service, came to the following resolutions, which they inclosed to the General in a Letter, a copy of which is hereunto annexed.

That an attempt on Philadelphia with the present Force under Gen' Washington, either by storming the Lines and Redoubts, crossing the Schuylkill, or by regular approaches to the City, is an enterprise under the circumstances of the Army attended with such a variety of difficulties, as to render it ineligible.

That the Season is so far advanced as to render very precarious large reinforcements of Militia from the distant States to cooperate with the regular Army in any attempt across the Schuylkill upon the Ice, and it is apprehended sufficient reinforcements cannot be obtained from the neighbouring States.

That there being time for Congress to determine on the properest mode of reinforcing the Army before the intended enterprise can be carryed into execution, it is expedient for the Committee to adopt measures for that purpose.

That until sufficient reinforcements can be obtained, such a post should be taken by the Army as will be most likely to overawe the Enemy, afford supplies of provision, wood, Water, and Forage, be secure from surprise, and best calculated for covering the Country from the ravages of the Enemy, as well as provide comfortable Quarters for the Officers and Soldiers.[32]

⚜

In France, Ben Franklin continued to impress as he worked on behalf of the new nation. Henri-Maximilien Grand, a French banker who supported the American cause, wrote Franklin from Nantes, France, pouring on the praise and seeking praise from Franklin.

Grand wrote that in the same manner as people brag about lodging in the house of a king or other royalty of their connection to them, even if tenuous, he would forever boast that the great Franklin called him "your affectionate friend, even if he was" not deserving of that honorable name. Nevertheless, this very pleasing illusion, he continued, was dear to him. "The Honour you do me on the one Hand, and the very great Service you render me on the other by your Letters of Recommendations, are Obligations, Sir, that will not be easily blotted out from my Memory; but that will on the contrary raise in me the greatest Desire of proving you the grateful Sense I have of them." Grand ended the letter with more praise in his salutation: "Nothing can equal the Sentiments of Veneration with which I have the Honour to be Sir Your most obedient and most devoted Servant."[33]

Silas Deane, who was in Paris, wrote Franklin that he wanted to meet with him to handle several business matters. Deane told Franklin that Marechal Maillebois gave him a memoir of Millin de la Brosse, who had been imprisoned in England for sending dispatches to the Continental Congress last September. Deane asked Franklin to relay to Maillebois, so that he did not think that Deane ignored him, that, at Deane's request, de la Brosse would be meeting with him in the next few days. As if to tempt Franklin to come and attend to pressing business, Deane closed his letter, "I have a Fire on the first Floor…"[34]

Lastly, Captain John Young, a member of the Continental Navy, wrote to the American Commissioners from Nantes, which was France's largest port. Young wrote, "I received Yours of the 2d instant from Mr. Mahlon [Moylan] along with the Dispatches for Congress which I will secure ready for Sinking in case of danger according to Your Orders. When the dispatches came to hand I was all clear for sea, and now only wait for a favourable opportunity." Apparently, the American Commissioners were disturbed by the delay in Young's vessel being able to safely leave France for the United States.[35]

So, December 16 ended with the soldiers now in tents, and the United States one step closer to having in place its first governing document, the Articles of Confederation.

CHAPTER 9

Washington Announces the Move to Winter Quarters, December 17

When all is said and done about pivotal days in the Revolutionary War, December 17, 1777, is one. Two of the major questions looming over the Continental Army, the new nation, and the Revolutionary War were resolved on this day.

First, Washington announced to the troops, in stirring and inspirational prose, his decision to move the Continental Army into winter quarters. He did not state the exact location of the winter quarters, only that they would "be in the neighborhood of this camp." However, he eloquently explained to his troops why they were going into winter quarters, how they would live when they arrived there, and what he hoped to accomplish in those cold winter months. Importantly, he gave his troops heartfelt thanks and recognition for their service and sacrifice.

Second, the French King Louis XVI announced his decision, to the delight of the American Commissioners, that France would henceforth officially recognize the United States as a nation and would begin the negotiation of treaties that so stated.

These two events provided great stability and inspiration to the Continental Army, the Continental Congress, the Pennsylvania General Assembly, the people of Pennsylvania and the other 12 states, France, and the other countries that had been watching the Revolutionary War, largely cheering on the United States. These two events contrasted with the unease and uncertainty that was shown in other events and writings of the day. However, as word of these two events made its way around the globe, the new United States's path forward became even more clear.

First, Washington's momentous General Orders:

> The Commander in Chief with the highest satisfaction expresses his thanks to the officers and soldiers for the fortitude and patience with which they have sustained the fatigues

of the Campaign—Altho' in some instances we unfortunately failed, yet upon the whole Heaven hath smiled on our Arms and crowned them with signal success; and we may upon the best grounds conclude, that by a spirited continuance of the measures necessary for our defence we shall finally obtain the end of our Warfare—Independence—Liberty and Peace—These blessings worth contending for at every hazard—But we hazard nothing. The power of America alone, duly exerted, would have nothing to dread from the force of Britain—Yet we stand not wholly upon our ground—France yields us every aid we ask, and there are reasons to believe the period is not very distant, when she will take a more active part,[1] by declaring war against the British Crown. Every motive therefore, irresistibly urges us—nay commands us, to a firm and manly perseverance in our opposition to our cruel oppressors—to slight difficulties—endure hardships, and contend every danger—The General ardently wishes, it were now in his power, to conduct the troops into the best winter quarters—But where are those to be found? Should we retire to the interior parts of the State, we should find them crowded with virtuous citizens, who, sacrificing their all, have left Philadelphia and fled thither for protection. To their distresses humanity forbids us to add—This is not all, we should leave a vast extent of fertile country to be despoiled and ravaged by the enemy, from which they would draw vast supplies, and where many of our firm friends would be exposed to all the miseries of the most insulting and wanton depredation—A train of evils might be enumerated, but these will suffice—These considerations make it indispensably necessary for the army to take such a position as will enable it most effectually to prevent distress & to give the most extensive security; and in that position we must make ourselves the best shelter in our power—With activity and diligence Huts may be erected that will be warm and dry—In these the troops will be compact, more secure against surprises than if in a divided state and at hand to protect the country. These cogent reasons have determined the General to take post in the neighbourhood of this camp; and influenced by them, he persuades himself, that that the officers and soldiers, with one heart, and one mind, will resolve to surmount every difficulty, with a fortitude and patience, becoming their profession, and the sacred cause in which they are engaged: He himself will share in the hardship, and partake of every inconvenience.

Tomorrow being the day set apart by the Honourable Congress for public Thanksgiving and Praise; and duty calling us devoutly to express our grateful acknowledgements to God for the manifold blessings he has granted us—The General directs that the army remain in it's present quarters, and that the Chaplains perform divine service with their several Corps and brigades—And earnestly exhorts, all officers and soldiers, whose absence is not indispensably necessary, to attend with reverence the solemnities of the day.[2]

Since Washington did not exactly state where the army was going for winter quarters, the rank-and-file soldier was left to speculate. One can probably assume that the generals knew exactly where the army was going. Other clues led to the belief that at least one general knew in advance.

According to the journal of Hessian soldier Bauermeister, General "Potter had been stationed with the Pennsylvania and Virginia militia" at Valley Forge before the main army marched in.[3] Perhaps that is why Potter's letters since December 15 were written from Chester County, the county in which Valley Forge was located.

Besides Washington's eloquent General Orders, Major Platt's Orderly Book also contained additional information that the Major General for tomorrow would be Sullivan, with Huntington as Brigadier General, First Officers Colonel Chambers and Lieutenant Colonel Caslton; with the Brigadier Major as Day. Platt's entry contained the additional line, "The Detail for Guards the same as yesterday, only Weedon's, Learned's, Varnum's, Scott's Brigade give captains instead of those which gave them yesterday."[4]

The Orderly Book of Col. Philip Van Courtland of the 2nd New York Regiment, for December 17 also contained additional detail. At the end of his record of the General Orders, the book noted, "Detail for Guards the Same as yesterday only Weedons, Learneds, Varnums & Schott's Brigades give Capts instead of those who gave them yesterday."[5]

Other entries showed that the troops performed regular military duties while in Gulph Mills. The book included brigade orders that noted their "Adjutant Sergt for Headquarters' from the 2 NY Regiment—Cherry." It then read, "The Brigade will assemble with their Arms at Eleven o'Clock tomorrow morning at the most Convenient Place on the top of the Hill. Every Officer and Soldier will pay Particular attention to this Order." It concluded, "The Regt. to parade with their Arms Tomorrow morning at Eleven O'clock in the morning in front of the Incampment."[6]

Reactions from the soldiers to the announcement of winter quarters were mixed, perhaps because of the poor weather and conditions in which they found themselves. Colonel Dearborn expressed discouragement as to what the army would find wherever it went into winter quarters. "The weather remains very uncomfortable—our General Officers are consulting what winter Quarters we are to have, which I fear will be very Poor."[7] Lieutenant Armstrong wrote that "nothing extraordinary" happened but some rain which deterred their marching."[8]

Lieutenant Colonel Angell wrote that the troops received orders at 7 a.m. for the wagons to "march off" immediately and the troops to march at 10 a.m. "But it begun to Storm and the orders were Countermanded. So we continued in our Encampment this day and the night following."[9]

Captain Paul Brigham of the 4th Connecticut Regiment wrote that it was wet and bad for them and that last night, some of them had fits and digestive problems from lying on the wet ground. He wrote that he bought a colonel's horse to use to ride home on an upcoming furlough. He expected that the army was going to march this day but did not.[10]

James Parker, the loyalist from Virginia who served in the British Army, wrote this from Philadelphia, as he contemplated the state of the men left in the Carolinas and Virginia and his having a quieter existence as the armies moved into winter quarters. "Almost all the men from Carolina & Virginia who had any Virtue left, have come to N York & this place rather than take the Oaths of Abjuration, & Allegiance to the States." One of the men who remained in Virginia and supported the American forces was his acquaintance, Colonel Palmer.

Parker's colleague Samuel Johnston must have had a major position in Virginia, given what Parker wrote about him: "The mighty are fallen." Johnston, who was in the Virginia militia, apparently was "divested of his honors." Johnston drew lots with the other militia men, whom Parker called "rabble," to see who would be drafted to join the Continental forces. "He drew No. 1, so he goes amongst the first that is draughted from the Militia to supply the Rebel Army, a common soldier."

In further news, Parker explained that the rivers would freeze soon, which would stop the mail from getting to England, so his correspondent, Charles Stewart, would not hear from him for a while. Anyway, James did not expect to have much to report in the way of war stories since the fighting would cease with both armies in winter quarters. "Surely their Generalships with a thousand alarms...and rascalls will not have the impudence to disturb our winter entertainments."[11]

The news of the Continental Army's movements and the British Army's December 11 forage in Gulph Mills was front and center in local newspapers. *The Pennsylvania Ledger, or the Philadelphia Market Day Advertiser*, printed this article on December 17:

> By some persons come in since writing the above, we learn, that the Congress, upon hearing that part of the Royal army had crossed the Schuylkill, tho't proper to decamp to Fredericktown in Maryland, in the greatest hurry.
> Last Week a part of the Royal army crossed the Schuylkill, and having cleared the country of the rebel militia infesting those parts have returned with a number of prisoners and a large number of cattle, &c.
> We learn that Mr. Washington with his army have removed from Whitemarsh, and encamped about the Gulph mills over Schuylkill, about 14 or 15 miles from this city. We have reason to hope his continuance there will not be of long duration.[12]

Now that he announced the move to winter quarters, Washington turned to other business at hand, specifically the troops: smallpox inoculation for the troops, provision for the troops, the need to draft or re-enlist more troops, the arrival of a French shop with supplies for the troops, and even the annoyance of Burgoyne and his troops.

He wrote to Major General William Heath in response to Heath's letters of November 23 and 27. Heath, whose botched attack of Fort Independence in New York in January 1777 earned him a censure by Washington and a decision to never again give Heath the command of troops in combat, was in Cambridge, Massachusetts. Heath was in charge of Burgoyne and his almost 6,000 troops who were captured at Saratoga, now named the Convention Army after the Convention of Saratoga that set the terms for the surrender and disposition of Burgoyne's troops.[13]

Washington ordered Heath to ensure that all new recruits who were intended for General Lee and General Jackson's regiments were inoculated for smallpox as soon as they enlisted and certainly before they joined the main army at camp. Washington wrote that he was "not less surprised than mortified" that men intended for Lieutenant Colonel Smith's unit were rendered unfit for duty because, by the time they reached the camp, so many had smallpox that he sent all of the men to the hospital.

Washington confirmed that he sent General Howe the letters that General Burgoyne wrote to him, which were delivered through Heath. Ever politic, Washington also stated that he did not think that he had the authority to grant Burgoyne's request to leave the prison before his army did. However, Washington made it clear that he opposed Burgoyne's request. "I think it would have been highly improper to have allowed him the liberty of visiting your Seaport Towns—a man of his sagacity and penetration would make many observations upon situations & c. that might prove detrimental to us in the future." Washington advised Heath that, in the future, if he had decisions that had to be made regarding Burgoyne and his troops, Heath should write Congress directly "as they alone must determine in all cases which refer to them."

Regarding provisions, Washington wrote that Heath, from his position in New York, "felt but a small share of the inconvenience arising from the ill regulation in the Commissary's department." Washington hoped that conditions would improve soon, but confirmed to Heath that he acted properly by appointing his own persons for that purpose.

Additionally, Washington was pleased to receive Heath's December 4 letter in which he advised Washington that a French ship had arrived with artillery and other supplies. Washington called it "fresh proof of the friendly disposition of that Court towards us." Troop strength, with soldiers coming on from enlistments and leaving on furlough or enlistments ending, and the various states fulfilling their responsibilities to supply troops to the Continental Army, always remained one of Washington's main concerns.

The enlistments of some 240 Massachusetts troops expired in a few weeks, at the end of December. General Patterson had informed Washington that the legislature would replace them, but Washington was not so sure. He wrote, "Lest they may be forgetful of it, I beg you will remind them not only of the necessity of reenlisting or supplying the place of the above number, but of filling their Regiments against the next Campaign," a matter which Washington also wrote Congress about.

Washington wrote to Burgoyne to confirm that he received Burgoyne's requests regarding his and his captured troops' movements back to England. Washington advised Burgoyne that he forward his letters to Howe for information and to the Continental Congress for a determination on Burgoyne's request.

Burgoyne's requests apparently were on a lot of minds. Continental Congress President Henry Laurens wrote to Washington on this date that the Congress had considered and passed a resolution regarding Burgoyne's request to Washington of December 14 and 15. The resolution confirmed what Washington had communicated to Heath, namely that it would not "receive nor consider any proposition for indulgence or altering the terms of the convention of Saratoga, unless immediately directed to their own body."[14]

Heath's letter included even more detail about Burgoyne's schemes and machinations. Heath wrote that Burgoyne was disappointed when he received the Continental Congress's December 1 resolve that restricted his troops' embarkation to the port that was stipulated in the Convention of Saratoga. Heath told Burgoyne that "an alteration would never be allowed but he flattered himself otherwise." Burgoyne now anxiously awaited an answer to this request that he and his immediate party be permitted to leave before his troops. Burgoyne wanted to send a letter to General Pigot, the British Army officer who was in command of the British troops in Rhode Island, to order the transport to Boston, but he deferred, pending an answer to his request.

Due to the hazardous condition of the waterways in the winter, even General Friedrich Riedsel, the commander of the Braunschweiger Jagers, who fought the British, and who commanded the German soldiers at Saratoga, observed that it was doubtful whether the troops would be able to sail this winter. Heath also gave Washington the cheery news that the "purchases of Lead and Cloathing have been very successful here, considerable Quantities of both are now on the road, forwarding to you."[15]

Heath's letter concluded, "Enclosed is a Letter[16] from Baron de Steuben, who is here with two French Gentlemen."[17] Heath was referring to Baron Friedrich von Steuben, who was a lieutenant general in the revered army of King Frederick the Great, the King of Prussia.[18] Von Steuben's letter also included a September 1777 letter from Ben Franklin and Silas Deane,

> *Extract of a letter from a gentleman at Camp, on Schuyl-kill, dated Dec. 17, 1777.*
> "We have been for several days past posted on the mountain near the gulph mill, and yesterday a party of the enemy, to the number of forty five, were surprised and made prisoners."
> Several vessels have lately arrived in James River, from Nantz; among the many valuable articles they brought, are 250 pair of blankets, a quantity of coarse cloth, and between 2 and 3000 bushels of salt.

"Extract of a letter from a gentleman at Camp, on Schuylkill, dated Dec. 17, 1777," describing activities at the Gulph Mills Encampment. (*Continental Journal and Advertiser,* January 22, 1778; courtesy of Historical Society of Pennsylvania)

from Passy, France, to General Washington, where they recommended Von Steuben for service in the Continental Army. It read, "He goes to America with a true Zeal for our Cause, and a View of engaging in it, and rendering it all the Service in his Power. He is recommended to Us, by two of the best Judges of Military merit in this Country; Mr Le Comte de Vergennes, and Mr Le Comte de St Germain, who has long been personally acquainted with him." Those two gentlemen were promoting von Steuben's "Voyage from a full persuasion that the Knowledge and Experience he has acquired by twenty Years Study and practice in the Prussian School, may be of great use in our Armies. I therefore cannot but recommend him warmly to Your Excellency, wishing that our Service may be made agreeable to him."[19]

Washington eagerly accepted von Steuben into the Continental Army due to his great respect for the military skills of the King of Prussia and his officers. Von Steuben had attended the King of Prussia in all of his campaigns and also served as his aide-de-camp and quartermaster. Von Steuben arrived at the Valley Forge Encampment in February and began drilling the Continental Army in the system of military discipline to which he was accustomed. This was widely credited with turning around the Continental Army and molding them into an army that could defeat the British. Von Steuben earned the title of "the Drillmaster of the Continental Army."

The Continental Navy Board wrote to Washington from Bordentown, New Jersey. They informed Washington that they were going to conduct "with Secrecy & Dispatch" an "important Experiment."[20] The experiment was an attempt to use floating mines to damage British vessels that were anchored near Philadelphia. Those mines, which could be triggered on contact, were invented and would have been constructed by David Bushnell who, in 1775, invented "the Turtle," the first submarine used in combat, and floating torpedoes. Bushnell, while a student at Yale University, proved that gunpowder could be exploded underwater.[21] Bushnell would be assisted in this effort by Lieutenant Colonel William Worthington, of the Connecticut Militia. The Continental Army had essentially ceded the Delaware and Schuylkill rivers to the British after the Continental Army lost Fort Mifflin and Fort Mercer and because the rivers froze in the winter.

On this date, Washington also received the resignation of Major Morgan Alexander, of the 8th Virginia Regiment. Many Continental Army soldiers went back and forth from military service to their homes to assist their families. "The Smallness of my Fortune, and the confused Situation of my affairs, obliges me to offer you my commission, could my family Subsist without me, I would by no means think of parting with the honour of holding a commission in so very desirable a Service."[22]

In Pennsylvania, the Supreme Executive Council and General Assembly was apoplectic at the thought of Washington establishing winter quarters at this time, but especially winter quarters that might be too far away from Philadelphia to protect them and the majority of the citizens in the Commonwealth from the British, such as in Wilmington, Delaware; the Jerseys, or further into central Pennsylvania. Perhaps they did not know that Washington had decided on Valley Forge and announced it that day. Apparently, Washington kept this decision, as he did many of his decisions, close to his vest, so that the enemy did not find out.

Its Remonstrance of Council and Assembly to the Continental Congress, on this date, detailed the fears of the Supreme Executive Council and General Assembly. The remonstrance concerned and was against the "Proposed Cantoonment [cantonment] of the Army of the United States," and it detailed four major reasons.

1st. The army's removal to the west side of the Schuylkill with some troops posted in Wilmington left too much of Pennsylvania, particularly the east side of the Schuylkill, "in the Power of the Enemy, subject to their Ravages." The Pennsylvanians would either have to "fly to the neighbouring states, or submit to such Terms as the Enemy may prescribe."

2nd. The Pennsylvania Assembly had levied a tax of five shillings on all persons' estates, both real and personal, to raise some $620,000 to support the war for the next year. If the army went into winter quarters, especially at a distance from Pennsylvania where its people could be not be protected from the British in Philadelphia, the Pennsylvania government would never raise this money. Too many citizens were already disaffected, and only the army's presence kept them obedient to the government. If the army was not around, "the Whigs, & those who have taken the most active Part in support of our Cause, will be discouraged & give up all as lost."

3rd. It would be "impossible to recruit the Regiments of this State" if the army left the state. "Those who would be active and zealous in promoting that measure will be obliged to leave the state." On the other hand, "the Torys & Disaffected will gain strength, in many places perhaps declare openly for the Enemy." These Tories would then likely be able to supply and strengthen the British Army.

4th. The already tenuous value of the Continental currency would crash if the army left. That is because farmers would be able to freely trade with the British "where they will receive at least a promise of hard money." The assembly noted, "It is a melancholy truth, that it is very Difficult to purchase from many of our most able Farmers the necessary provisions of our Army, owing to their fear of the money."

In addition, the Council reprimanded Colonel Clement Biddle, Commissary of Forage, who wrote the Council on December 14 with his concerns about the Council's canceling of their forage ordinance. The Council stated that Biddle misunderstood the Council's ordinance because "it was only a recommendation to the purchasing Commissarys." The Council informed Biddle that prior to repealing the ordinance, they entered into a Resolve that authorized Washington to empower the Commissaries to collect provisions and forage and, if Biddle had not seen that Resolve, the Council took the liberty of enclosing another copy. The reprimand ended, "If, after the Powers that his Excellency is therein vested, the Army should be in want of Victual or Forage, the fault must lay with the Persons so employed."[23]

The Continental Congress received a letter on this day that would also enmesh their actions with the Supreme Executive Council of Pennsylvania. The enmeshment started when Owen Jones, Jr., a Quaker, wrote a letter dated December 17 to James Duane, a Continental Congress member from New York, in which he asked Duane to help him and his fellow Quakers whom the Continental Congress moved from Philadelphia to exile in Winchester, Virginia because the Quakers did not support the war.

First, Jones stated that he was unjustly accused of not supporting the United States. Jones argued that his support would have been revealed if he had been given a chance to defend himself before an "impartial jury of my Country."

Major Holmes, who had watch over the Quakers in Winchester, had just informed Jones and the other Quakers that they would be moved to Staunton, Virginia, 97 miles away, and that they would be generally confined without use of paper, pen, or ink.

Holmes also informed Jones that only Jones would be put in the county jail in Staunton because Jones sent sixteen "half Joes," which is a Portuguese gold coin, "down the Country to be exchanged for continental money." Jones argued that he was not trying to nor did he diminish the value of the Continental money by trading in his half Joes. Jones explained that he made the exchange to get Continental money to pay for items to support himself and his companions while they were in exile since the support that Pennsylvania promised them when they were driven out of Pennsylvania did not materialize. The half Joes "were an Article of merchadize in my native Country, & were bought & sold daily by persons who were esteemed good Whigs," Jones wrote.

Jones informed Duane that he would not have even written to him if he was treated the same as his fellow Quakers, but he hoped Duane would help him because of their former friendship. Even now, Jones wrote that his father had helped the American army and "does it not merit a return"? Jones's father obtained the release of several American officers whom the British had imprisoned. He even had a letter from a Captain Willis, a relative of George Washington, "acknowledging my father's kindness in obtaining his Liberty." In the conclusion of his letter to Duane, Jones asked that his letter go before the Continental Congress at the same time that the Congress received and considered the Joint Remonstrance of the other Quakers.[24]

Jones also enclosed a copy of his letter to Duane in a December 18 letter to his "respected friend," Timothy Matlack, Secretary to the Supreme Executive Council of Pennsylvania. Jones asked Matlack to "lay the copy of my letter to Duane" before the Supreme Executive Council." Jones wanted the council to be fully informed of the "cruel & for such a crime unparalleled situation" that he and other Quaker prisoners were subjected to in Winchester. Jones asked Matlak to "back my request with thy Influence," and stated that he hoped Matlack would "take the same pleasure in rendering me a service, as be assured I should do to thee, were it in my power."[25]

⚜

Finally, on this day, the French King, Louis XVI, recognized the United States as an independent nation and directed his ministers to negotiate a Treaty of Amity and Commerce with the new country. This is after over a year of France providing informal aid to the new country against a common archenemy, Britain. The formal treaties would be signed in 1778, but Ben Franklin memorialized the significance of this day in a letter from the American Commissioners to the Continental Congress's Committee for Foreign Affairs on December 18 from Franklin's home in Passy.

First, Franklin stated that the American victory at Saratoga occasioned "as much general Joy in France, as if it had been a Victory of their own Troops over their own Enemies; such is the universal warm and sincere Goodwill and Attachment to us and our Cause in this Nation." With that, the American Commissioners took the opportunity to "press the Ministry" to a decision on the proposed treaty between France and the United States "which had so long lain under their Consideration and been from time to time postponed."

The parties met on December 12. Some difficulties were mentioned and removed, and explications asked and given in satisfaction. The French told the American Commissioners that Spain's concurrence was necessary, but that they would dispatch a courier the next day with an answer likely in about three weeks. Because both France and Spain were ruled by members of the royal Bourbon family, the nations had a defensive alliance called a *Pacte de Famille*. This meant that the French King, Louis XVI, and the Spanish King, Charles III, would generally seek cooperation to have their countries support the same causes. The American Commissioners, however, explained to the French minister that Britian probably was making the same propositions of accommodation to the Spanish, and that the Continental Congress should be explicitly informed "what might be expected from France and Spain."

M. Gerard, one of the French secretaries, visited the American Commissioners the day before,

> to inform us by order of the King, that after a long and full Consideration of our Affairs and Propositions in Council, it was decided and his Majesty was determined to acknowledge our Independence and make a Treaty with us of Amity and Commerce; that in this Treaty no Advantage would be taken of our present Situation to obtain Terms from us which otherwise would not be convenient for us to agree to, his Majesty desiring that the Treaty once made should be durable, and our Amity subsist forever, which could not be expected if each Nation did not find its Interest in the Continuance as well as in the Commencement of it.

The French King intended that the terms of the treaty would be the same as if the United States had been a long-established nation.

> That his Majesty was fix'd in his Determination, not only to acknowledge but to support our Independence, by every means in his Power. That in doing this he might probably be soon engag'd in War, with all the Expences, Risque and Damage usually attending it; yet he should not expect any Compensation from us on that Account, nor pretend that

he acted wholly for our Sakes, since besides his real Goodwill to us and our Cause, it was manifestly the Interest of France that the Power of England should be diminish'd by our Separation from it.

King Louis XVI also stated that the United States could make a separate peace with England. "He would have us be at full Liberty to make a peace for ourselves, whenever good and advantageous Terms were offered to us; The only Condition he should require and rely on would be this, that we in no Peace to be made with England should give up our Independency, and return to the Obedience of that Government."

The King also stated that as soon as he received notice from the courier that Spain concurred, the American Commissioners could give Congress "the strongest assurances in our Dispatches." Until then, he cautioned, the Congress should "keep the whole for the present a dead secret, as Spain had three reasons for not immediately declaring," although the King thought these matters would be resolved soon. First, "her Money Fleet had not yet come home." Second, her army and fleet in Brazil had not come home either. Third, her peace with Portugal had not yet been completed.

The American Commissioners then told the King that they perceived and admired equally his "magnanimity and his wisdom; That he would find us faithful and firm Allies," and that they wished "that the Amity between the two Nations might be eternal."

There was more good news. It had been some time since the United States had obtained a promise of three million livres coming from France, but the French notified them that the United States would receive the funds in January. The Commissioners were also told that Spain would send additional funds. "What we receive here will help get us out of Debt."

Supply ships had been delayed or seized by the English ships that "swarm in the Bay and channel." At some point, all the supply ships would sail together because now the French will use "a King's ship to convoy them out of the Channel, and we hope quite to America. They will carry we think to the amount of 70,000 Pound Sterling and Sailing in a few days." The Commissioners had also obtained a frigate to carry their dispatches, which were frequently lost. "The extraordinary Favors, of a Nature provoking to Great Britian, are marks of the sincerity of this Court, and seem to demand the thanks of Congress."

Reporting further, the letter noted that "the French Ambassador at London has desired to be recalled, being affronted there, where the late News from America has created a violent Ferment." There was also talk that Lord Stormont, the British Ambassador to France, would be recalled to England.

"The Stocks in England fall fast; and on both sides, there is every Appearance of an approaching War."

The Commissioners also had received numerous reports that the American prisoners in England were being treated inhumanely. They wrote a letter of objection to Lord North and sent someone to England to deliver it in person while also instructing the agent to visit the prisoners and alleviate some of the prisoners' discomfort. The Commissioners advised Congress that they put out a "very considerable" amount of money on this issue, and that they had incurred other expenses for which they had received repeated "assurances of payment" but no payment yet.

Lastly, the Commissioners explained that the supplies in the ships and what they have sent and are sending from Spain "though far short of your Orders (which we have executed as far as we are able)" will put the country "into pretty good Circumstances as to Cloathing, Arms, &c if they arrive." They promised to "continue to send, as Ability and opportunity may permit." Their standard greeting, in this very important letter, seemed all the more poignant: "believe us, with sincere Esteem, Gentlemen, Your most obedient humble Servant."[26]

Thus, the long mission of the American Commissioners was accomplished. This decision by the French King Louis XVI would turn the tide of the Revolutionary War. On February 6, 1778, France, whose signatory on behalf of "the most Christian King" was Conrad Alexander (C. A.) Gerard, noted as royal syndic of the city of Strasbourg and secretary of his majesty's Council of State; and the United States, whose signatories were Benjamin Franklin, noted in the treaty as Deputy to the General Congress from the State of Pennsylvania and President of the Convention of the same state; Silas Deane, noted as Deputy from the State of Connecticut, and Arthur Lee, noted as Counsellor at law, signed the Treaty of Alliance.[27]

Franklin's company continued to be sought by the French lovers of liberty. Anne-Robert-Jacques Turgot, Baron De L'Aulne, a French economist, statesman, and Controller-General of Finances under King Louis XVI,[28] wrote to Franklin, "Mr. Turgot accepts with great pleasure the proposal made to him by Mr. Franklin by Mr. Quesnai of St. Germain to compensate him on Saturday for the pleasure of which Mr. Franklin's engagements deprive him for Friday. Every opportunity of seeing Mr. Franklin is precious, and he is anxious to express his joy at their successes to the friends of liberty."[29]

Charles Millon, the French sculptor of a bust of Franklin, who also achieved a "distinguished career as a man of letters and as a teacher of legislation, ancient languages, and philosophy,"[30] also wrote from Paris to Franklin in the spirit of continued dialogue and sharing of ideas between intellectuals. Millon gave his critical opinion about some sections of the Pennsylvania Constitution that Franklin had a part in drafting. He wrote, "I render you homage as the man whom the public credits with authorship of the Pennsylvania constitutions."

Millon's ideas included: intolerance as "the most destructive force in any society," caution about giving religious orders too much power lest they end up "convincing themselves that they are God's agents," the conviction that there should be a ban on usury because it "afflicts the poorest and most numerous and thereby undermines social cohesion," the role of law in promoting the general welfare, how to divide offenses into categories, and how to divide punishments.[31]

While the Articles of Confederation had been adopted by the Virginia House of Delegates on December 15 and the Senate on December 16, Thomas Jefferson, who, since October 1776 was a member of the Virginia House of Delegates, thought it important to write John Adams about a part of the Articles that generated debate and possible rejection.

That part was Article 9, which reserved to Congress the power of entering into treaties and alliances and that they should not give exemptions from imposts to foreigners. Jefferson said that some members of the House of Delegates interpreted this to mean that Congress would have the whole regulation of and a monopoly on trade. Jefferson did not read the language that way, but he suggested that Congress pass an explanatory amendment to make its intentions clearer. That article was the one that almost caused adoption to fail in Virginia, Jefferson stated, and he did not want that to be a stumbling block for other state legislatures.[32]

Jefferson thought this issue was important enough to ask Adams to get Congress to clarify part of Article 9. Perhaps other states did, too, and perhaps this was one reason that all states did not adopt the Articles until 1781. Perhaps Jefferson was prescient in trying to get Congress to resolve this issue. However well-meaning his concerns, Jefferson was unaware that Adams had left Congress by that time to go to France to become one of the American Commissioners.

So, December 17 ended with chaplains throughout the Continental Army sharpening their quills as they wrote the sermons that they would deliver to the weary troops on the great Day of Thanksgiving. The officers, no doubt, wondered what on earth they were going to feed their soldiers for a Thanksgiving feast when there was so little food in camp. Likely, all of the soldiers were cheered at the announcement that they would soon be in winter quarters where they could get at least some measure of rest before they had to go back out and fight another day.

CHAPTER 10

Thanksgiving, December 18

General Washington delayed the march to winter quarters so the troops could rest and celebrate the Day of Thanksgiving that the Continental Congress, in a November 1 resolution, called to be held on December 18. The Thanksgiving was to celebrate the October victory of the Northern Army of the Continental Army, under the command of General Henry Gates, over England's General Burgoyne at Saratoga. Massachusetts's Son of Liberty and Continental Congress member, the firebrand Sam Adams, drafted the Thanksgiving Resolution in the spirit of New England Thanksgivings. The Day of Thanksgiving was the first national holiday of the new United States.

The resolution read:

> First National Thanksgiving Proclamation issued by the Continental Congress on November 1, 1777:
>
> FORASMUCH as it is the indispensable Duty of all Men to adore the superintending Providence of Almighty God; to acknowledge with Gratitude their Obligation to him for Benefits received, and to implore such farther Blessings as they stand in Need of: And it having pleased him in his abundant Mercy, not only to continue to us the innumerable Bounties of his common Providence; but also to smile upon us in the Prosecution of a just and necessary War, for the Defense and Establishment of our unalienable Rights and Liberties; particularly in that he hath been pleased, in so great a Measure, to prosper the Means used for the Support of our Troops, and to crown our Arms with most signal success: It is therefore recommended to the legislative or executive Powers of these UNITED STATES to set apart THURSDAY, the eighteenth Day of December next, for SOLEMN THANKSGIVING and PRAISE: That at one Time and with one Voice, the good People may express the grateful Feelings of their Hearts, and consecrate themselves to the Service of their Divine Benefactor; and that, together with their sincere Acknowledgments and Offerings, they may join the penitent Confession of their manifold Sins, whereby they had forfeited every Favor; and their humble and earnest Supplication that it may please GOD through the Merits of JESUS CHRIST, mercifully to forgive and blot them out of Remembrance; That it may please him graciously to afford his Blessing on the Governments of these States respectively, and prosper the public Council of the whole: To inspire our Commanders, both by Land and Sea, and all under them, with that Wisdom and Fortitude which may render them fit Instruments, under the Providence of Almighty GOD, to secure for these United States, the greatest of all human

Blessings, INDEPENDENCE and PEACE: That it may please him, to prosper the Trade and Manufactures of the People, and the Labor of the Husbandman, that our Land may yield its Increase: To take Schools and Seminaries of Education, so necessary for cultivating the Principles of true Liberty, Virtue and Piety, under his nurturing Hand; and to prosper the Means of Religion, for the promotion and enlargement of that Kingdom, which consisteth "in Righteousness, Peace and Joy in the Holy Ghost."[1]

Adams drafted the resolution with two of his Freemason brothers, Continental Congress delegates Richard H. Lee, the Virginia plantation owner who made the motion in the Second Continental Congress to declare independence from Britain, and Daniel Roberdeau, a Philadelphia merchant who also happened to be his landlord in York. The Continental Congress passed the resolution so that there would be one day of national celebration of the victory at Saratoga rather than a hodgepodge of different days that the various states had designated to celebrate the victory. Citizens everywhere understood the importance of what happened at Saratoga. Continental Congress Secretary Laurens sent the resolution to the states on the first day that it passed.[2]

Some commentators alleged that the Thanksgiving resolution was a slap in the face to Washington from General Gates's supporters Sam Adams, John Adams, and Richard H. Lee.[3] At the time these men drafted the resolution, Washington had suffered losses during most of the Philadelphia Campaign at the battles of Brandywine, Paoli, and Germantown.

While Thanksgiving conjures up memories of bountiful food today, the reality on December 18, 1777 at Gulph Mills was vastly different.

Lieutenant Colonel Henry Dearborn, of the 1st New Hampshire Regiment, who was at Saratoga with his battalion when Burgoyne surrendered, described the day this way:

>...the weather still Remains uncomfortable—this is Thanksgiving Day thro the whole [Continent of America]—but god knows We have very Little to keep it with this being the Third Day we have been without flouer or bread—& are Living on a high uncultivated hill, in huts & tents Laying on the Cold Ground, upon the whole I think all we have to be thankful for is that we are alive & not in the Grave with many of our friends—we had for thanksgiving breakfast some Exceeding Poor beef which has been boil.d & Now warm.d in an old short hndled frying Pan in which we ware Obliged to Eat it having No other Platter.[4]

Dearborn ate his Thanksgiving dinner with General Sullivan.

Lieutenant Samuel Armstrong also fought at Saratoga, and his diary gave a detailed account of the British soldiers who were captured, sick, wounded, or killed at Saratoga. Armstrong wrote this Thanksgiving Day that they had "Thick Cloudy Weather. We had neither Bread nor meat 'till just before night when we had some fresh Beef, without any Bread or flour." The beef could have made minced pie if it was tender enough, but it seemed like "Mr. Commissary did not intend that we Shou'd keep a Day of rejoicing." However, his men "Sent out a Scout for some fowls and by Night he Return'd with one Dozen; we distributed five of them among our fellow sufferers three we Roasted, two we boil'd, and Borrowed a few Potatos." They ate this "without any Bread or anyting stronger than Water to drink!"[5]

Lieutenant Ebenezer Wild wrote that the men "had orders to turn out to roll call at 9 o'clk, but it began to rain so fast we did not turn out then. About 12 o'clk we turned out to roll call with arms. We had orders read to us that the Genl. determined to take up winter quarters in this place. The troops are to make Huts for them Selves and Make our Selves as comfortable as We Can, in Order to keep the Armey together. We Should have Moved to Day but this Being the Day Set apart by the Congress for A Day of Publick Thanksgiving." He wrote that the troops were ordered to stay still, and the chaplains of the various brigades were to provide "divine services," while officers and soldiers were urged to attend. However, he added, "We had not Chaplin and We had but A poor Thanksgiven,—nothing but Fresh beef and Flour to Eate, without aney Salt & but Very Scant of that."[6]

November 1, 1777 Continental Congress Proclamation for a General Thanksgiving, throughout the United States of America, to be held on December 18, 1777.

Colonel Angell wrote about the day, "This day being Appointed by the Honourable Continental Congress as a day of thanksgiving through All the Continent we had orders to Still Continue in our present encampments and it was Strongly Recommended to all the Officers and Soldiers of the Army to attend Divine Servis. The troops attended Servis at three oClock in the afternoon."[7]

Captain Paul Brigham wrote of his miserable day, "On ye 18th Being the Continental Thanksgiving Lay Still and Did not march it Still continued Rainy and Dull weather I kept Thanksgiving without Eateing any Bread all Day our Beaf was Poor and no Sauce and allowance Very Short."[8]

Dr. Waldo, feeling better, had a roasted pig for his day of "Universal Thanksgiving." He added, "God be thankful for my health which I have pretty well recovered. How much better should I feel, were I assured my family were in health. But the same good being who graciously preserves me, is able to preserve them & bring me to ardently wish'd for enjoyment of them again." He continued to complain about the lack of provisions for the army. "The Army are poorly supplied with Provision, occasioned it is said by the Neglect of the Commissary of Purchases." It was not just the Commissary of Purchases who did a poor job. Waldo thought that Congress did not pay the Continental Army officers enough to make them want to stay. "Much talk among Officers about discharges. Money has become of too little consequence. The Congress have not made their Commissions valuable Enough. Heaven avert the bad consequences of these things!!"[9]

Joseph Plumb Martin's Day of Thanksgiving remembrance was even more stark, but he wrote about it with a little sense of humor as he looked back.[10]

> While we lay here there was a Continental thanksgiving ordered by Congress; and as the army had all the cause in the world to be particularly thankful, if not for being well off, at least, that it was no worse, we were ordered to participate in it. We had nothing to eat for two or three days previous, except what the trees of the fields and forests afforded us. But we must now have what Congress said—a sumptuous thanksgiving to close the year of high living, we had now nearly seen brought to a close.

Martin quipped that the nation was so kind as to give every soldier "the extraordinary superabundant donation" of a half a gill, or about ¼ a cup, of rice and a tablespoon full of vinegar. Then the men were ordered to attend a Thanksgiving sermon. When the sermon was over, they returned to camp, passing by the Commissary's quarters. They saw a sentinel guarding a barrel full of hocks of fresh beef. "One of my messmates purloined a piece of it, five or six pounds, perhaps," which, Martin thought, "might help to eke out our Thanksgiving supper; but alas!" The sentinel saw the man take the beef and made him return it. "So I had nothing else to do but go home and make out my supper as usual, upon a leg of nothing and no turnips."

Martin's thoughts turned serious when he wrote about the state of the army that day.

> The army was now not only starved but naked; the greatest part were not only shirtless and barefoot, but destitute of all other clothing, especially blankets. I procured a small piece of raw cowhide and made myself a pair of moccasins, which kept my feet (while they lasted) from the frozen ground, although, as I well remember, the hard edges so galled my ankles, while on a march, that it was with much difficulty and pain that I could wear them afterwards; but the only alternative I had, was to endure this inconvenience or to go barefoot, as hundreds of my companions had to, till they might be tracked by their blood upon the rough frozen ground. But hunger, nakedness and sore shins were not the only difficulties we had at that time to encounter;—we had hard duty to perform and little or no strength to perform it with.[11]

One of the Thanksgiving sermons preached at Gulph Mills was by Rev. Israel Evans, who was chaplain to General Enoch Poor's Brigade. Evan's sermon was later published "at the request of the general and officers of said brigade, to be distributed among the soldiers, gratis," by Francis Bailey of Lancaster, Pennsylvania. Evans sent the published sermon to Washington on February 17, 1778, but Washington did not receive it until March 12. On March 13, 1778, Washington read the sermon and wrote a letter of thanks to Reverend Evans:

> I have read this performance with equal attention and pleasure, and at the same time that I admire, and feel the force of the reasoning which you have displayed through the whole, it is more especially incumbent upon me to thank you for the honorable, but partial mention you have made of my character; and to assure you, that it will ever be the first wish of my heart to aid your pious endeavours to inculcate a due sense of the dependance we ought to place in that all wise and powerful Being on whom alone our success depends.[12]

Reverend Evans's sermon was an inspirational mix of religion that was based, he noted, on the words of David in the 115th Psalm in the Bible and facts about the victory at Saratoga and the other battles in which the soldiers in the brigade to which he was assigned had fought. Evans included lofty praise and prayers for Washington and for all of the officers and soldiers who fought the much-better equipped, prepared, and experienced British Army.

Evans's sermon is worth reading in full, but here are some excerpts.[13] Evans extolled the happy sight of soldiers from different states coming together as one army. "The happiness of the one state, is the happiness of the other; and as we have seen the good effects of that perfect harmony which has prevailed among us; let us cultivate it more and more…"[14]

To strengthen the troops as they prepared to go into winter quarters, Evans preached:

> Are any of you startled at the prospect of hard winter quarters? Think of liberty and Washington, and your hardships will be forgotten and banished. Let Europe, nay let the world hear, that the American army, in the defence of their country, cheerfully submitted to the inconvenience of having no other houses of accommodation, than such as their own hands reared in the depth of winter. Be encouraged, therefore, to undertake all that has been proposed to you, in the generals orders.

Having taken to winter quarters himself in three previous campaigns, Evans assured the soldiers "that what has appeared hard and impracticable, at a distance, has been found tolerable and easy, when the worst that could be imagined has arrived." Many of them endured the entire winter during the campaign in Quebec. Surely, "[you] will not complain of the winter's cold in the state of Pennsylvania." He went on to state that few of them were "not inured to war, who are not veterans in hardships, and losses, as well as in the service of their country." Therefore, he urged the men to be "firm and exact in the discharge of our several duties," and render themselves "respectable and honourable in the fight of our leader, and make it seem a pleasure to command us."[15]

Further, Evans addressed the negative comparisons of Washington's skills as commander to those of General Gates, whose victory at Saratoga still lodged in the hearts and minds of these soldiers who fought with Gates there. He started off pleading, "Regret not your removal from the late successful command of the honourable general Gates, for here is his excellency general Washington." Then he exhorted, "Look on him, and catch the genuine patriot fire of liberty and independence. Look on him, and learn to forget your own ease and comfort; like him resign the charms of domestic life, when the genius of America bids you grow great in her service, and liberty calls you to protect her. Look on your worthy general, and claim the happiness and honour of saying, he is ours. Like him love virtue, and like him, reverence the name of the great Jehovah." Evans reiterated, "Learn of him to endure watchings, cold and hardships, for you have just heard that he assures you, he is ready and willing, to endure whatever inconveniences and hardships may attend this winter."[16]

The auction house Christies, on a page advertising an auction of a vintage copy of the Thanksgiving Proclamation, noted that Rev. Timothy Dwight, who preached from Stamford, Connecticut, compared Burgoyne's defeat to Hezekiah's successful defense of Jerusalem against the Assyrians. Christies added that Reverend Dwight gave a lengthy recounting of the entire Revolutionary War, starting with the Battles of Lexington and Concord. Reverend Dwight demonstrated each victory and loss as a sign of divine intervention.[17]

Further, he exhorted the soldiers to remember that it was the Lord who was the answer to the questions he raised about how the Americans secured the victory at Saratoga.

> Who united us at first in a general and vigorous opposition to our enemies, and thus thwarted every expectation of the most boasted human foresight? Who directed our enemies at first to that province, and town, where alone, perhaps, they could have been confined, 'till we could furnish ourselves with materials for carrying on the war? Who hath raised up those powerful armies, with which we now resist our foes? Who gave us a person to direct our military affairs, whom the tongue of envy acknowledges to be thoroughly qualified for so difficult and dangerous a station? Who, when our hearts died within us, at the success of our enemies, the last campaign, dispelled the gloom by the timely and illustrious victories of TRENTON and PRINCETON? Who, in a manner still more extraordinary, enabled us, with a handful of troops, to keep the field against a mighty force, during the last winter? Who collected a sufficient body of militia to destroy Colonel BAUME's detachment, by the glorious and most beneficial victory of BENNINGTON.

Dwight continued, "Who gave into our hands the whole army of General BURGOYNE, and inflicted such a wound upon BRITISH pride, as it hath scarcely received, during our present century? Who, finally, hath so infatuated the counsels of our enemies, that their measures have, almost in every instance, been advantageous to us, as our own?"[18]

Reverend David Avery, who preached from Greenwich, Connecticut, used part of his sermon to praise and thank the Virginians for standing up for liberty by opposing the Stamp Act in 1772 and "being the first in petitioning for a redress of this grievance." Then he called on the Virginians, with their "well-known character," magnanimity, and "patriotic, humane principles" to end slavery. He preached, "May we not hope they will go on to set the most illustrious example, in emancipating all their African Slaves? This would at once give a pleasing omen of the happy issue of our present struggle for LIBERTY, and procure to them the high approbation and applause of all future generations."[19] Alas, that was not to be.

We have no idea where or what Washington ate on this Thanksgiving. He probably heard a sermon himself, like his soldiers. Yet, he set about the business of preparing his army for winter quarters, using most of his General Orders to instruct the army in great detail how it should go about constructing and locating their huts.

Washington's General Orders for the day began with confirmation of various court martials, one for a soldier in the 1st Pennsylvania Brigade, the 1st Pennsylvania Regiment, and the 11th Virginia Regiment, that were held in the past month. Washington then went on to detail how the Valley Forge Encampment should be set up, including the role of specific officers, the

> FIRST NATIONAL THANKSGIVING
> CELEBRATED BY WASHINGTON'S ARMY
>
> HERE AT "THE GULPH" ON THURSDAY, DECEMBER 18, 1777 WASHINGTON'S ARMY DELAYED THEIR MARCH INTO VALLEY FORGE BY ONE DAY TO CELEBRATE THE FIRST THANKSGIVING OF THE UNITED STATES PROCLAIMED BY THE CONTINENTAL CONGRESS WITH CHAPLAINS PERFORMING THE DIVINE SERVICE. THIS THANKSGIVING IN SPITE OF SUFFERING THE DAY BEFORE THE MARCH INTO VALLEY FORGE SHOWED THE REVERENCE AND CHARACTER THAT WAS FORGING THE SOUL OF A NATION.
>
> BY VARIOUS HISTORICAL AND PATRIOTIC SOCIETIES
> AND
> THE NATIONAL THANKSGIVING FOUNDATION

Historical Marker, First National Thanksgiving Celebrated by Washington's Army, in Gulph Mills.

dimensions and locations of all huts, and cash rewards for the first groups of soldiers in each regiment who constructed their huts, and another reward for any officer or soldier who devised a cheaper and quicker material than wood board to cover the huts. The very important bulk of those General Orders follow in full:

> The Major Generals and officers commanding divisions, are to appoint an active field officer in and for each of their respective brigades, to superintend the business of hutting, agreeably to the directions they shall receive; and in addition to these, the commanding officer of each regiment is to appoint an officer to oversee the building of huts for his own regiment; which officer is to take his orders from the field officer of the brigade he belongs to, who is to mark out the precise spot, that for every hut, for officers and soldiers, is to be placed on, that uniformity and order may be observed.
>
> An exact return of all the tools, now in the hands of every regiment is to be made immediately, to the Qr Mr General, who, with the Adjutant General, is to see that they, together with those in store, are duly and justly allotted to the regimental overseers of the work; who are to keep an account of the men's names, into whose hands they are placed, that they may be accountable for them—The Superintendents and Overseers are to be exempt from all other duty, and will moreover be allowed for their trouble.
>
> The Colonels, or commanding officers of regiments, with their Captains, are immediately to cause their men to be divided into squads of twelve, and see that each squad have their

proportion of tools, and set about a hut for themselves. And as an encouragement to industry and art, the General promises to reward the party in each regiment, which finished their hut in the quickest, and most workmanlike manner, with *twelve* dollars—And as there is reason to believe, that boards, for covering, may be found scarce and difficult to be git—He offers *One hundred* dollars to any officer or soldier, who in the opinion of three Gentlemen, he shall appoint as judges, shall substitute some other covering, that may be cheaper and quicker made, and will in every respect answer the end.

The Soldier's huts are to be of the following dimensions—viz—fourteen by sixteen each—sides, end and roofs made with logs, and the roof made tight with split slabs—or in some other way—the sides made tight with clay—fire-place made of wood and secured with clay on the inside eighteen inches thick, this fire-place to be in the rear of the hut—the door to be in the end next to the street—the doors to be made of split oak-slabs, unless boards can be procured—Side-walls to be six and a half-feet high—The officers huts to form a line in the rear of the troop, one hut to be allowed to each General Officer—one to the Staff of each brigade—one to the field officers of each regiment—one to the staff of each regiment—one to the commissioned officers of two companies—and one to every twelve non-commissioned officers and soldiers.

After Orders. The army and baggage are to march to morrow in the time and manner already directed in the orders of the 15th instant, Genl Sullivan's division excepted, which is to remain on its present ground 'till further orders.[20]

Washington's reference to his General Orders for December 15 is puzzling. His December 15 General Orders only included the following about the time and manner of the march for the army and its baggage: "After Orders. The baggage of the army is to move at seven, and the whole army at ten o'clock, to morrow morning, in such routes and order, as shall be previously directed."[21]

However, one of the regimental Orderly Books for December 18 listed a *distinct* Order of March for the march to Valley Forge. It was not, as written in Washington's General Orders, the "manner already directed in the orders of the 15th instant."[22]

The Orderly Book of Lt. Col. Joseph Storer, York County, Massachusetts Regiment, listed at the bottom of the page, "The Order for the March of the Army," as it left Gulph Mills and marched on to Valley Forge, as:

1. North Carolina
2. Genl McDugal's Division
3. Marquis la Fayett's d.
4. Lord Sterling's Division
5. Park of Artillery
6. Genl Green's Division
7. Genl De Kalb's do ["do" meaning ditto]
8. Genl Glover's Brigade
9. Genl Sullivan's Division

December 18, 1777 entry, Orderly Book of Lt. Col. Joseph Storer's York County, Massachusetts Regiment, showing the Order of March from the Gulph Mills Encampment to Valley Forge. (Library of Congress)

10. Genl Wayne's do
11. Genl Poor's Brigade
12. Brigade of Light Dragoons
13. The Waggons in this order
14. Forage Master's Waggons
15. Commissary's do
16. Spare Ammunition
17. Baggage of the Troops, in the order the Troops march.
18. The whole March on the road to the Valley Forge.[23]

Paintings and descriptions of the march to Valley Forge are seared into our collective consciousness. Yet, if it is to be trusted, Storer's Orderly Book revealed exactly how that march was to take place. The above was the only document that this author could locate on how the troops who were encamped in Gulph Mills were to march to Valley Forge. Why was the Order of March in this Orderly Book but not others? Did Washington want to keep the Order of March a secret from others so that the British did not find out? Further research is in order.

Major Platt's Orderly Book recorded that Washington named General Greene as the Major General of the Day for tomorrow, Brigadier General as Smallwood, Field Officers as Lt. Col. Morgan Conner, who had served as Adjutant General from April to June 1777, and Lt. Col. Ebenezer Sproat, of Col. William Shepard's 4th Massachusetts Regiment, a man who was said to be the tallest in his regiment, and Brigadier Major as Hitchcock. Platt's book also included the line that all persons who had papers from Maj. Gen. John Clark, whose spies regularly went into British-occupied Philadelphia, were to pass all guards.

The Orderly Books from Capt. Peter Brown's Company of the Philadelphia Militia Artillery, thought to be written by soldier Jesse Williamson, and Col. Philip Van Courtland, 2nd New York Regiment, both contain a section marked "Advertisements." Brown's Orderly Book read, "A Silver mounted hanger with Ivory handles and Circular guard was found some days ago. The owner by applying to Capt. [Laurens] of the 5th Mary. Regiment may have it again. The said Capt. have also a large Country made Blanket taken from a soldier who it is supposed Stole it." It continued as "Found," some type of item with money in it. "The owner may have it by applying to Capt. Shumway in Col. Prentice's Regt. Gen. Huntington's Brigade."[24]

There are no other letters attributed to Washington's writing on this day. Undoubtedly, the upcoming Valley Forge Encampment consumed him. Of course, people continued to write to him.

From Philadelphia, a Joseph Galloway, who was married to a Pennsylvania Supreme Court justice's daughter, wrote to Washington to allow Galloway's daughter, with her "Household furniture and Effects to remove from my Seat in the Country to Philadelphia." Continental patrols restricted access into Philadelphia so that the Tories, spies, and merchants could not get to the British. Galloway realized that his request was trivial when compared to the war, but he wrote that "the Business of War by no Means excludes the Feeling of Humanity, and relying on that Candor and Liberality of Sentiment which those who are best acquainted with your Excellency agree you possess."[25] Another letter in Washington's papers came from Colonel John Gunby, who explained how he claimed the rank of colonel.[26]

⚜

In France, Franklin received a letter from Pageant Veuve Rivaud, from Tournus in the Burgundy region of France, asking for his help in contacting her son, who was in New England. "I beg you to forward a letter to my son in New England. I have received two of his, and he is extremely uneasy at having heard nothing from me and my family. He is one of the engineers that the government selected to send to America. I am a mother who has lost her companion in joy and sorrow; the only pleasure left me is in my family. Allowing him to go grieved me, but he had a good offer."[27]

French citizen Doerner Jur wrote to Franklin and asked him to provide letters of introduction and other assistance as he traveled to Charlestown, Maryland, and Virginia in the United States to establish his business as a general merchant.[28]

Franklin continued to receive letters from citizens and friends who wanted to send their young relatives or relatives of their friends to the United States to assist in the war, as he did with Lafayette, Pulaski, Von Steuben, and Duportail, among other stalwart officers and soldiers. The Duchess De Deux-Ponts, a friend of Franklin's, wrote him in support of the nephew of her friend, the Dowager of the Duke of the Two Bridges, "in bringing one of her nephews to America and obtaining for him a military post in the army of the Republic." The Dowager's nephew, named M. De Fontevieux, "had a decided vocation for arms, and especially for the service of the valiant Americans." Well born and well educated, his parents wanted him to enter the civil service, but "his passion for the military got the better of him." Currently, the nephew worked in the French Army Engineer's Office, where he received "the best testimonials" from his superiors. Handsome, "well made" and robust, the nephew also spoke German, French, and a little Latin. Not to worry about the expense of this young man getting to the United States. The Dowager of the Duke of the Two Bridges would pay for her nephew's transportation to the United States and for his equipment because the Dowager "ardently desires to see at least someone who belongs to her" in the service of the brave United States' citizens who began their own country. The Dowager herself would "hasten to shed her blood for their cause, which is that of all generous men." The Duchess closed her letters asking that Franklin "undertake to bring him to America, and to recommend him to the kindness of Congress, that the young man may be honorably placed."[29]

Now that the Day of Thanksgiving concluded, 11,000 soldiers packed up their meager belongings for the morning's march to winter quarters.

CHAPTER 11

The Army Leaves the Gulph and Marches to Valley Forge, December 19

If they found any food at all, most soldiers had a meager breakfast, their last in Gulph Mills for all but a small percent of them. That food had to hold them because the vast majority of them would eat nothing else for the rest of the day. Thousands of soldiers started and ended the day starving, with nothing to eat at all, on a day when they would have to march some nine miles to a place called Valley Forge.

At least, the sun was shining. The soldiers pulled themselves and their few belongings together—water canteens, blankets if they had them, axes, and guns. They put the baggage that could not fit in their individual backpacks into the baggage wagons designated for their individual regiments.

At 10 o'clock, they lined up, ready to march and to end the Gulph Mills Encampment.

First, the North Carolina troops. Then General McDougall's Division, followed by General Lafayette's Division, and Lord Stirling's. Behind them, the Park of Artillery, General Greene's Division, General De Kalb's Division, General Glover's Brigade, General Sullivan's Division, General Wayne's Division, and General Poor's Brigade. Bringing up the rear of the troops was the Brigade of Light Dragoons. Then the wagons lined up. First, the Forage Master's wagons, then the Commissary's, followed by Spare Ammunition, and, lastly, the Baggage of the Troops in the order that they marched. Then, "the whole March[ed] on the road to Valley Forge."[1]

The soldiers described the march in grueling detail.

Private Elijah Fisher wrote, "Thare Come orders for all the sick to be sent the Hospital and I with the others of the sick belonging to the Reg't was sent to the hospital at Reading but when we come there the sick belonging to the other Right had taken up so we was sent to Dunkertown to the hospital there."[2]

Lieutenant Armstrong wrote of his last moments in Gulph Mills, "The Sun Shone out this morning being the first time I had seen it for days, which seem'd to put new Life into every thing—we took the Remains of 2 Days Allowance of Beef...and 2 fowls we had left, of those we made a broth upon which we Breakfasted with a half a loaf of Bread we Begg'd and bought, of which we should have made a tolerable Breakfast, if there had been Enough!!" Then, Armstrong was on the move:

> By ten O'Clok we were to march to a place Call'd Valley Forge being about five or six miles—and about Eleven OCk we sit out, but did not arrive there 'till after SunSit. During this march we had nothing to Eat or to drink, but when we arrived, our Boys went to work to Bake bread and of this we Eat like Insatiate Monsters 'till they had made some Lilley P[3] of which we eat 'till our Guts began to Ake when we thought it was time to quit and lay down to sleep.[4]

Colonel Dearborn wrote, "The Army marched ab. 5 mile & incamp.d Near a height where we are to build huts to Live in this winter."[5]

Lieutenant Colonel Laurens recorded, "On the 19th inst., we march'd from the Gulph to this camp, headquarters at the Valley Forge."[6]

Private Plumb Martin wrote, "we marched for the Valley Forge in order to take up on winter-quarter. We were now in a truly forlorn condition,—no clothing, no provisions and as disheartened as need be...Our prospect was indeed dreary. In our miserable condition, to go into the wild woods and build us habitation to stay (not to live) in, in such a weak, starved and naked condition, was appalling in the highest degree, especially to a New Englander, unaccustomed to such kind of hardships at home."[7]

Colonel Israel Angell of the 2nd Rhode Island Regiment wrote:

> This morning was a Severe Cold one, as it Cleared off last Evening with a Strong Norwest wind which blew So that it blew our fires into Some of our huts and burnt them Down, it broke down one tree across a tent where five men lay asleep but providently hurt but one man and he had his thigh broke. We Recd. orders this morning to march as Soon as possible and before ten oClock the whole Army was a marching, pleased with the thoughts of going into winter Quarters. Though in the woods, we marched all the day without provisions as there was none to be drawn in this morning and neither Could we get any at night, we marched but about Eight miles this day, being plagued so bad With our waggons as the Roads was Excessive Bad and our horses very poor and weak.

Despite their condition, Angell and his men made it to Valley Forge. "We Turned into the woods about Sunset, where we built us fires, and encampt by them that night often Eating our Supper of raw Corn which we got out of a field man by our encampment." He added that "one Accident happened this Day." Sadly, a wagon turned over and killed one woman.[8]

This is one of the rare entries from this encampment where women are mentioned, even though there were likely some 400 women "camp followers" in Gulph Mills. The camp followers were women who followed the army from place to place. Many were wives of the soldiers who came with them, often with their children in tow, to help their husbands. Others were women who worked at the camp to cook and wash clothes for the soldiers in exchange for food, shelter, clothing, or whatever they might be paid. Some of the women were enslaved women who were forced to accompany their enslavers. And then, there were prostitutes who also worked their trade in the camps. Scholars have documented at least one woman who was at the Gulph Mills Encampment, working as a laundress as she traveled with her family. That is Mary Geyer, who, with her 11-year-old son, who is not named in the source material, went to camp with her husband, Peter, a rifleman, and another son, John, a drummer, with the 13th Pennsylvania Regiment. While Peter and John were discharged January 1, 1778, at Valley Forge, Geyer remained there to work as a washerwoman—the family needed the money.[9]

Captain Brigham of Connecticut's 4th Regiment wrote, "On ye 19th Last night it Cleared off Cold this morning and loaded our Tents and prepared to march at a moments warning and about 9 marched through ye mud 5 or 6 miles and Pitched our Tents. I went a little out of the Road and staid all night."[10]

Corporal Ebenezer Wild of the 1st Massachusetts wrote, "This Morning Clear and Cold & very Windy. About 12 OClock we Marchd off for the place Where we Was to take our Winter Quarters. We Marched about 6 Miles up Lancaster rode and encamped in the Woods."[11]

Lieutenant McMichael wrote, "At 10 A.M., we marched from the Gulph and took post near the Valley Forge, where our ground was laid out for cantonments."[12]

Then, there is a description that many of us are familiar with—Washington Irving's description from *The Life of Washington*: "Sad and dreary was the march to Valley Forge; uncheered by the recollection of any recent triumph, as was the march to winter-quarters in the preceding year. Hungry and cold were the poor fellows who had so long been keeping the field; for provisions were scant, clothing worn out, and so badly off were they for shoes, that the footsteps of many might be tracked in blood." Yet at this very time, we are told, "hogsheads of shoes, stockings, and clothing were lying at different places on the roads in the woods, perishing for want of teams, or of money to pay the teamster."[13] Irving also wrote that when the troops arrived at Valley Forge, they "had still to brave wintry weather in their tents until they could cut down trees and construct huts for their accommodation. Those who were on the sick list had to seek temporary shelter, wherever it could be found, among the farmers of the neighborhood."[14]

Brigadier General Anthony Wayne's December 19 letter from "Camp at the Gulf" to Richard Peters, Secretary and Member of the Continental Board of War, reflects some of the hardship and illness that he and his fellow soldiers had experienced over the past many months, hardship that they hoped could be improved. Wayne hoped that Peters could convince the Continental Congress to give Wayne a furlough for five or six weeks. Wayne apparently did not think that Washington would give him a furlough for that long. Wayne insisted that he needed the furlough to "effect a Radical cure."

He explained, "After struggling with a stubborn cold for near two months [and] pain in my breast Occasioned by a fall at Germantown...the [Illness] has taken hold in my lungs and throat and unless I am permitted to change my Ground I dread the Consequences." Wayne added that his doctor wanted him to go to an inland town where he could "properly attend and procure a suitable Regimen." He added that he had been "in Constant duty" for 23 months, 16 of which he served in Canada and Ticonderoga and the remainder with Washington, "during which period I have never had one single moment respite." Finally, he stated that his financial interests were suffering and, if something happened to him, there was no one else who could attend to them. Hopeful, Wayne wrote, "I am Confident that when they Reflect on the length of time I have served them together with the hard duty I have underwent they will not hesitate to grant me this Indulgence at being the first I ever asked."[15]

Wayne's biographer noted that Washington gave Wayne a month-long leave of absence on January 1, 1778, after Washington initially turned him down, despite the army doctors' conclusion that Wayne's condition was serious enough that he should see his family physician. After Wayne's troops got settled at Valley Forge, Wayne returned to Waynesborough during this leave, but he soon went to see Philadelphia's Benjamin Rush, "the leading physician of the time," for treatment.[16]

While the Continental Army marched into its winter quarters, the British Army did likewise. Hessian Captain Ewald wrote, "Since the ten redoubts constructed upon the heights from Kensington up to the Schuylkill River at the Morris house were considered suitable defensive positions to protect Philadelphia, a part of the army marched today to its quarters in the city." Ewald described his quarters on December 30: "My quarters, along with thirty men, were with an old Strassburger who could give me a spacious room and

THE ARMY LEAVES THE GULPH • 153

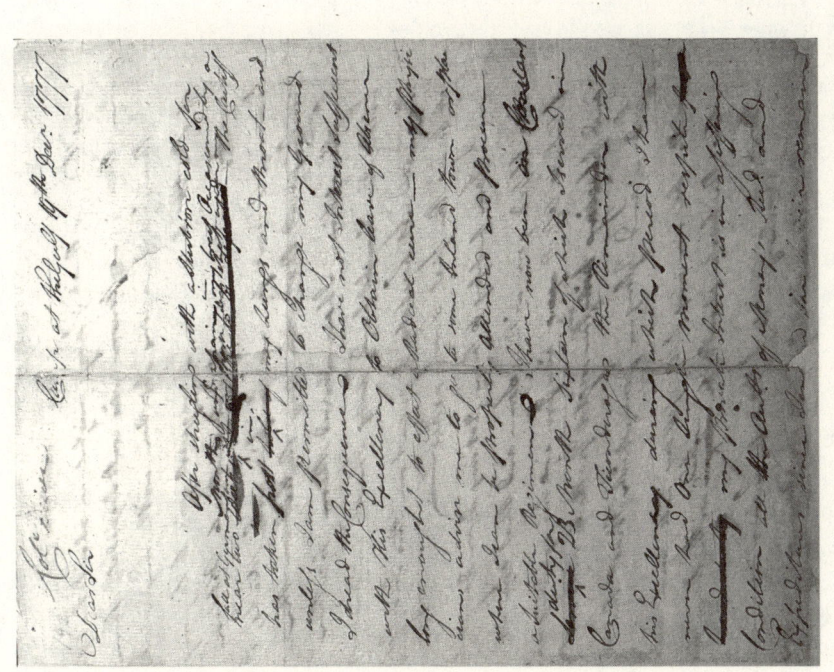

December 19, 1777 letter from General Anthony Wayne at Camp at the Gulph to Richard Peters, Secretary of the Continental Board of War, requesting that he intervene with General Washington to secure Wayne a leave of absence for five or six weeks due to sickness and the rigors of the recent campaign. (Courtesy of Historical Society of Pennsylvania)

a bed. I was heartily glad that I had arrived safely under cover after two very hard campaigns, and could stretch my bones peacefully in a bed again—How sweet is rest, when one seldom enjoys it!"[17]

So, the Continental Army finally marched on to winter quarters at Valley Forge. Some leading sources of Washington's writings, such as the Library of Congress, Washington Papers, and Founders Online, do not attribute any General Orders to Washington for December 19. However, Major Platt's Orderly Book contains orders for December 19 from "Headquarters at Valley Forge." Some of the leading sources attributed the same orders to Washington for December 20. Perhaps Washington dictated the orders on the 19th but did not have them distributed until the 20th because his first priority was to let his tired army complete the grueling march to Valley Forge and get themselves settled.

The December 19 orders as recorded by Major Platt, from Headquarters Valley Forge, which would be the first from Valley Forge or the last from Gulph Mills, were as follows:

> Major General for tomorrow is Lord Stirling, with Brigadier as Weedon, Field Officers Lt. Cols. Butler and Lt. Col Davis from North Carolina, with Brigadier Major as Minnis.
> The Guards are to parade at ½ Past 3 O'Clock in the afternoon near the Artillery Park—
> Genl. McIntosh is appointed to the Command of the North Carolina Brigade—
> The Major Generals accompanied by the Engineers are to view the Ground attentively & fix upon the proper spot & made for Hutting so as to render the Camp as Strong & as inaccessible as possible. The Engineers after this are to mark the Ground out & direct the Field Officer appointed to Superintend the Buildings for each Brigade where they are to be placed.
> The Soldiers in cutting their firewood are to save such Parts of each Tree as will do for building, reserving sixteen & eighteen feet of the Trunk for logs to rear their Huts with. In doing this such Regiment to reap the Benefit of their own Labour.—
> All those who in consequence of the Orders of the 18th Instant have turned their Thoughts to easy & expeditious method of covering the Huts are requested to communicate their plans to Major Generals Sullivan, Green or Lord Stirling who will cause Experiments to be made and assign the proffered Reward to the best projector.
> The Q M Genl is to Delay no Time, but use his utmost Exertions to procure large Quantities of Straw, either for covering the Huts, if it should be found necessary or for beds for the Soldiers. He is to assume...that unless they get their Grain out immediately, the Straw will be taken with the Grain in it, & paid for as Straw only—
> The Qr Mr Genl is to collect as soon as possible all the Tents not used by the Troops, & as soon as they are hutted all the Residue of the Tents and have them washed & well dried & then laid up in store such as are good for the next Campaign, the others for the uses as shall be directed—The whole are to be carefully preserved.
> The Colonels & Officers commanding Regiments are forth with to make Returns to the Qr Mr Genl of every Tent belonging to their Corps.

> The Army being now come to a fixed station—The Brigadiers & Officers Commanding Brigades are immediately to take effectual means to collect & bring to Camp all the Officers and Soldiers at present scattered about the Country.
>
> All Officers are enjoined to see that their men do not wantonly or needlessly burn and destroy rails & never to fire their Sheds or Huts when they leave them.[18]

Before Washington joined his troops on the march to Valley Forge, he addressed important business in his last letters from Gulph Mills. Key among them were two letters regarding his plans for how the Continental Army would protect Wilmington, Delaware, where his spies told him that the British would soon move to occupy. He decided to send Brigadier General William Smallwood and his brigade to Wilmington for the winter, rather than canton them with the rest of the army at Valley Forge.

He informed George Read, governor of Delaware, about his plans as follows:

> I have recd information, which I have great reason to believe is true, that the Enemy mean to establish a post at Wilmington for the purpose of countenancing the disaffected in the Delaware State, drawing supplies from that Country and the lower parts of Chester County, and securing a post upon Delaware River during the Winter. As the advantages resulting to the Enemy from such a position are most obvious I have determined, and shall accordingly, this day, send off Genl Smallwood with a respectable Continental Force to take post at Wilmington before them. If General Howe thinks the place of that importance to him, which I conceive it is, he will probably attempt to dispossess us of it.

Washington explained that the "the Force which I can at present spare, is not adequate to making it perfectly secure, I expect that you will call out as many Militia as you possibly can," to get to Wilmington and put themselves under General Smallwood's command. He hoped that the men of Delaware would "turn out cheerfully, when they consider that they are called upon to remain within and defend their own State."

In the rest of the letter, Washington advised Read that he could not do a prisoner exchange of former Delaware Governor John McKinley because Washington did not have any prisoner of war that was proper for such an exchange. McKinley served as governor of Delaware during the Battle of Brandywine on September 11, 1777. The day after the battle, British forces pulled McKinley out of his bed at the Governor's Residence and imprisoned him on a British ship that was docked in the Delaware River.[19] Washington told Read to send the prisoner exchange request to the Continental Congress because they had a number of prisoners under their direction for whom Howe would probably agree to an exchange.

Washington added a warning postscript—"let the Militia march to Wilmington by Companies or even parts of Companies from their Battalions there. Because if the enemy move it will be quickly."[20]

Washington's letter to General Smallwood ordering him to march from Gulph Mills straight to Wilmington follows.

> With the Division lately commanded by Genl Sullivan, you are to March immediately for Wilmington, and take Post there. You are not to delay a moment in putting the place in the best posture of defense, to do which, and for the security of it afterwards, I have written in urgent terms to the President of Delaware State to give every aid he possibly can of Militia—I have also directed an Engineer to attend you for the purpose of constructing, and superintending the Works, and you will fix with the Quarter Master on the number of Tools necessary for the business—but do not let any neglect, or deficiency on his part, impede your operations, as you are hereby vested with full power to seize & take (passing receipts) such articles as are wanted. The Commissary & Forage Master will receive directions respecting your Supplies, in their way; but I earnestly request that you will see these Supplies are drawn from the Country between you and Philadelphia, as it will be depriving the Enemy of all chance of getting them; and in this point of view, becomes an object to us of importance.

Washington ended the letter exhorting Smallwood to "keep both Officers and men to their duty and to avoid furloughs" except where absolutely necessary. He ordered Smallwood to "collect all the stragglers" from both brigadiers and clothe the men "in the most comfortable manner" as he could. Importantly, he ordered Smallwood to be particularly observant "of everything passing on the river" and to communicate everything of importance to him."[21]

Washington also wrote to Virginia Governor Patrick Henry, thanking him for sending sorely needed clothing for the Virginia troops, although it would not meet the needs of all of them. "It will be a happy circumstance, and of great saving, if we should be able in future to cloath our Army comfortably. Their sufferings hitherto have been great, and from our deficiencies in this instance, we have lost many Men & have generally been deprived of a large proportion of our Force." Washington realized that "many desertions have proceeded from" the lack of clothing and other necessaries.

Evidently, Henry had written to the Marquis de Lafayette and asked to meet him. Washington replied, "I shall present you to him according to your wishes. He is certainly amiable & highly worthy of esteem." Finally, Washington informed Henry that a Boston newspaper and other letters have reported that "a Ship has arrived from France at One of the Eastern ports with Fifty pieces of Brass Artillery—5000 Stand of Arms and other Stores."[22]

One of the most important letters that was sent to Washington this day was from Brigadier General Casimir Pulaski, the experienced general from Poland who was an expert at and who commanded the cavalry. The letter concerned and enclosed Pulaski's recommendations to create a cavalry corps to further organize and strengthen the Continental Army's cavalry.

Pulaski had previously written to Washington that he should create a Cavalry Regiment, but he stated that the need was more urgent now. "The advantages that would arise from a superiority in Cavalry are too obvious to be unnoticed." As the war progressed, he continued, there would be fewer woods and fences in areas where the army found itself. That is because the army constantly cuts down trees and fences to use for building and burning. These open fields and lands would be "better adapted to the maneuvers and services of the Cavalry."

Whether braggadocio or speaking from experience, Pulaski wrote that if the army was "superior in Cavalry the enemy will not dare to extend their force." Yet, he warned, if the enemy increased their cavalry, the Continental cavalry would "diminish & dwindle away." He outlined a doomsday scenario should that happen. One battle could cause the Continental Army to lose it all. "Our Army once dispersed & pursued by their Horse will never be able to fully rally, thus on retreat may early be cut off, our baggage lost, our principal Officers taken & many other events occur not less Fatal."

It seems that at some point, Washington expressed dissatisfaction that Pulaski did not attend to one of Washington's orders. Pulaski wrote that he would like to carry out every order "but the weak state of the Corps I command renders it impossible to perform every Service required." Pulaski closed the letter by stating that if Washington agreed with Pulaski's request, Pulaski would even take Washington's letter to establish the cavalry directly to Congress because "we want So many things there is not time to be lost."[23]

Pulaski went on to form the cavalry, and he was honored with the name "the Father of the Cavalry" in the United States Army.

Major General John Armstrong, whom Washington had sent to the area of the camp at Whitemarsh to check on and move the sick, the weapons, and the supplies that the army left behind, wrote to Washington about what he found and his thoughts for moving forward.

Armstrong informed Washington that he planned to move over the Bethlehem and Easton roads near Neshaminy, but that he was impeded by the weather and the inability to move out of camp the sick soldiers and leftover fragments of the Whitemarsh Encampment. "The scarcity of wagons to procure Our provisions have stood in the way."

Armstrong stated that Colonel Pickering wrote to him that the Pennsylvania Militia's 200–300 arms, tents, and other items were left at the Morris house. Armstrong asserted that the Pennsylvania Militia did not leave those items, but that it was probably used and left by the Maryland or Virginia Militia. Surely, his fellow Pennsylvanians would not leave their arms like that or, if they did, he would "early attend to & remove them."

Armstrong reported that several good wagons and other important items were left at Mr. Emlen's house near the Whitemarsh Encampment and various other places nearby. He warned that neighbors would take the arms and the equipment if the army did not send for it. While he did not have the time to attend to these things "without neglecting things of greater importance," he agreed to send a guard from his battalion to the bridge on Egypt Road to safeguard the items.

There were also 10–15 wagon loads of entrenching tools and horseshoes left, which were to go to Major Rice, who was uneasy that such important items had been left behind. Armstrong stated that those supplies would be moved over to the rear of the main army.

Area residents from Delaware and Whigs from Neshaminy and the area crossroads now moved closer to Armstrong's encampment, likely for protection from the British. Armstrong felt that he had to "immediately attend" to their situation. He intended to "attempt the best General arrangement or disposition for the winter" for them, including posting troops on the nine main roads in the area as well as some by-roads.

These troops would need to be supported with some sort of central camp or headquarters, but Armstrong did not yet have a plan on "how to feed or supply these various detachments with any regularity & certainty." Before he dispersed troops under this plan, he wanted to get some cattle from the area that are now "convenient to the enemy if any such are to be found."

Armstrong had already sent a battalion to the Newtown Road. He planned to leave another battalion to maintain the picket at the Whitemarsh church. He stated that the picket at Barren Hill had to be held by the regiment at a nearby bridge. He welcomed Washington's thoughts and corrections on his plans "when leisure admits." Lastly, Armstrong noted that he waited for word from the "Hyde-Master" in Germantown about the number of tan fats, the state of the leather there, and such.[24]

And, finally, Major John Clark, Jr., from William Lewis's home at Newtown Square, which had also served as an outpost for General Potter, wrote to Washington about a report of a person who had spied on the British, the conditions of citizens in Pennsylvania, activities in the city of Philadelphia, and problems that Clark had with getting a good and much-needed horse from the army quartermaster.

Clark wrote that the Philadelphia residents expected the British to remain quiet in their winter quarters. Presently, the British were shoring up the roads by extending a ditch from the center city to the Upper Ferry. His spy thought that the British would "most easily be caught" while they were out cutting wood near the Schuylkill. His spy had already brought him some papers to present to Washington, and Clark expected "further information any moment, which will be perfectly satisfactory with respect to the Enemy's future intentions."

Meanwhile, Clark reported that "the Country people carry in provision constantly" to the British, despite the Continental Army's attempts to stop them on the roads. One of the "country people" pulled his spy's coat and called him a "damned Rebel" in front of a British advance sentry. But, before the sentry could catch him, the spy clapped his spurs on his horse and sped away, leaving the sentry lying in the road. As the country man returned, one of Clark's horsemen caught the country man, whom he learned was Edward Hughes, "a Papist" who lived in Springfield. He appealed to Clark's soldier, but Clark hoped that an example would be made of Hughes "to deter others."

The area needed a troop of two Horse stationed there, patrolling the roads. Speaking of horses, Clark noted that Washington told him to ask General Potter's quartermaster for a horse, which he did. However, the quartermaster told Clark that he would not give him a horse because "his Horses were too poor." Consequently, Clark used his own horses "and nearly ruined three."

He purchased a pony "to send Expresses," but "it is wore down, & I am obliged to return it to the Quartermaster" and use someone else's horse. Clark said that he had to "ride from 20 to 60 miles a Day to meet my Friends to prevent suspicion (the people being Quakers)." He asked for permission to purchase a horse, which he would return to the quartermaster. He added, "Otherwise, I must do it out of my own pocket, & my pay won't afford it." He concluded that if the quartermaster had any horses, "they are nearly worn out & won't do for my business."[25]

With all urgency, Deputy Commissary General Thomas Jones, at the Camp at the Gulph, wrote to Pennsylvania Council President Wharton about the poor condition of the troops and the desperate need for Pennsylvania to prioritize their support. "Honoured Sir, The approaching Calamity that Threatens our Army for want of Provisions (occasion'd by the scarcity of wagons now employ'd to hall the same to Camp) emboldens me to address you on the occasion, hoping your honour will take the same into consideration. At present there is not half teams employ'd in halling flowr, & c. to supply the great army now at camp."

Jones continued, "this present time there is not one single Barrell of flour to deliver out to the troops in Camp, nor cannot tell when I shall receive any; some Brigades have not Receiv'd flour for this day." He stated that he sent express riders to the Issuing Commissary at the Pennsylvania cities of

Lancaster, York, and Reading to get supplies down to the main army as soon as possible. However, the Commissaries at Lancaster and Reading said that they could not "procure wagons sufficient" to transport the supplies. "Unless an immediate step is taken to send daily 200 to 250 barrels of flour to Camp, the army will not be able to exist one week longer. I remain, Sir, In the greatest Distress..."[26]

Jonathan Bayard Smith, a Philadelphia merchant and member of the Continental Congress, wrote to George Bryan, Vice President of the State of Pennsylvania, about how the Continental Congress responded to Pennsylvania's general concerns about the Continental Army's winter quarters. He stated that on this date, Congress passed a resolution of this matter, which he did not enclose, but presumed would be sent more formally by the Pennsylvania congressional delegates. Yet, he did want Bryan to inform both houses of the Pennsylvania legislature what Congress did "for the present satisfaction." The letter ended, "We hear that the army are about putting in the Gulph Valley. This is the wish of Congress as far as I can judge."[27]

The December 19 Resolution that the Continental Congress passed, to which Smith referred, read:

> Congress resumed the consideration of the remembrances from the Council & Assembly of Pennsylvania, whereupon
>
> Resolved, That a copy of the remembrances be transmitted by express to general Washington, & that he be desired to inform Congress whether he has come to a fixed resolution to canton the army; & if he has, what line of cantonment he has proposed; In particular, what measures are agreed on for the protection of that part of Pennsylvania which lies on the easterly side of the Schuylkill & of the State of New Jersey.[28]

Importantly, the Pennsylvania Supreme Executive Council and General Assembly, and the Continental Congress, were now on one accord.

⚜

Across the sea in France, Franklin and the other American Commissioners continued to receive congratulatory letters regarding the American victory at Saratoga. Charles-Guillame-Frederic Dumas, States General for the Dutch, wrote to the American Commissioners from Algemeen Rijksarchief, The Hague, on behalf of the committee for foreign affairs. He wrote that he "sent messengers to all the provinces, undoubtedly, to carry the news of Saratoga and to suggest the probable consequences in Europe."[29]

Benjamin Sowden, in Holland, wrote to Franklin, in part, "Most heartily do I congratulate you on the late brilliant Success of the Provincial Arms at

Saratoga, hoping it will produce the most salutary events in favor of your Army under the Command of Genl. Washington, to the speedy emancipation of N. America from her present cruel Invaders and all tyrannical claims and the establishment of her Liberty and prosperity upon a solid and lasting Basis."[30]

He then wrote about a visit he had from Franklin's "worthy Friend" Dr. Ingenhausen, who planned to leave Brussels for England to spend most of the winter there: "I could not help observing to him that his having been lately with you, if known in London, would be no recommendation of him at the west end of Town. His Answer, accompanied with a Smile, was that tho' he gloried in the honor of Dr. Franklin's acquaintance and Friendship, prudential consideration would prevent his boasting of it in the Region of St. James [the English Royal palace]."[31]

And, Jean-Francois, Count de Reynaud, noted directly, "My congratulations on the glory that the brave Americans have deserved, I am myself American, though French, and would have wished with all my heart to share that glory on the famous day of General Burgoyne's capture. May the Howe brothers have the same fate."[32] The "Howe brothers" was a reference to William Howe, Commander in Chief of the British Army in America, and his brother, Richard, Commander of the Royal Navy in America.

So, on December 19, General Washington joined a long line of poorly clothed, often barely shoed, and hardly fed soldiers, down the Gulph Road, past the Gulph Mill that had provided them with what flour and cornmeal it could during the last six days. They marched past a large shale rock that protruded 8 feet over the Gulph Road, the rock that came to be widely known as the "Hanging Rock." The Hanging Rock, which the owner of the property on which it sits donated to the Valley Forge Historical Society in 1924 to ensure the rock's preservation, became nationally recognized as the symbol of the Gulph Mills Encampment when it was entered into the National Register of Historic Places in 1997.[33]

Thus ended the Gulph Mills Encampment. During that encampment, the relevant parties answered all five questions that were posed at the beginning of the encampment.

One, George Washington and the Continental Army leadership decided not to engage in a winter campaign against the British in Philadelphia.

Two, George Washington decided to establish winter quarters in Valley Forge, a place that would come to be revered for what occurred and what was accomplished there.

Three, the major existential concerns of the national and state legislative bodies were settled. The Continental Congress advanced one step further

1900s photo of the Hanging Rock, on Gulph Road by the Gulph Creek, in the defile called "the Gulph" or "the Gulf." George Washington and the Continental Army marched by the Hanging Rock during the Gulph Mills Encampment, and Washington was said to have climbed up on the top of it to watch his troops parade by. The Hanging Rock, which the owner of the property on which it sits donated to the Valley Forge Historical Society in 1924 to ensure the rock's preservation, is the symbol of the Gulph Mills Encampment that was entered into the National Register of Historic Places in 1997. Various historical societies and the community saved the rock from being cut back in part or in full to make it easier for modern cars to pass on Gulph Road. (Courtesy of the King of Prussia Historical Society)

towards the adoption and establishment of its proposed governing structure for the United States when Virginia became the first state to adopt the Articles of the Confederation. Washington quashed the fears of the Pennsylvania Supreme Executive Council and General Assembly that its citizens would be abandoned by the Continental Army if it established winter quarters in another state and left them to the depredations of the British in Philadelphia.

Four, the American Commissioners in France—Benjamin Franklin, Silas Deane, and Arthur Lee—finally persuaded King Louis XVI of France to publicly support the new United States in its war for freedom against their common archenemy, Britian.

Five, the British Army would not be able to run roughshod over the people of the Commonwealth of Pennsylvania all winter because the Continental Army would be right in their backyard, within a day's striking distance of the British winter quarters in Philadelphia.

All of these five monumental matters concluded by the end of the day, December 19, when the Continental Army marched out of its six-day encampment at a little place called Gulph Mills, on and in the shadow of the Conshohocken Hills, its highest point aptly called Rebel Hill.

CHAPTER 12

Gulph Mills During the Valley Forge Encampment

Gulph Mills maintained an important role during the Valley Forge Encampment, which lasted six months from December 19, 1777 to June 19, 1778. One reason was because of Gulph Mill's strategic location. The Gulph Road was a main road that was used by travelers to reach the Valley Forge area from the city of Philadelphia. It certainly was one of two main roads that the British could have used to get to the Continental Army's Winter Quarters at Valley Forge, the other being the Lancaster Road, which was a few miles away.

General Washington set up a picket post at Gulph Mills early on in the encampment, exactly when is not known, but it appears that it was not before the soldiers finished constructing their huts at Valley Forge. It is well-known that the site of the Gulph Mills picket post was at Jonathan Sturgis' home, directly across from the Gulph Mill. That location was important to the Valley Forge Encampment for several reasons. A section called "The Historical Picket Post" in a menu from the restaurant called the Picket Post, that was located in the Sturgis home from the 1960s to the 1990s, read, "The moment he decided on Valley Forge, Jonathan Sturgis' stone home guarding the defile to it became the most important post in his chain of defense. Thus, it became known as The Picket Post. Gulph Creek traversed a section through which the British would first have to penetrate should they decide to chase his army further inland. Placing an officer in charge at Gulph Mills, he set up a picket line which extended from Lancaster Pike to the Schuylkill River."[1]

The picket post had a rotating group of soldiers and officers who commanded it. The soldiers at that picket had to be aware at all times whether the British were headed in their direction.

As described herein in Chapter 5, on December 13 Lord Stirling commanded a picket post in Gulph Mills and stayed there on Rebel Hill at the home of John Rees during the first few weeks of the Valley Forge Encampment.[2] Washington called Stirling back to Valley Forge in early January, where he was headquartered at the home of William Currie.[3]

By early January, Captain Henry Lee, Jr., after following Washington's orders to acquaint himself "with the roads which communicate with the left of the army," recommended to Washington that a true picket post be set up at the Gulph Mill.[4] On January 9, Lee wrote to Washington from Scotts-farm, Pennsylvania, that, "If a post of infantry was established at the gulph-mill, (where a body of troops might be commodiously quartered, it would completely secure the left of the army,) tho' an accident should befall the patrole of hourse, & would be an additional security to the post at Radnor meeting."[5]

Richard Kidder Meade, a colonel in the 14th Virginia Regiment and aide-de-camp to Washington, replied to Lee that Washington was "struck with the propriety of taking a Post at the Gulph, but that our present situation renders it impossible, to be done at this time, as soon as the Huts are finished, and some other matters accomplished, your proposition will take place." Yet, recognizing the Gulph's strategic importance, he instructed Lee that "your attention to that part of the Country must be the greater, as you will be without the aid of any Patroles."[6]

A few weeks later the Gulph Mills picket post existed. Brigadier General Edward Hand's Orderly Book for January 10 included these After Orders: "A detachment of 300 men are to parade to-morrow morning at 9 o'clock, on the grand parade, to relieve Colo. Morgan's corps,[7] and prepare for a week's command. Colo. Stevens & Major Ledyard are appointed field officers for the detachment. Another detachment of one hundred & fifty men are to parade at the same time & place, to take post at the Gulph Mill for one week. Lt. Colo Rhea will take the Command of this detachment…"[8] Hand's notes about the detail for Gulph Mills shows that various generals contributed troops to reach the number of 150 guards. The numbers are: Huntington—19; Varnum—16; Muhlenberg—8; Weedon—10; Woodford—4; Scott—6; 1st Pennsylvania Regiment—8; 2nd Pennsylvania Regiment—7; Maxwell, Conway, Learned, and Glover—11 each; and Poor and Patterson—14 each.[9]

Washington's January 12 General Orders, read: "The detachments ordered to relieve Coll. Morgan & to take post at Gulph-Mill are to be on the grand parade and ready to march at sunrise tomorrow morning with their provisions completed to next Wednesday inclusively."[10]

One of the officers who commanded the picket post at Gulph Mills was Aaron Burr, the third Vice President of the United States, under President Thomas Jefferson. Burr is infamously known as the man who killed Alexander

Hamilton in a duel in 1804, rather than the man who lost the 1800 election for President of the United States to Thomas Jefferson by one vote.[11] At the time of the Valley Forge Encampment, Burr was a lieutenant colonel who commanded Malcolm's Additional Continental Regiment.

The exact dates that Burr commanded the Gulph Mills picket are unknown, but his actions during his command are legendary. The soldiers who were initially stationed at the picket were members of the militia, most likely Pennsylvania Militia. They were not well disciplined or well trained, and that caused problems for the main army.

Washington stationed a "strong body of militia" at the Gulph to warn the main army at Valley Forge if the British approached. These largely untrained and undisciplined soldiers thought that they heard the British Army approaching with every noise at night. Consequently, the militia men kept sending alarms—false ones—to the headquarters at Valley Forge, causing Washington to keep the main army up and on alert all night. The leadership soon determined that the militia did not have the proper discipline or observation skills. General Alexander McDougal from the 1st New York Regiment, a Scottish-born merchant-seaman, recommended to Washington that he put Colonel Burr in charge of the picket.

Immediately, Burr established more rigorous and severe discipline. He often showed up at the picket when he was not expected to be there, keeping the militia men on their toes. Burr's system of discipline and command grew intolerable to the militia men. In the past, while they were in winter quarters, these members of the militia were accustomed to idleness, practically coming and going as they pleased, and to taking whatever goods they needed for their pleasure from area residents, without regard to the residents' comfort and existence, all under cover of duty and patriotism.

Most of the militia "were exceedingly discontented, and finally resolved at any cost to rid themselves of" Burr. However, Burr learned about their plot and devised his own. One evening, before sending the soldiers out on patrol, Burr removed the cartridges from their muskets. Holding "a well-sharpened sword," Burr marched down the line and looked the ringleaders in the face, observing their smallest movement. One soldier stepped out of line and shouted, "Now is your time, my boys," while he pointed his musket at Burr. In a flash, Burr raised his sword and hit that ringleader on his arm, above his shoulder, with all the force he could muster. The force from Burr's sword broke the ringleader's bone and left his arm hanging by mere bits of skin. Cooly, Burr looked the man dead in the eye and quietly said, "Take your place in the line, sir."

The ringleader stepped back in line, Burr dismissed the rest of the soldiers, and they went to bed. The next morning, the ringleader's arm was amputated. Burr heard no more talk about mutiny, and there were no more false alarms under his command.[12]

The Gulph Mills picket would necessarily be involved in any Continental Army activity that occurred in the area of the Gulph. On April 16, Washington wrote to Colonel Henry Beekman Livingston in response to Livingston's idea to engage in a surprise maneuver to capture British troops that were located around Barren Hill in Whitemarsh Township and to monitor the movements of those British troops from the high hills in Gulph Mills. Livingston led the 4th New York Regiment, which was part of General Gates's left wing in the successful Battle of Saratoga. The regiment later joined the main army at Valley Forge. Livingston's children went on to claim, after his death in 1828, that Livingston was actually the author of the famous poem "The Night Before Christmas," not Clement Clark Moore.[13]

Washington told Livingston that he supported his plan and that he should work it out while being "exceedingly cautious, & secret, in the scheme." Washington also told Livingston, "It will be necessary for you to inform Lt Colo. Smith of your design as his aid may be wanted." Lieutenant Colonel William Stephens Smith commanded a detachment of troops from Lee's, Henley's, and Jackson's regiments that had been stationed at the Gulph since at least April 11.[14] Also, Washington told Livingston to inform and get the cooperation of Colonel Morgan, who commanded a picket post in Villanova, Radnor Township, on the grounds of a 400-foot hill called Camp Woods.[15]

The return for Colonel Henry Jackson's regiment, called Jackson's Additional Continental Regiment, for May 2, 1778, is registered with his location as Gulph Mills, with 131 active and present for duty officers and rank-and-file soldiers, 15 sick present, and 55 sick absent. The return also noted the number of prisoners who were wounded, "Prisoner wounded in Phila/ on Road/ at Grist Mill/ Upper Merion." Jackson also filed a return from May 9 as "Advanced Piquet Gulph Mills" showing 123 rank-and-file present and fit for duty, along with 44 officers, seven soldiers sick absent, and 34 soldiers sick present. Similarly, Jackson filed a return from June 15 marked "Gulph Picquet," with 236 active rank-and-file, 31 officers, 32 sick absent, and 21 sick present.

The National Archives' Revolutionary War records for May 1778 show a number of soldiers at the Gulph from the muster rolls for the 16th Massachusetts Regiment, Captain Brown's Company of the Regiment of Foot, and Lt. Thomas Lamb's Company in the Regiment of Foot, commanded by Col. Henry Jackson.[16]

Strength return from Henry Jackson's regiment from the Gulph Mills picket, May 2, 1778. (Library of Congress)

At least one pension application on behalf of a deceased soldier noted that he served at the Gulph Mills picket during the Valley Forge Encampment. The pension application for Melancthon Lloyd Woolsey, who served at the

Gulph Mills picket post during the Valley Forge Encampment, was made by his widow Alida. The application stated that in June 1777, Lloyd was in Boston until December following, "when he marched with a detachment to be moved taking an amount of fixed ammunition for Carlisle, but stopped at Lancaster, where his men were inoculated (such as had not had it) for the small pox; after which the Regiment was ordered to Valley Forge and were immediately detailed in advance to the Gulf Mills, whose possessions continually harassed until Sir Henry Clinton evacuated Philadelphia."[17]

Another function that Gulph Mills served during the encampment was as a site for court martials. There were several.

One of the first court martials must have been for some of the Pennsylvania Militia troops who fought in the Battle of Matson's Ford. General Potter appointed Colonel Lacey, who performed so admirably in that battle, as the Judge Advocate to oversee the court martial trial of some of those men who threw away their arms during the retreat in the battle.

Lacey described the experience this way: Several of the men were found guilty of throwing away their muskets, their cartouch boxes that they used to store and carry cartridges, and their knapsacks. Some were ordered to pay for the items they threw away. Others were judged to be publicly whipped. Lacey was gratified to find that there was not a single missing gun, knapsack, cartouch box, or blanket in his regiment, which he said went to their honor.

General Potter ordered the sentence to be carried out. Several men were actually given "fifteen to thirty lashes which caused much murmuring among the Militia." Lacey wrote, "the General was highly censured for it" and that the men "became so exasperated." Lacey thought that the rest of the brigade might mutiny because of the harsh sentences. However, they were sent to join the other part of the militia under General Armstrong in North Wales, where "the men became tranquil and pacified."[18]

On January 28, 1778, Armstrong, then back in Carlisle, in central Pennsylvania, even wrote to Lacey so that Lacey could understand "what effect the severity of this Discipline had on the minds of the people whose friends were suffered by the Judgment of the Court Martial inflicted by order of General Potter."

The letter from General Armstrong read, "a great deal of heat and publik clamour hath gone abroad against Genl. Potter and the Member of a Certain Court Martial held by his Orders, the sentence of which they say was to punish with whip[ping] & also paying for the Arms thrown away, which they consider as a double Punishment for one offence. In this piece of discipline, its like some persons where Whipped who in other respects had been well behaved, and when at home are Creditable People." He added that "the whole matter is not fairly stated," and that the "discipline was no doubt too high." Even if some of the men deserved punishment, it was not good policy.

Armstrong stated that he was grieved that "an Officer possessed of many good Qualities as General Potter is, should have such a Clamour raised against him on this occasion."

One good point, Armstrong noted, was that it was chiefly people who lived in the western part of Pennsylvania, where Potter and many of the involved militia came from, "who have been offended," not those in the eastern part of the state, where Lacey came from. Armstrong added that there was no mention made of Lacey, "so that I suppose you will escape the Censure."[19]

Another court martial is mentioned in Washington's May 1 General Orders. It stated, "A General Court Martial whereof Major Tyler is appointed President is ordered to sit tomorrow ten oClock in the forenoon at the Gulph to try such Persons as shall be brought before them, six Captains and eight Subalterns will attend as Members." The May 5 General Orders refer to that court martial as having been held where a soldier in Col. Henry Jackson's Regiment, which was posted at the Gulph Mills picket, was tried for desertion from his post while on sentry duty, found guilty of a breach of the Articles of War, and "sentenced to be hung by the Neck 'till he is dead."[20]

Interestingly, the same day, the After Orders noted how the army would celebrate on the next day the signing of the French Alliance of February 1778. Word of the alliance, which began to be negotiated on that momentous day of December 17, as noted in Chapter 9 of this book, took months to reach the United States. On May 6, the whole army was ordered to shout, "Huzza! Long Live the King of France!" "Huzza! And long live the friendly European powers!" and then "Huzza! To the American States!" amid marching, pomp and circumstance, feasting, and drinking in a "feu de joie." No doubt the soldiers rejoiced also that "Each man is to have a Gill of rum."[21]

Again, local residents interacted with the Continental Army soldiers who were at the Gulph Mills picket, right in their own backyard. The picket took its toll on local residents as citizen and soldier alike struggled with scarce resources.

Washington aide-de-camp Captain Tench Tilghman, of the Continental Army's Flying Camp, on May 14, sent to Washington a complaint from Gulph Mills resident Phillip Reese about Col. Henry Jackson, of Jackson's Additional Continental Regiment, who commanded the Gulph Mills picket.

"Phillip Reese an inhabitant of the Gulf has been at Head Quarters with a complaint that some of the Officers of your detachment have forcibly put some sick into his House altho' there is an empty House, an empty School

House and a Church, all more suitable for sick, in the Neighbourhood."[22] He further says that they took his "Feather Beds, Sheets & pillows from him." Tilghman continued, "This is Mr. Reese's story, but as his Excellency does not chuse ever to give judgment ex parte, he desired me to inform you of it, with a wish that you would enquire into it, and if the man has been aggrieved, redress him."[23]

Also, Gulph Mills and the soldiers at the picket post there played a role in the Battle of Barren Hill, on May 18–20. General Washington had ordered General Lafayette to Barren Hill, near the site of the former Whitemarsh Encampment, to keep an eye on and obtain intelligence regarding the British. Washington's intelligence showed that, since it was spring, the British were ready to leave Philadelphia, but maybe not without first trying to attack the army in Valley Forge.[24]

The soldiers at the Gulph Mills picket post were ordered to join the 2,200 men that Lafayette had with him, which included about 40 members of the Oneida Indian Nation who had marched down from New York and just arrived three days earlier, on May 15, to support the Continental Army at Valley Forge. At the time, Colonel Jackson had command of the picket.

The British, who had eyes and spies everywhere, found out that Lafayette was at Barren Hill. Commander in Chief General Howe went out himself with a group of troops, as did General Henry Clinton, Major General James Grant, and Major General Charles "No Flint" Grey to engage with and capture Lafayette and his men. However, the Continental Army had its eyes, too. Lafayette's scouts warned him about the British movement. Generals Howe and Grey reached their positions without discovery. Grant learned where Lafayette's forces were posted and prepared to attack. The quick-thinking Lafayette evaded Grant "with a combination of swift marching, good discipline, and bluff,"[25] and retreated back over the Matson's Ford.

There were reports that Washington was on his horse, on the heights of the Conshohocken Hills, watching what played out at Barren Hill, ready to call out all of the forces at Valley Forge if necessary. Some speculated that Washington raced to the Conshohocken Hills to observe what was going on, from a distance, out of concern for Lafayette, with whom he had developed a father-son type relationship.[26] Equally probable was that Washington learned that British Commander in Chief Howe was out with his forces, so Washington went out to join his Continental forces, in what could have been one last engagement before both armies left their winter quarters.

Later that month, on May 23, Washington warned Brigadier General Smallwood of intelligence that the British might try to attack him at his headquarters in Wilmington. Washington advised Smallwood to fall back towards the Schuylkill should this happen. Again, given Gulph Mills' strategic location, Washington ordered Colonel Morgan, who was alternately posted both at Radnor and at Gulph Mills, to be ready.

Richard Kidder Meade, one of Washington's aides-de-camp,[27] sent a letter by Light Dragoons to Colonel Morgan "at the Gulf." It read, "His Excellency has this Instant received intelligence that the Enemy mean very shortly to move your way, you are therefore desired to keep the most vigilant watch, & that, as near their Bridge & other places as you possibly can, Should you make discoveries of the sort, you will give the very earliest notice of it. This you will please to communicate to Colo. Smith at the Gulf, & also to Colo. Van Schaick."[28]

Washington's aide-de-camp, Tilghman, also sent a letter to Colonel Morgan "at Radnor," and stated, "We have fresh reason to believe that the Enemy are prepared to move, perhaps this Night. If they come out in force, General Smallwood will expect to have the intelligence from you, you are therefore to keep two of your best Horse ready mounted, and dispatch them to him; one a little while after the other for fear of accident."[29]

June was also a busy time at the Gulph. In his June 7 General Orders, Washington stated that "A General Court-Martial to sit tomorrow at nine oClock at the Gulph-Mill to try such Persons as shall be brought before them—Lieutt Coll Smith will Preside—Four Captains and eight Subalterns from Colonel Jackson's detachment to attend as Members."[30]

On June 9, Gulph Mills resident John Johnston wrote Washington about how the "Guards at the Gulph" were damaging his property and requested that Washington do something to stop it. Johnston also took the liberty of telling Washington how he had suffered during the Gulph Mills Encampment and the British foraging expedition of December 11.

He wrote, "on the Eleventh of Decr last your Petitioner was Plundered by the Brittish Army of almost every thing I had, (to a Considerable amount,)—Except my working horses. that when the army under Your Excellencie's Command Marched from White Marsh to the Gulf a Number of them Encamped on my Land, & burnt upwards of Ten thousand Rails." The result of those soldiers' actions in December was that "my Winter Crop is entirely ruined, & my Meadow & three Orchards are left without any fence, that the Guards at the Gulph or Some of them make a Common Practice of taking my horses out of the Gears from me & riding them about two or three days, & Never less than One day & Night, by which Severe hard usage my horse are not able to Do my own Work neither can I keep them one Whole day together at home."[31]

Johnston pleaded, "May it Please Your Excellency to Put a Stop to the Practice of Officers impressing my horses & taking them by night, I have no Grain left To reap this next harvest & if I am deprived of Getting a fall Crop in for another Season, I Shall be utterly ruined and distresed." In closing, Johnston prayed as "Your greatly distressed Petitioner," that Washington would "be so kind as to Grant me a Protection for my horses & for three Yearling heifers which I Have Purchased lately (which is all my Stocks) that none of them be taken From me."[32]

Washington's aide-de-camp Alexander Hamilton took Johnston's petition and wrote on the bottom of it, ostensibly to Colonel Henry Jackson, who still commanded the picket post at the Gulph at that time. Hamilton wrote, "Sir—His Excellency desires you will put a stop, by every mean in your power to the above practice. Any officer who shall be found impressing this man's horses without proper authority will be most severely dealt with."[33]

Colonel Jackson drew complaints about his command at the Gulph picket just about up until the end of the Valley Forge Encampment. In General Orders on June 16, 1778, Washington ordered, "A Court of Enquiry with Colonel Cortlandt presiding to sit the next day at Cortlandt's Quarters to consider and report upon a Complaint by Capt. Jarvis against Colonel Jackson." Members of the court were to include Lieutenant Colonel North, Major Porter, and a captain from Muhlenberg's and Paterson's brigades.[34]

Thus ends the recitation of the role of Gulph Mills during the Valley Forge Encampment.

⚜

This ends this story about the importance of what happened during the Gulph Mills Encampment of the Revolutionary War, how the events of those six days in December shaped the foundation and set the future for the Continental Army, the new United States of America and its government, the Commonwealth of Pennsylvania, its people, and its government.

A forgotten and overlooked period in American history—the Gulph Mills Encampment—is forgotten and overlooked no more.

Appendix

Letter from General George Washington to Henry Laurens, President of the Continental Congress, December 10, 1777[1]

I have the honor to inform you, that in the course of last week from a variety of intelligence I had reason to expect that Genl Howe was preparing to give us a general Action. Accordingly on Thursday night he moved from the City with all his Force, except a very inconsiderable part left in his Lines & Redoubts, and appeared the next morning on Chestnut Hill in front of, & about three miles distant from our Right wing. As soon as their position was discovered, the Pennsylvania Militia were ordered from our Right to skirmish with their light advanced parties, and I am sorry to mention, that Brigadr Genl Irvine, who led them on, had the misfortune to be wounded and to be made prisoner. Nothing more occurred on that day. On Friday night the Enemy changed their Ground and moved to our left within a mile of our line, where they remained quiet and advantageously posted the whole of the next day. On Sunday they inclined still further to our left, and from every appearance there was reason to apprehend they were determined on an Action. In this movement, their advanced and flanking parties were warmly attacked by Colo. Morgan & his Corps, and also by the Maryland Militia under Colo. Gist. Their loss I cannot ascertan, but I am informed [I]t was considerable, having regard to the number of the Corps who engaged them. About Sunset, after various marches and countermarches they halted, and I still supposed from their disposition and preceding manuvres that they would attack us in the Night, or early the next morning, but in this I was mistaken. On Monday afternoon, they began to move again and instead of advancing filed off from their Right, and the first certain account, that I could obtain of their intentions was, that they were in full march towards Philadelphia by Two or Three Routs. I immediately detached light parties after them to fall upon their Rear, but they were not able to come up with 'em. The Enemy's loss, as I have observed, I cannot ascertain. One account from the City is, that Five hundred wounded had been sent in: Another is that Eighty two Waggons had gone in with Men in this situation. These I fear are both exaggerated and not to be depended upon. We lost Twenty Seven Men in Morgans Corps killed & wounded, besides Major Morris, a Brave & gallant Officer, who is among the latter: Of the Maryland Militia, there were also Sixteen or Seventeen wounded. I have not received further Returns yet. I sincerely wish, that they had made an attack, the Issue in all probability, from the dis[positi]on of our Troops and the strong situ[ation] of our Camp, would have been for[tunate] and happy. At the same time, I m[ust add,] that reason, prudence, and every principle of policy forbad us quitting our post to attack them. Nothing but success would have justified the measure, and this could not be expected from their position.

Resolution of the Continental Congress to General George Washington, December 10, 1777[2]

Resolved, That General Washington be informed, that Congress have observed, with deep concern, that the principal supplies for the army under his command have, since the loss of Philadelphia, been drawn from distant quarters, whereby great expence has accrued to the public, the army has been irregularly and [often] scantily supplied, and the established magazines greatly reduced, while large quantities of stock, provision and forage, are still remaining in the counties of Philadelphia, Bucks and Chester, which, by the fortune of war, may be soon subjected to the power of the enemy:

That Congress, firmly persuaded of General Washington's zeal and attachment to the interest of these states, can only impute his forbearance in exercising the powers vested in him by Congress, by their resolutions of the 17 September and 14 November, to a delicacy in exerting military authority on the citizens of these states; a delicacy, which though highly laudable in general, may, on critical exigencies, prove destructive to the army and prejudicial to the general liberties of America: That from these considerations, it is the desire and expectation of Congress, that General Washington should, for the future, endeavour as much as possible to subsist his army from such parts of the country as are in its vicinity, and especially from such quarters as he shall deem most likely to be subjected to the power or depredations of the enemy: and that he issue orders for such purpose to the commissaries and quarter masters belonging to the army:

That General Washington be directed to order every kind of stock and provisions in the country above-mentioned, which may be beneficial to the army or serviceable to the enemy, to be taken from all persons without distinction, leaving such quantities only as he shall judge necessary for the maintenance of their families; the stock and provisions so taken to be removed to places of security under the care of proper persons to be appointed for that purpose; and that he issue a proclamation, requiring all persons within seventy miles of head quarters, forthwith to thresh out their grain within such limited periods of time, as he shall deem reasonable, on penalty, in case of failure, of having the same seized by the commissaries and quarter masters of the army and paid for as straw:

That General Washington be directed to cause all provisions, stock, forage, waggons and teams, which may be, at any time, in the route of the enemy, and which cannot be seasonably removed, to be destroyed. Whereas, it is essentially necessary, that magazines should be seasonably provided in the interior part of the country, and many inhabitants, through motives of avarice or disaffection, refuse to thresh out their grain.

Resolved, That it be earnestly recommended to the legislature of the commonwealth of Pennsylvania, forthwith to enact a law, requiring all persons within the county of York their State, at the distance of seventy miles and upwards, from General Washington's head quarters, and below the Blue Mountains, to thresh out their wheat and other grain, within as short a period of time as the said legislature shall deem sufficient for that purpose; and, in case of failure, to subject the same to seizure by the commissaries and quarter masters of the American army, to be paid for at the price of straw only, excepting from such penalty, such families only, who, from the absence of the master, sons or servants, in the service of their country, can give good proof that their compliance with the said law was not practicable.

Extract from the minutes, CHA. THOMSON, Sec'y.

Resolution of the Supreme Executive Council & General Assembly of the Commonwealth of Pennsylvania, December 17, 1777[3]

At a Conference with the Supreme Executive Council & Gen'l Assembly of this State, held in the Assembly Room Resolv[d], that a Remonstrance be Immediately drawn up & forwarded to Congress, against the Propos'd Cantoonment of the Army of the United States, under command of his Excell[r] Gen[l] Washington, & that the following reasons be urged.

1st. That by the Armys removal to the West side of the Schuylkill, as far as Wilmington & in its neighbourhood, great part of this State, particularly that on the East side, together with the State of New Jersey, must be left in the Power of the Enemy, subject to their Ravages—the Inhabitants be obliged either to fly to the neighboring States, or submit to such Terms as the Enemy may prescribe.

2d. That the State Assembly, at their last session, had laid a tax of 5s, in the Pound on all Estates, real & Personal, in order to call in & Sink the monies Issued by this Government, & at this Session had Resolv'd over & above [said] Tax to raise the sum of 620,000 [Dollars] for support of the War for the Ensuing Year, agreeable to resolve of Congress—both [which] Taxes must infalliably fail, provided the Army go into Cantoonment, at such a Distance as will prevent their covering the Country from the Depredations of the Enemy, it being a melancholly truth, that too many of our People are so disafected already that nothing but the neighborhood of the Army keeps them subjet to Government, whilst the Whigs, & those who have taken the most active Part in support of our Cause, will be discouraged & give up all as lost.

3d. By the removal of our Army it will be impossible to recruit the Regiments of this State, as those who would be active & Zealous in promoting that measure will be obliged to leave the State, whilst the Torys & Disafected will gain Strength, in many places perhaps declare openly for the Enemy, by [which] means there will be a probablility of their not only Supplying their Exausted Magazines, but greatly strengthening their Arm.

4th. The Army removing at a Distance from the Enemy must give a fatal Stab to the Credit of the Continental Currency throughout this State. It is a melancholy truth, that it is very Difficult to purchase from many of our most able Farmers the necessary Provisions of our Army, owing to their fear of the money—but this difficulty must be greatly Encreaed when another Market without Interruption, will open to them where they will receive at least a promise of hard money.

Letter from the American Commissioners Benjamin Franklin, Silas Deane, and Arthur Lee to the Continental Congress's Committee for Foreign Affairs, December 18, 1777, from Franklin's Residence in Passy, France[4]

Since our last of Nov. 30, a Copy of which is herewith sent you, we receive your Dispatches of Oct. 6. from York Town. They came to us by a Packet from Boston, which brought the great News of Burgoynes Defeat and Surrender, News that apparently occasion'd as much general Joy in France, as if it had been a Victory of their own Troops over their own Enemies; such is the universal warm and sincere Goodwill and Attachment to us and our Cause in this Nation.

We took the Opportunity of pressing the Ministry by a short Memorial to the Conclusion of our propos'd Treaty which had so long lain under their Consideration, and been from time to time postponed: A Meeting was had accordingly on Friday the 12th Inst. In which some Difficulties were mention'd and remov'd, some Explications ask'd and given, to Satisfaction. As the Concurrance of Spain is necessary, we were told, that a Courier should be dispatch'd the next Day to obtain it, which we are since assured was done; and in three Weeks from the Time the Answer is expected.

On signifying to the Ministry the Importance it might be of at this Juncture, when probably Britain would be making the same Propositions of Accommodation, that the Congress should be inform'd explicitly, what might be expected from France and Spain, M. Gerard, one of the Secretaries, came Yesterday to inform us *by order of the King, that after a long and full Consideration of our Affairs and Propositions in Council, it was decided and his Majesty was determined to acknowledge our Independence and make a Treaty with us of Amity and Commerce* [emphasis added]; that in this Treaty no Advantage would be taken of our present Situation to obtain Terms from us which otherwise would not be convenient for us to agree to, his Majesty desiring that the Treaty once made should be durable, and our Amity subsist forever, which could not be expected if each Nation did not find its Interest in the Continuance as well as in the Commencement of it. It was therefore his Intention that the Terms of the Treaty should be such as we might be willing to agree to, if our State had long since established, and in the fullness of Strength and Power, and such as we shall approve of when that time shall come. That his Majesty was fix'd in his Determination, not only to acknowledge but to support our Independence, by every means in his Power. That in doing this he might probably be soon engag'd in War, with all the Expences, Risque and Damage usually attending it; yet he should not expect any Compensation from us on that Account, nor pretend that he acted wholly for our Sakes, since besides his real Goodwill to us and our Cause, it was manifestly the Interest of France that the Power of England should be diminish'd by our Separation from it. He should moreover not so much as insist, that if he engag'd in a War with England on our Account we should not make a separate Peace, he would have us be at full Liberty to make a peace for ourselves, whenever good and advantageous Terms were offered to us; The only Condition he should require and rely on would be this, that we in no Peace to be made with England should give up our Independency, and return to the Obedience of that Government. That as soon as the Courier [returned] from Spain with the Concurrence expected, the Affair would be proceeded in and concluded; and of this we might give the Congress the strongest Assurances in our Dispatches, only cautioning them to keep the whole for the present a dead Secret, as Spain had three Reasons for not immediately declaring; her Money Fleet had not yet come home; her Brasil Army and Fleet the same; and her Peace with Portugal not yet quite completed; but these Obstacles would probably soon be removed. We answered, that in what had been communicate to us, we perceiv'd and admir'd equally the King's magnanimity and his Wisdom; That he would find us faithful and firm Allies, and we wish'd with his Majesty that the Amity between the two Nations might be eternal. And mentioning that Republicks were usually steady in their Engagements, for Instance the Swiss Cantons, the Secretary remarked, that France had been as steady with Regard to them two hundred Years having pass'd since their first Alliance for 50 Years had commenc'd which had been renew'd from time to time and such had been her uniform good Faith towards them that as it appear'd in the last renewal, the Protestant Cantons were free from their ancient Prejudices and Suspicions and join'd readily with the rest in the League, of which we herewith send you a Copy.

It is sometime since we obtain'd a Promise of an additional Aid of three Million of Livres, which we shall receive in January. Spain we are told will give an equal Sum but finding it inconvenient to remit here, she purposes sending it from the Havana in specie to the Congress. What we receive here will help get us out of Debt.

Our Vessels laden with Supplies have by various means been delay'd, particularly by fear of falling into the Hands of the English cruizing Ships, who swarm in the Bay and Channel. At length it is resolv'd they shall sail together, as they are all provid'd for Defence, and we have obtain'd a King's Ship to convoy them out of the Channel, and we hope quite to America.

They will carry we think to the amount of L70,000 Sterling and sail in a few Days. Also, in Consideration of the late frequent Losses of our Dispatches and the Importance of the present, we have apply'd for and obtain'd a Fregate to carry them. These extraordinary Favours, of a Nature provoking to Great Britian, are marks of the Sincerity of this Court, and seem to demand the Thanks of Congress.

We have accepted 5 bills drawn on us by the President, in favour of some return'd Officers, and shall pay them punctually. But as we receive no Remittances for our Support, and the Cargo in the Amphitrite is claimed from us by M. Beaumarchais and we are not certain that we can keep it, we hope Congress will be sparing in their Drafts, except for the Interest mentioned in our former Letters, of which we now repeat the Assurances of payment: Otherwise we may be much embarrassed and our situation rendered very uncomfortable.

It is said the French Ambassador at London has desired to be recalled, being affronted there, where the late News from America has created a violent Ferment. There is also Talk here of Lord Stormont's recall. The Stocks in England fall fast; and on both sides there is every Appearance of an approaching War.

Being informed by the concurring Reports of many who had escaped, that our People, Prisoners in England are treated with great Inhumanity, we have written a Letter of Expostulation on the Subject to Lord North, which is sent over by a Person express, whom we have instructed to visit the Prisons, and (under the Directions of Mr. Hartley) to relieve as much as may be the most necessitous. We shall hereafter acquaint you with the Result. The Expences we are put to by those who get to us are very considerable.

The Supplies not going out from hence, and what we have sent and are sending from Spain, tho' far short of your Orders (which we have executed as far as we are able) will be we hope, with private Adventurs encourag'd by us, and others, put you into pretty good Circumstances as to Clothing, Arms, &c, if they arrive: And we shall continue to send, as Ability and Opportunity may permit. Please to present our Duty to Congress, and believe us, with sincere Esteem, Gentlemen, Your most obedient humble Servant.

B. Franklin
Silas Deane
Arthur Lee

Letter from Brigadier General Casimir Pulaski, who came from Poland to volunteer for the Continental Army, to General Washington, advocating for the creation of a United States Cavalry, December 19, 1777[5]

In my preceding representations I have been particular respecting the present State of the Cavalry, the means by which it may be augmented & completed—but on this head I must necessarily know your Excellencys determination—The advantages that would arise from a Superiority in Cavalry are too obvious to be unnoticed—It may be further observed that during this war, the Country will daily become more open & Clear of woods & fences Consequently better adopted to the manoevres & Service of the Cavalry.

While we are superiour in Cavalry the enemy will not dare to extend their force, and, Notwithstanding we act on the defensive we Shall have many Opportunitys of attacking & destroying the enemy by degrees, whereas if they have it in their power to augment their Cavalry & we Suffer ours to diminish & dwindle away. It may happen that the loss of a Battle will terminate in our Total defeat—Our Army once dispersed & pursued by their Horse will never be able to fully rally, thus our retreat may early be Cutt off, our baggage lost, our principal Officers taken & many other events occur not less Fatal.

Your Excellency must be too much Occupyed, to take Cognizance of the detail of every department—a workman requires proper Tools to Carry on his business & if he does not use them in their place he Can never be perfect. Your Excellency is undoubtedly acquainted with yours, therefore, a person possessing your Confidence & properly authorised is essentially necessary to answer decisively Such proposals as I have made in my late representations respecting the Cavalry.

I must not omit to mention here the dissatisfaction you have expressed at my seemingly in attention to your order—Your Excellency may be assured that the good of the Service is my Constant Study but the Weak State of the Corps I command renders it impossible to perform every Service required Nay my reputation is exposed as being an entire Stranger in the country the least accident would suffice to injure me but Notwithstanding, I Cannot avoid hazarding every thing that is valuable in life.

Signed C. Pulaski Gl of Cavalry.

[Postscript]
If you think that my request is important & Right and that You Would before expect the Resolution of Congress; I Would be glad to be the bearer of Your letters, to Congress I hope to obtain sooner by that way their Resolved as we want So many things there is not time to be lost.

Endnotes

Front Matter

1. Extracts of poem from Phillis Wheatly to General George Washington; "Enclosure: Poem by Phillis Wheatley, 26 October 1775," *Founders Online,* National Archives, https://founders.archives.gov/documents/Washington/03-02-02-0222-0002. [Original source: Philander D. Chase, ed., *The Papers of George Washington*, Revolutionary War Series, Vol. 2, *16 September 1775–31 December 1775*, Charlottesville: University Press of Virginia, 1987, 242–44.] Note from Founders Online: *The Pennsylvania Magazine: or, American Monthly Museum*, 2 (April 1776), 193.
2. Charles Henry Browning, *Welsh Settlement of Pennsylvania* (Philadelphia, PA: W. J. Campbell, 1912), 2.
3. John Laurens and William Gilmore Simms, *The Army Correspondence of Colonel John Laurens in the Years 1777–8*, 1867: Introduction, no page number; *The antiquary. A comedy, acted by her majesties servants at the Cock-pit.* Written by Shackerly Mermion, 1603–1639. London, printed by F. K. for I. W. and F. E., 1641. https://hdl.handle.net/2027/gri.ark:/13960/t5jb2mz67.
4. Joseph Plumb Martin, *A Narrative of Some of the Adventures, Dangers and Sufferings of a Revolutionary Soldier* (Glazier, Masters & Co., 1830), https://www.google.com/books/edition/A_Narrative_of_Some_of_the_Adventures_Da/ZbdcAAAAcAAJ?hl=en.

Introduction

1. William Baker, "The Camp by the Old Gulph Mill," *Pennsylvania Magazine of History and Biography* 17, no. 4 (1893): 429. http://www.jstor.org/stable/20083558.
2. Baker, "Camp," 414.
3. For excellent books on the Philadelphia Campaign, see Thomas J. McGuire, *The Philadelphia Campaign Volume I: Brandywine and the Fall of Philadelphia* (Mechanicsburg, PA: Stackpole Books, 2006); Thomas J. McGuire, *The Philadelphia Campaign Volume II: Germantown and the Roads to Valley Forge* (Mechanicsburg, PA: Stackpole Books, 2006); and Thomas J. McGuire, *Battle of Paoli* (Mechanicsburg, PA: Stackpole Books, 2006).
4. Gulph Mills became part of Montgomery County when the county was created in 1784 out of part of Philadelphia County.
5. "Conshohocken (/ˌkɒnʃəˈhɒkən/ kon-shə-HOK-ən; Lenape: Kanshihàkink) is a borough on the Schuylkill River in Montgomery County, Pennsylvania, in suburban Philadelphia. The name 'Conshohocken' comes from the Unami language, from either Kanshi'hak'ing, meaning 'Elegant-ground- place', or, more likely, Chottschinschu'hak'ing, which means 'Big-trough-ground-place' or 'Large-bowl-ground-place', referring to the big bend in the Tulpe'hanna (Turtle

River, or modern Schuylkill River). Conshohocken has also been translated from the Lenape Native American word for 'pleasant valley' due to the area's natural beauty." From "About Conshohocken | Conshohocken Historical Society," Conshohocken HS, accessed February 6, 2024, https://www.conshohockenhistoricalsociety.org/about-conshohocken. William Penn purchased the land from the Lenni Lenape. Conshohocken Register (Conshohocken, PA: Recorder Publishing Company, 1920).

6   S. Paul Teamer, "The Welsh Tract," *TEHS Quarterly Archives (Tredyffrin Easttown Historical Society)* 2, no. 1 (January 1939): 19–24, https://www.tehistory.org/hqda/html/v02/v02n1p019.html.

7   "Battle of Brandywine—Brandywine Battlefield Park Associates," Brandywine Battlefield, accessed February 12, 2024, https://brandywinebattlefield.org/battle.

8   "Brandywine," American Battlefield Trust, accessed February 14, 2024, https://battlefields.org/learn/revolutionary-war/battles/brandywine.

9   Michael Bertram, ed., "The Revolutionary War," *Tredyffrin Easttown Historical Society Quarterly Archives* 44, no. 1 & 2, The History of Tredyffrin Township (2007): 22–26, https://www.tehistory.org/hqda/html/v44/v44n1+2p022.html.

10 Thomas J. McGuire, *Battle of Paoli* (Mechanicsburg, PA: Stackpole Books, 2006), 133–34, 185–86.

11 "Milestones: 1776–1783—Office of the Historian," n.d. History.state.gov. https://history.state.gov/milestones/1776-1783/secret-committee.

12 "E Pluribus Unum—History of Motto Carried by Eagle on Great Seal," n.d. Greatseal.com. https://greatseal.com/mottoes/unum.html.

13 "Howe hoped that by seizing Philadelphia, he would rally the Loyalists in Pennsylvania, discourage the rebels by capturing the capital, and bring the war to a speedy conclusion." "Revolutionary War: The Turning Point, 1776–1777 | the American Revolution, 1763–1783 | U.S. History Primary Source Timeline | Classroom Materials at the Library of Congress | Library of Congress," Library of Congress, n.d. https://www.loc.gov/classroom-materials/united-states-history-primary-source-timeline/american-revolution-1763-1783/revolutionary-war-turning-point-1776-1777.

14 Darlene Emmert Fisher, "Social Life in Philadelphia during the British Occupation," *Pennsylvania History: A Journal of Mid-Atlantic Studies* 37, no. 3 (1970): 237, https://www.jstor.org/stable/27771875.

15 McGuire, *Philadelphia Campaign*, Vol. 2, 222.

16 Charles R. Barker, "The Gulph Mill," *Pennsylvania Magazine of History and Biography* (April 1, 1929): 168–83, https://journals.psu.edu/pmhb/article/view/28158.

17 M. Regina Supplee, "Gulph Mills and Rebel Hill," *Bulletin of the Historical Society of Montgomery County* 6 (1947): 17.

18 Howard H. Peckham, *The Toll of Independence: Engagements & Battle Casualties of the American Revolution* (Editorial: Chicago, London: The University Of Chicago Press, 1974), 45; Fort Washington Historical Society, *The Heritage of Fort Washington* (Fort Washington, PA: Historical Society of Fort Washington, 1976).

19 "Buildings of the Department of State—Buildings—Department History—Office of the Historian," State.gov., 2023, https://history.state.gov/departmenthistory/buildings/section1.

20 "The American Revolution | Timeline | Articles and Essays | George Washington Papers | Digital Collections | Library of Congress," Library of Congress, accessed January 28, 2024, https://www.loc.gov/collections/george-washington-papers/articles-and-essays/timeline/the-american-revolution.

21 William Bradford Reed, *Life and Correspondence of Joseph Reed*, Vol. 1 (Philadelphia: Lindsay & Blackiston, 1847), 342–43.

22 Worthington Ford, ed., *Journal of the Continental Congress*, Vol. 9 (Washington, DC: Government Printing Office, 1907), 972.
23 Elias Boudinot, *Journal or Historical Recollections of American Events during the Revolutionary War* (Philadelphia: F. Bourquin, 1890), 52–53.
24 Pennsylvania uses the designation Commonwealth, instead of state; however, there is no difference for all practical purposes in the United States. Virginia used the term Commonwealth in its new constitution of June 29, 1776, "most likely to emphasize that Virgina's new government was based upon the sovereignty of the people united for the common good, or common weal… Pennsylvania followed Virginia, also using the official designation of commonwealth when it adopted its constitution a short time later in September 1776." Library of Congress, blogs.loc.gov, "What's In a Name? The Four U.S. States That Are Technically Commonwealths," posted by Anna Price, August 16, 2023. Kentucky and Massachusetts also use the term Commonwealth.
25 In southeastern Pennsylvania, two additional counties were created shortly after the Revolutionary War—Montgomery County, named for General Richard Montgomery, in 1784, from several townships in Philadelphia County, including Whitemarsh and Upper Merion. "The History of Montgomery County—Historical Society of Montgomery County, PA," hsmcpa.org, accessed February 14, 2024, https://hsmcpa.org/index.php/learn/the-history-of-montgomery-county. Delaware County, from the southeastern part of Chester County, in 1789. "History—at a Glance—Delaware County, Pennsylvania," www.delcopa.gov, n.d., https://www.delcopa.gov/departments/history.html.
26 "Pennsylvania Constitution (1776) | the National Constitution Center," National Constitution Center, constitutioncenter.org, n.d., https://constitutioncenter.org/the-constitution/historic-document-library/detail/pennsylvania-constitution.
27 Anne Wharton, "Thomas Wharton, Jnr.," *Pennsylvania Magazine of History and Biography* 5, no. 4 (1881): 426–39, https://jstor.org/stable/20084522.
28 Ford, *Journal of the Continental Congress*, 263.
29 Ibid, 269.
30 Boudinot, *Journal*, 29.
31 Edward St Germain, "Pierre-Augustin Caron de Beaumarchais Biography & Facts," AmericanRevolution.org, accessed April 17, 2024, https://www.americanrevolution.org/pierre-augustin-caron-de-baumarchais-biography/; Merriam-Webster Dictionary, https://www.merriam-webster.com/dictionary/polymath#:~:text=polymath%20noun%20poly%C2%B7%E2%80%8Bmath%20%CB%88p%C3%A4-l%C4%93-%CB%8Cmath%20Synonyms%20of,polymath%20%3A%20a%20person%20of%20encyclopedic%20learning.
32 Boudinot, *Journal*, 29.
33 Ibid.
34 "America's First Rock Star: Benjamin Franklin in France," National Constitution Center, December 17, 2015, https://constitutioncenter.org/blog/americas-first-rock-star-benjamin-franklin.
35 Edward Everett Hale, and Edward Everett Hale, Jr., *Franklin in France* (Boston, MA: Roberts Brothers, 1887), 159–60.

Chapter 1: The Continental Army and the New Nation

1 The term "band of brothers" is from William Shakespeare's play *Henry V*, when King Henry used the term in a speech that was designed to encourage his army, which was widely outnumbered by the French. The speech, read by Sir Lawrence Olivier, was also used to encourage British

troops in World War II. "From this day to the ending of the world, But we in it shall be remember'd; we few, we happy few, we band of brothers." William Shakespeare, *Henry V*, 1599. The phrase was also used in a 1789 song, "Hail Columbia, or the President's March," at Washington's inauguration as the first President. "Firm, united let us be, Rallying round our liberty, As a band of brothers joined, Peace & Safety we shall find." Joseph Hopkinson, "Hail Columbia," 1789, https://www.loc.gov/item/ihas.200000008.

2   Rufus Griswold, W. William Simms, and Edward Ingraham, *Washington and the Generals of the American Revolution*, Vols. 1 and 2, 2nd Edition (Philadelphia, PA: Edward Meeks, 1885).

3   Griswold, Simms, and Ingraham, *Washington's Generals*, Vol. 1, 164–82.

4   By "Duffrin," Alexander is thought to have referred to the Welsh name of Duffryn Mawr, which means Great Valley, which includes East and West Whiteland Townships, and Tredyffrin, which means Valley Town, in Tredyffrin Township, about 30 miles west of Philadelphia. McGuire, *Battle of Paoli*, 50.

5   "To George Washington from Major General Stirling, 1 December 1777," *Founders Online*, National Archives, https://founders.archives.gov/documents/Washington/03-12-02-0462. [Original source: Frank E. Grizzard, Jr. and David R. Hoth, eds., *The Papers of George Washington*, Revolutionary War Series, Vol. 12, *26 October 1777–25 December 1777* (Charlottesville: University Press of Virginia, 2002), 483–85.]

6   "US History," www.ushistory.org, accessed January 28, 2024, https://ushistory.org/valleyforge/served/Armstrong2.html.

7   "To George Washington from Major General John Armstrong, 1 December 1777," *Founders Online*, National Archives, https://founders.archives.gov/documents/Washington/03-12-02-0442. [Original source: Grizzard, Jr. and Hoth, *The Papers of George Washington*, Vol. 12, 455–56.]

8   Ushistory.org, "Biography of General Chevalier Louis Lebegue DePresle Duportail," n.d., https://www.ushistory.org/valleyforge/served/duport.html; Griswold, Simms, and Ingraham, *Washington's Generals*, Vol. 2, 262–64.

9   "To George Washington from Brigadier General Duportail, 1 December 1777," *Founders Online*, National Archives, https://founders.archives.gov/documents/Washington/03-12-02-0444. [Original source: Grizzard, Jr. and Hoth, *The Papers of George Washington*, Vol. 12, 457–59.] Duportail liked Gulph Mills so much that, after the Revolutionary War, he bought property and settled in Gulph Mills in the Swedesburg/Swedeland area. See William Joseph Buck, *History of Montgomery County within the Schuylkill Valley* (Norristown, PA: E. L. Acker, 1859), 49.

10 At the time, New Jersey was divided into East and West Jersey. "The Province of New Jersey, Divided into East and West, Commonly Called the Jerseys," Library of Congress, n.d. Accessed January 28, 2024, https://www.loc.gov/item/74692515.

11 Griswold, Simms, and Ingraham, *Washington's Generals*, Vol. 1, 62–104; "To George Washington from Major General Nathanael Greene, 1 December 1777," *Founders Online*, National Archives, https://founders.archives.gov/documents/Washington/03-12-02-0445. [Original source: Grizzard, Jr. and Hoth, *The Papers of George Washington*, Vol. 12, 459–63.]

12 "James Irvine," n.d., University Archives and Records Center. Accessed January 28, 2024, https://archives.upenn.edu/exhibits/penn-people/biography/james-irvine/.

13 "To George Washington from Brigadier General James Irvine, 1 December 1777," *Founders Online*, National Archives, https://founders.archives.gov/documents/Washington/03-12-02-0446. [Original source: Grizzard, Jr. and Hoth, *The Papers of George Washington*, Vol. 12, 463–64.]

14 Griswold, Simms, and Ingraham, *Washington's Generals*, Vol. 2, 269–71; "Biography of General Baron Johan DeKalb," n.d., https://www.ushistory.org/valleyforge/served/dekalb.html.

15 "To George Washington from Major General Johann Kalb, 1 December 1777," *Founders Online*, National Archives, https://founders.archives.gov/documents/Washington/03-12-02-0447. [Original source: Grizzard, Jr. and Hoth, *The Papers of George Washington*, Vol. 12, 464–65.]

16 Griswold, Simms, and Ingraham, *Washington's Generals*, Vol. 1, 235–42; "Biography of General Henry Knox," ushistory.org, 2019, https://www.ushistory.org/valleyforge/served/knox.html; "To George Washington from Brigadier General Henry Knox, 1 December 1777," *Founders Online*, National Archives, https://founders.archives.gov/documents/Washington/03-12-02-0448. [Original source: Grizzard, Jr. and Hoth, *The Papers of George Washington*, Vol. 12, 465–66.]

17 "To George Washington from Colonel Henry Emanuel Lutterloh, 1 December 1777," *Founders Online*, National Archives, https://founders.archives.gov/documents/Washington/03-12-02-0453. [Original source: Grizzard, Jr. and Hoth, *The Papers of George Washington*, Vol. 12, 472–73.]

18 Griswold, Simms, and Ingraham, Vol. 2, 213–29; "To George Washington from Major General Lafayette, 1 December 1777," *Founders Online*, National Archives, https://founders.archives.gov/documents/Washington/03-12-02-0449. [Original source: Grizzard, Jr. and Hoth, *The Papers of George Washington*, Vol. 12, 466–68.]

19 Griswold, Simms, and Ingraham, Vol. 2, 265; "To George Washington from Brigadier General William Maxwell, 1 December 1777," *Founders Online*, National Archives, https://founders.archives.gov/documents/Washington/03-12-02-0454. [Original source: Grizzard, Jr. and Hoth, *The Papers of George Washington*, Vol. 12, 473–74.]

20 Griswold, Simms, and Ingraham, Vol. 2, 332; "To George Washington from Brigadier General Peter Muhlenberg, 1 December 1777," *Founders Online*, National Archives, https://founders.archives.gov/documents/Washington/03-12-02-0455. [Original source: Grizzard, Jr. and Hoth, *The Papers of George Washington*, Vol. 12, 474–75.]

21 Griswold, Simms, and Ingraham, Vol. 1, 313; To George Washington from Brigadier General Enoch Poor, 1 December 1777," *Founders Online*, National Archives, https://founders.archives.gov/documents/Washington/03-12-02-0456. [Original source: Grizzard, Jr. and Hoth, *The Papers of George Washington*, Vol. 12, 475.]

22 "To George Washington from Brigadier General James Potter, 16 October 1777," *Founders Online*, National Archives, https://founders.archives.gov/documents/Washington/03-11-02-0539. [Original source: Philander D. Chase and Edward G. Lengel, eds., *The Papers of George Washington*, Revolutionary War Series, Vol. 11, *19 August 1777–25 October 1777* (Charlottesville: University Press of Virginia, 2001), 530–31.]

23 Ibid.

24 Note 3, "To George Washington from Brigadier General James Potter, 16 October 1777," *Founders Online*, National Archives, https://founders.archives.gov/documents/Washington/03-11-02-0539. [Original source: Chase and Lengel, *The Papers of George Washington*, Vol. 11, 530–31.]

25 "From George Washington to Brigadier General James Potter, 1 December 1777," *Founders Online*, National Archives, https://founders.archives.gov/documents/Washington/03-12-02-0457. [Original source: Grizzard, Jr. and Hoth, *The Papers of George Washington*, Vol. 12, 476.]

26 "From Benjamin Franklin to George Washington, 29 May 1777," *Founders Online*, National Archives, https://founders.archives.gov/documents/Franklin/01-24-02-0072. [Original source: William B. Willcox, ed., *The Papers of Benjamin Franklin*, Vol. 24, *May 1 through September 30, 1777* (New Haven and London: Yale University Press, 1984), 98.]

27 "To George Washington from Brigadier General Casimir Pulaski, 1 December 1777," *Founders Online*, National Archives, https://founders.archives.gov/documents/Washington/03-12-02-0458. [Original source: Grizzard, Jr. and Hoth, *The Papers of George Washington*, Vol. 12, 476–77.] Pulaski also later formed the Pulaski Cavalry Legion and became known as the "Father of American Cavalry." Griswold, Simms, and Ingraham, Vol. 2, 232–41.

28 Reed was also elected to the Continental Congress in 1778 while serving as President (Governor) in Pennsylvania's Supreme Executive Council; he went on to become one of the five delegates from Pennsylvania to sign the Articles of Confederation in 1778. He was elected President of the Supreme Executive Council on December 1, 1778; Griswold, Simms, and Ingraham, Vol. 1, 58–82.

29 "To George Washington from Joseph Reed, 1 December 1777," *Founders Online*, National Archives, https://founders.archives.gov/documents/Washington/03-12-02-0459. [Original source: Grizzard, Jr. and Hoth, *The Papers of George Washington*, Vol. 12, 477–81.]

30 "From George Washington to Joseph Reed, 2 December 1777," *Founders Online*, National Archives, https://founders.archives.gov/documents/Washington/03-12-02-0474. [Original source: Grizzard, Jr. and Hoth, *The Papers of George Washington*, Vol. 12, 500.]

31 "To George Washington from Brigadier General Charles Scott, 1 December 1777," *Founders Online*, National Archives, https://founders.archives.gov/documents/Washington/03-12-02-0460. [Original source: Grizzard, Jr. and Hoth, *The Papers of George Washington*, Vol. 12, 482.] Scott became chief of intelligence by late 1778. Griswold, Simms, and Ingraham, Vol. 2, 312.

32 "To George Washington from Brigadier General William Smallwood, 1 December 1777," *Founders Online*, National Archives, https://founders.archives.gov/documents/Washington/03-12-02-0461. [Original source: Grizzard, Jr. and Hoth, *The Papers of George Washington*, Vol. 12, 482–83.]; Griswold, Simms, and Ingraham, Vol. 1, 274.

33 Charles Whittemore, *A General of the Revolution: John Sullivan of New Hampshire*, March 27, 2016 (New York, Columbia University Press, 1961), 20; "John Sullivan," American Battlefield Trust, n.d., https://www.battlefields.org/learn/biographies/john-sullivan.

34 "To George Washington from Major General John Sullivan, 1 December 1777," *Founders Online*, National Archives, https://founders.archives.gov/documents/Washington/03-12-02-0463. [Original source: Grizzard, Jr. and Hoth, *The Papers of George Washington*, Vol. 12, 485–88.]; Griswold, Simms, and Ingraham, Vol. 1, 194–214.

35 "To George Washington from Brigadier General James Mitchell Varnum, 1 December 1777," *Founders Online*, National Archives, https://founders.archives.gov/documents/Washington/03-12-02-0464. [Original source: Grizzard, Jr. and Hoth, *The Papers of George Washington*, Vol. 12, 488–89.] Griswold, Simms, and Ingraham, Vol. 1, 287–89. Varnum, in early 1778, as soldiers continually deserted and died at Valley Forge, recommended allowing freed African American enslaved persons to enlist in the Continental Army and this resulted in the 1st Rhode Island Regiment, under his command, as a racially integrated unit in 1778; also enslaved persons were promised their freedom. Rhode Island could not fill its enlistment requirements to the Continental Army on free white men alone. Farrell Evans, "America's First Black Regiment Gained Their Freedom by Fighting against the British," HISTORY, February 3, 2021, https://www.history.com/news/first-black-regiment-american-revolution-first-rhode-island.

36 Griswold, Simms, and Ingraham, Vol. 1, 105–32; "To George Washington from Brigadier General Anthony Wayne, 1 December 1777," *Founders Online*, National Archives, https://founders.archives.gov/documents/Washington/03-12-02-0465. [Original source: Grizzard, Jr. and Hoth, *The Papers of George Washington*, Vol. 12, 489–91.]

37 "To George Washington from Brigadier General George Weedon, 1 December 1777," *Founders Online,* National Archives, https://founders.archives.gov/documents/Washington/03-12-02-0466. [Original source: Grizzard, Jr. and Hoth, *The Papers of George Washington,* Vol. 12, 491–93.] Griswold, Simms, and Ingraham, Vol. 1, 286–87.

38 "To George Washington from Brigadier General William Woodford, 1 December 1777," *Founders Online,* National Archives, https://founders.archives.gov/documents/Washington/03-12-02-0467. [Original source: Grizzard, Jr. and Hoth, *The Papers of George Washington,* Vol. 12, 493–94.]; Griswold, Simms, and Ingraham, Vol. 1, 289–90.

39 "From George Washington to Joseph Reed, 2 December 1777," fn. 1, *Founders Online,* National Archives, https://founders.archives.gov/documents/Washington/03-12-02-0474. [Original source: Grizzard, Jr. and Hoth, *The Papers of George Washington,* Vol. 12, 500.]

40 "Brigadier General John Cadwalader's Plan for Attacking Philadelphia, 24 November 1777," *Founders Online,* National Archives, https://founders.archives.gov/documents/Washington/03-12-02-0368. [Original source: Grizzard, Jr. and Hoth, *The Papers of George Washington,* Vol. 12, 371–73.]

41 Ford, *Journal of the Continental Congress,* 972.

42 Ford, *Journal of the Continental Congress,* 975–76.

43 "Circular to the General Officers of the Continental Army, 3 December 1777," *Founders Online,* National Archives, https://founders.archives.gov/documents/Washington/03-12-02-0478. [Original source: Grizzard, Jr. and Hoth, *The Papers of George Washington,* Vol. 12, 506.]

44 "To George Washington from Major General Stirling, 3 December 1777," *Founders Online,* National Archives, https://founders.archives.gov/documents/Washington/03-12-02-0491. [Original source: Grizzard, Jr. and Hoth, *The Papers of George Washington,* Vol. 12, 529–30.]

45 "To George Washington from Major General John Armstrong, 4 December 1777," *Founders Online,* National Archives, https://founders.archives.gov/documents/Washington/03-12-02-0495. [Original source: Grizzard, Jr. and Hoth, *The Papers of George Washington,* Vol. 12, 536–38.]

46 In 1778, Cadwalader shot former General Thomas Conway, whose efforts to undermine Washington's command in 1777 were called the Conway Cabal. "John Cadwalader," n.d., George Washington's Mount Vernon, https://www.mountvernon.org/library/digitalhistory/digital-encyclopedia/article/john-cadwalader/.

47 Griswold, Simms, and Ingraham, 188–93.

48 "To George Washington from Brigadier General John Cadwalader, 3 December 1777," *Founders Online,* National Archives, https://founders.archives.gov/documents/Washington/03-12-02-0479. [Original source: Grizzard, Jr. and Hoth, *The Papers of George Washington,* Vol. 12, 507–10.]

49 "To George Washington from Brigadier General John Cadwalader, 3 December 1777," *Founders Online,* National Archives, https://founders.archives.gov/documents/Washington/03-12-02-0479. [Original source: Grizzard, Jr. and Hoth, *The Papers of George Washington,* Vol. 12, 507–10.]

50 "To George Washington from Brigadier General Duportail, 3 December 1777," *Founders Online,* National Archives, https://founders.archives.gov/documents/Washington/03-12-02-0485. [Original source: Grizzard, Jr. and Hoth, *The Papers of George Washington,* Vol. 12, 515–16.]

51 "To George Washington from Major General Nathanael Greene, 3 December 1777," *Founders Online,* National Archives, https://founders.archives.gov/documents/

52. "To George Washington from Brigadier General James Irvine, 4 December 1777," *Founders Online*, National Archives, https://founders.archives.gov/documents/Washington/03-12-02-0498. [Original source: Grizzard, Jr. and Hoth, *The Papers of George Washington*, Vol. 12, 542–43.]

53. "To George Washington from Major General Johann Kalb, 3 December 1777," *Founders Online*, National Archives, https://founders.archives.gov/documents/Washington/03-12-02-0487. [Original source: Grizzard, Jr. and Hoth, *The Papers of George Washington*, Vol. 12, 522–24.]

54. "To George Washington from Brigadier General Henry Knox, 3 December 1777," *Founders Online*, National Archives, https://founders.archives.gov/documents/Washington/03-12-02-0488. [Original source: Grizzard, Jr. and Hoth, *The Papers of George Washington*, Vol. 12, 524–25.]

55. "To George Washington from Major General Lafayette, 3 December 1777," *Founders Online*, National Archives, https://founders.archives.gov/documents/Washington/03-12-02-0489. [Original source: Grizzard, Jr. and Hoth, *The Papers of George Washington*, Vol. 12, 525–28.]

56. "To George Washington from Brigadier General William Maxwell, 4 December 1777," *Founders Online*, National Archives, https://founders.archives.gov/documents/Washington/03-12-02-0499. [Original source: Grizzard, Jr. and Hoth, *The Papers of George Washington*, Vol. 12, 543.]

57. "To George Washington from Brigadier General Peter Muhlenberg, 4 December 1777," *Founders Online*, National Archives, https://founders.archives.gov/documents/Washington/03-12-02-0500. [Original source: Grizzard, Jr. and Hoth, *The Papers of George Washington*, Vol. 12, 543–45.]

58. "To George Washington from Brigadier General John Paterson, 4 December 1777," *Founders Online*, National Archives, https://founders.archives.gov/documents/Washington/03-12-02-0501. [Original source: Grizzard, Jr. and Hoth, *The Papers of George Washington*, Vol. 12, 545.]

59. "To George Washington from Brigadier General Enoch Poor, 4 December 1777," *Founders Online*, National Archives, https://founders.archives.gov/documents/Washington/03-12-02-0503. [Original source: Grizzard, Jr. and Hoth, *The Papers of George Washington*, Vol. 12, 545–46.]

60. "To George Washington from Brigadier General James Potter, 4 December 1777," *Founders Online*, National Archives, https://founders.archives.gov/documents/Washington/03-12-02-0504. [Original source: Grizzard, Jr. and Hoth, *The Papers of George Washington*, Vol. 12, 546–47.]

61. "To George Washington from Joseph Reed, 4 December 1777," *Founders Online*, National Archives, https://founders.archives.gov/documents/Washington/03-12-02-0506. [Original source: Grizzard, Jr. and Hoth, *The Papers of George Washington*, Vol. 12, 548–52.]

62. "To George Washington from Brigadier General Charles Scott, 4 December 1777," *Founders Online*, National Archives, https://founders.archives.gov/documents/Washington/03-12-02-0507. [Original source: Grizzard, Jr. and Hoth, *The Papers of George Washington*, Vol. 12, 553.]

63. "To George Washington from Brigadier General William Smallwood, 4 December 1777," *Founders Online*, National Archives, https://founders.archives.gov/documents/Washington/03-12-02-0508. [Original source: Grizzard, Jr. and Hoth, *The Papers of George Washington*, Vol. 12, 553–54.]

64　"To George Washington from Major General John Sullivan, 4 December 1777," *Founders Online*, National Archives, https://founders.archives.gov/documents/Washington/03-12-02-0509. [Original source: Grizzard, Jr. and Hoth, *The Papers of George Washington*, Vol. 12, 555–58.]

65　"To George Washington from Brigadier General James Mitchell Varnum, 3–4 December 1777," *Founders Online*, National Archives, https://founders.archives.gov/documents/Washington/03-12-02-0492. [Original source: Grizzard, Jr. and Hoth, *The Papers of George Washington*, pp. 530–34.]

66　"To George Washington from Brigadier General Anthony Wayne, 4 December 1777," *Founders Online*, National Archives, https://founders.archives.gov/documents/Washington/03-12-02-0510. [Original source: Grizzard, Jr. and Hoth, *The Papers of George Washington*, Vol. 12, 558–59.]

67　"To George Washington from Brigadier General George Weedon, 4 December 1777," *Founders Online*, National Archives, https://founders.archives.gov/documents/Washington/03-12-02-0511. [Original source: Grizzard, Jr. and Hoth, *The Papers of George Washington*, Vol. 12, 559–60.]

68　"To George Washington from Brigadier General William Woodford, 4 December 1777," *Founders Online*, National Archives, https://founders.archives.gov/documents/Washington/03-12-02-0512. [Original source: Grizzard, Jr. and Hoth, *The Papers of George Washington*, Vol. 12, 561.]

Chapter 2: Leaving Whitemarsh, December 10

1　The Editors of Encyclopedia Britannica, "Lydia Barrington Darragh | American War Heroine." In *Encyclopedia Britannica*, 2019. https://www.britannica.com/biography/Lydia-Barrington-Darragh.

2　Boudinot, *Journal*, 50–51.

3　"To George Washington from William Dewees, Jr., 4 December 1777," *Founders Online*, National Archives, https://founders.archives.gov/documents/Washington/03-12-02-0496. [Original source: Grizzard, Jr. and Hoth, *The Papers of George Washington*, Vol. 12, 538–41.]

4　For an extensive description of the Battle of Whitemarsh, see McGuire, *Philadelphia Campaign*, Vol. 2, 240–57.

5　Ibid, 240–57.

6　"Battle of White Marsh—American Revolutionary War," n.d., American Revolutionary War 1775 to 1783. Accessed February 6, 2024. https://revolutionarywar.us/year-1777/battle-white-marsh/#:~:text=Casualties%20-%20American%20casualties%20were%20estimated%20to%20be.

7　"To George Washington from a Continental Congress Camp Committee, 10 December 1777," *Founders Online*, National Archives, https://founders.archives.gov/documents/Washington/03-12-02-0536. [Original source: Grizzard, Jr. and Hoth, *The Papers of George Washington*, Vol. 12, 588–89.]

8　Ford, *Journal of the Continental Congress*, 1029–31.

9　"General Orders, 10 December 1777," *Founders Online*, National Archives, https://founders.archives.gov/documents/Washington/03-12-02-0533. [Original source: Grizzard, Jr. and Hoth, *The Papers of George Washington*, Vol. 12, 585.]

10　Buck, *History of Montgomery County*, 19.

11　Ibid, 33–34.

12. "Order of March from Whitemarsh, Pennsylvania, 10 December 1777," *Founders Online*, National Archives, https://founders.archives.gov/documents/Washington/03-12-02-0534. [Original source: Grizzard, Jr. and Hoth, *The Papers of George Washington*, Vol. 12, 585–87.]
13. Ibid.
14. Ibid.
15. At the time, New Jersey was divided into East New Jersey and West New Jersey. See William Faden's Map 1777, "The Province of New Jersey, Divided into East and West, Commonly Called the Jerseys."
16. "Order of March from Whitemarsh, Pennsylvania, 10 December 1777."
17. Ibid.
18. Harry Schenawolf, "Washington's Staff during the American Revolutionary War: Major General of the Day," *Revolutionary War Journal*, February 18, 2015, https://revolutionarywarjournal.com/washingtons-major-general. Schenawolf wrote that the purpose of the Major General of the Day was to "review troops, meet with the Brigadier Generals, check on supplies and regiments, attend hospitals, look to sanitary conditions, oversee disciplinary measures are carried out. In essence, he became the George Washington persona when viewing the troops and interacting with them."
19. The December 10 General Order did not list who was the Major General of the Day, but the Major Generals of the Day were assigned in a rotating order, and a review of that rotation made it likely that Stirling was assigned as Major General of the Day for December 10.
20. "Order of March from Whitemarsh, Pennsylvania, 10 December 1777."
21. "Out of Money, One—Symbols of Unity on State and Continental Currency," n.d., Greatseal.com. Accessed January 29, 2024. https://greatseal.com/unity/money.html.
22. "Order of March from Whitemarsh, Pennsylvania, 10 December 1777."
23. "From George Washington to Brigadier General Thomas Nelson, Jr., 10 December 1777," *Founders Online*, National Archives, https://founders.archives.gov/documents/Washington/03-12-02-0539. [Original source: Grizzard, Jr. and Hoth, *The Papers of George Washington*, Vol. 12, 593–94.
24. "From George Washington to Brigadier General Thomas Nelson, Jr., 10 December 1777," *Founders Online*, National Archives, https://founders.archives.gov/documents/Washington/03-12-02-0539. [Original source: Grizzard, Jr. and Hoth, *The Papers of George Washington*, Vol. 12, 593–94.]
25. "From George Washington to Henry Laurens, 10 December 1777," *Founders Online*, National Archives, https://founders.archives.gov/documents/Washington/03-12-02-0538. [Original source: Grizzard, Jr. and Hoth, *The Papers of George Washington*, Vol. 12, 591–93.]
26. Ibid. The Continental Congress Camp Committee did report the results of its visit to Henry Laurens and the rest of the Continental Congress on December 6.
27. Ford, *Journal of the Continental Congress*, 1014–15; Washington made a similar proclamation for the same purpose in his General Orders on December 20, 1777, the second day of the Valley Forge Encampment. See "General Orders, 20 December 1777," *Founders Online*, National Archives, https://founders.archives.gov/documents/Washington/03-12-02-0584. [Original source: Grizzard, Jr. and Hoth, *The Papers of George Washington*, Vol. 12, 641–44.]
28. Archibald Robertson, *Archibald Robertson, Lieutenant General Royal Engineers: His Diaries and Sketches in America, 1762–1780*, ed. Harry M. Lydenberg (1930; repr., New York: New York Public Library, 1971), 161, https://babel.hathitrust.org/cgi/pt?id=mdp.39015019750978&seq=11.

Chapter 3: The Battle of Matson's Ford, December 11

1. John Reed, "The Fight on Old Gulph Road," *Bulletin of the Historical Society of Montgomery County* XV (1 and 2) (1966): 32–36.
2. Ibid, 32.
3. *Pennsylvania Archives*, Vol. 6 (Philadelphia, PA: Joseph Severns & Co, 1853): 83.
4. "Battle of Matson's Ford—American Revolutionary War," n.d., American Revolutionary War 1775 to 1783. Accessed January 30, 2024. https://revolutionarywar.us/year-1777/battle-matsons-ford. This site provides a very good account of what led up to this battle, how the day started, and what transpired.
5. "A Revolutionary River Historical Marker," n.d., www.hmdb.org. Accessed January 30, 2024. https://www.hmdb.org/m.asp?m=203794.
6. Reed, "The Fight at the Old Gulph Road," 32–36; McGuire, *Philadelphia Campaign*, Vol. 2, 256–63.
7. John Andre, *Major Andre's Journal*. Edited by Henry Cabot Lodge. Vol. 1 (Boston, MA: The Bibliophile Society, 1903), hathitrust.com.
8. Andre, *Journal*, 131.
9. "To George Washington from John Johnston, 9 June 1778," *Founders Online*, National Archives, https://founders.archives.gov/documents/Washington/03-15-02-0380. [Original source: Lengel, *The Papers of George Washington*, Vol. 15, 366–68.]
10. Buck, *History of Montgomery County*, 67.
11. Ibid.
12. "Definition of TORY," n.d., www.merriam-Webster.com. https://www.merriam-webster.com/dictionary/Tory.
13. "John Roberts of the Mill," n.d., Lower Merion Historical Society. Accessed January 30, 2024. https://lowermerionhistory.org/home/full-text/schmidt-collection/john-roberts-of-the-mill/.
14. Descriptions of the Battle of Matson's Ford are from Baker, "The Camp by the Old Gulph Mill," 17: 422–29; Reed, "The Fight on Old Gulph Road," 32–36; and Samuel Gordon Smyth, "The Gulph Hills in the Annals of the Revolution," *Historical Sketches of Montgomery County* 3 (1905): 171–74.
15. "Battle of Matson's Ford—American Revolutionary War," *Revolutionary War US*, accessed January 30, 2024, https://revolutionarywar.us/year-1777/battle-matsons-ford.
16. Ibid.
17. To read the original, see "James Potter to Thomas Wharton," *Pennsylvania Archives*, Vol. 5: 97.
18. John Lacey and John Armstrong, "Memoirs of Brigadier-General John Lacey of Pennsylvania," *The Pennsylvania Magazine of History and Biography* 25, no. 1 (1902): 101–11, https://www.jstor.org/stable/20086016?seq=10.
19. Lacey was a colonel at the time of the Battle of Matson's Ford. He was later promoted to Brigadier General. Lacey and Armstrong, "Memoirs," 101–11.
20. "Inns, Restaurants, and Hotels," n.d., Lower Merion Historical Society. Accessed January 31, 2024. https://lowermerionhistory.org/home/full-text/lower-merion-and-narberth-postcards/inns-restaurants-hotels/.
21. John Laurens and William Gilmore Simms, contributor, *The Army Correspondence of Colonel John Laurens in the Years 1777–8* (New York: The Bradford Club, 1867), 94–98.
22. Samuel Armstrong and Joseph Boyle, ed., "From Saratoga to Valley Forge: The Diary of Lt. Samuel Armstrong," *The Pennsylvania Magazine of History and Biography*, Vol. 121, No. 3 (July 1997): 256. See also "Samuel Armstrong Diary Original Pages," digital.americanancestors.

org, accessed February 15, 2024, https://digital.americanancestors.org/digital/collection/p15869coll22/id/1225/rec/1.
23   Waldo, *Diary*, 305; see also Herbert Thoms, "Albigence Waldo, Surgeon," *Annals of Medical History* 10, no. 4 (December 1, 1928): 486–97, https://www.ncbi.nlm.nih.gov/pmc/articles/PMC7940074/.
24   Henry Dearborn, *Journals of Henry Dearborn 1776–1783*, (Cambridge, MA: J. Wilson & Son, 1887), 12.
25   Dave Roos, "How John Marshall Expanded the Power of the Supreme Court," HISTORY, November 30, 2021, http://www.history.com/news/supreme-court-power-john-marshall.
26   John Marshall, *The Life of George Washington*. Project Gutenberg. Vol. 2, https://www.gutenberg.org/files/18592/18592-h/18592-h.htm#CHAPTER_IX.
27   Israel Angell, *The Diary of Colonel Israel Angell: Commanding Officer, 2nd Rhode Island Regiment, Continental Army, 1 October, 1777–20 January, 1778*. Boston, MA, n.d. Transcribed from manuscripts at the Massachusetts Historical Society by Norman Desmarais, accessed January 31, 2024, 11. https://digitalcommons.providence.edu/cgi/viewcontent.cgi?date=1180547585&article=1000&context=primary&preview_mode=.
28   James McMichael, "Diary of Lieutenant James McMichael, of the Pennsylvania Line, 1776–1778." *The Pennsylvania Magazine of History and Biography* 16 (2) (1892): 129–59. https://www.jstor.org/stable/20083473.
29   Paul Brigham, "A Revolutionary Diary of Capt. Paul Brigham, Nov. 19, 1777 to Sept. 4, 1778," edited by Edward Hoyt. In *Vermont History* 34 (1) (1966).
30   McDonald, "Thro Mud & Mire into the Woods," https://www.revwar75.com/library/bob/smith2.htm.
31   Ebenezer Wild, *The Journal of Ebenezer Wild (1776–1781)* (Cambridge: John Wilson and Son, University Press, 1891): 29. https://babel.hathitrust.org/cgi/pt?id=chi.56986164&seq=1.
32   Archibald Robertson and Harry Miller Lyndenberg, ed., *Archibald Robertson, His Diaries and Sketches in America, 1762–1780* (New York: The New York Public Library and The New York Times & Arno Press, 1971); 161, originally published 1930 New York Public Library.
33   David Head, "George Washington's Mount Vernon," George Washington's Mount Vernon (Mount Vernon, 2019), https://www.mountvernon.org/library/digitalhistory/digital-encyclopedia/article/hessians/.
34   Johann Von Ewald, *Diary of the American War: A Hessian Journal*, ed. and trans. Joseph Philips Tustin (New Haven: Yale University Press, 1979), 110, https://archive.org/details/EwaldsDIARYOFTHEAMERICANWAR/page/n143/mode/2up.
35   Carl Leopold Baurmeister, *Revolution in America*. Trans. by Bernhard Uhlendorf (New Brunswick, NJ: Rutgers University Press, 2003), 139. https://archive.org/details/revolutioninamer00baur/page/139/mode/2up.
36   *Pennsylvania Archives*, Vol. 26, 30–44. See also "Abstracts of Pension Applications on File in the Division of Public Records," 499, for a number of references to the Battle of Matson's Ford, as well as "Revolutionary War Pension Files and Related Accounts, 1785–1809 | Psa," Powerlibrary.org, 2024, https://digitalarchives.powerlibrary.org/psa/islandora/object/psa%3Arwpfra.
37   Microfilm Publication M804, contains only the records of pensions granted or paid by the US government. Records for pension applications made before 1800 were lost in the fire at the US War Department on November 8, 1800. Congress provided pensions for Revolutionary War soldiers, widows, and orphans under various conditions in laws enacted from 1780 to 1832. See Jean Nudd, "Using Revolutionary War Pension Files to Find Family Information, Genealogy Notes," *Prologue Magazine*, Summer 2015, accessed January 31, 2024. https://www.archives.gov/publications/prologue/2015/summer/rev-war-pensions.html. Other reference sites

are "Case Files of Pension and Bounty-Land Warrant Applications Based on Revolutionary War Service, Ca. 1800–Ca. 1912"; National Archives Catalog, n.d., https://catalog.archives.gov/id/300022; and National Archives, War Department Collection of Revolutionary War Records, n.d., https://catalog.archives.gov/search-within/422?q=gulph.
38 Samuel Gordon Smyth, "Matson's Ford," *Bulletin of the Historical Society of Montgomery County* IV (1910): 67, https://archive.org/details/historicalsketch04hist; "Case Files of Pension and Bounty-Land Warrant Applications Based on Revolutionary War Service, Ca. 1800–Ca. 1912," National Archives Catalog, n.d., https://catalog.archives.gov/id/300022; NAID 53983580, Application W3068.
39 Smyth, "Matson's Ford," 67.
40 Ibid; "US, Revolutionary War Pensions, 1800–1900," Fold3, accessed February 24, 2024, https://www.fold3.com/publication/467/us-revolutionary-war-pensions-1800-1900; Application S9749.
41 Smyth, "Matson's Ford," 67; n.d., Fold3, US, Pennsylvania Revolutionary War Battalions and Militia Index, 1775–1783, accessed February 24, 2024, database and images, https://www.fold3.com/publication/1162/us-pennsylvania-revolutionary-war-battalions-and-militia-index-1775-1783.
42 Smyth, "Matson's Ford," 67; n.d., Fold3, US, Pennsylvania Revolutionary War Battalions and Militia Index, 1775–1783, accessed February 24, 2024, database and images, https://www.fold3.com/publication/1162/us-pennsylvania-revolutionary-war-battalions-and-militia-index-1775-1783.
43 Smyth, "Matson's Ford," 67.
44 Coyle, Manasseh, US, Revolutionary War Pensions, 1800–1900, Fold3; Application W2759; Coyle, Manassah, US, Pennsylvania Revolutionary War Battalions and Militia Index, 1775–1783, Fold3.
45 "Case Files of Pension and Bounty-Land Warrant Applications Based on Revolutionary War Service, Ca. 1800–Ca. 1912," National Archives Catalog, n.d., https://catalog.archives.gov/id/300022 Application W3643.
46 Fold3.com/memorial/65360125/henrich-herring/facts; File R.4925, Bounty Land Records.
47 "US, Revolutionary War Pensions, 1800–1900," Fold3, accessed February 24, 2024, https://www.fold3.com/publication/467/us-revolutionary-war-pensions-1800-1900.
48 Harriet J. Walker and JSTOR, *Revolutionary Soldiers Buried in Illinois*, Internet Archive (Journal of the Illinois State Historical Society (1908–1984), 1916), https://archive.org/details/jstor-40194379.
49 Richard Roberts, "Peter 'Johann Peter' Samsel (1734–1777), Find A..." www.findagrave.com. July 20, 2012. https://www.findagrave.com/memorial/93936585/peter-samsel.
50 National Archives, War Department Collection of Revolutionary War Records, n.d., https://catalog.archives.gov/search-within/422?q=gulph.
51 Smyth, "Matson's Ford," 62–72. https://archive.org/details/historicalsketch04hist. Accessed January 31, 2024.
52 Smyth, "The Gulph Hills in the Annals of the Revolution," 180.
53 Henry Melchior Muhlenberg and Theodore Tapput and John W. Doberstein, Trans., *The Journals of Henry Melchior Muhlenberg*, Vol. 3 (Philadelphia, PA: Muhlenberg Press, 1958), 112. https://babel.hathitrust.org/cgi/pt?id=mdp.39015011394700&seq=130.
54 William Howe, *William Howe Orderly Book, March 9, 1776–May 1, 1778* (University of Michigan, 1776), https://quod.lib.umich.edu/h/howew/howew.0001.001/1.
55 Thomas Simes, *A Treatise on the Military Science*, 1780.
56 "From George Washington to William Livingston, 11 December 1777," *Founders Online*, National Archives, https://founders.archives.gov/documents/Washington/03-12-02-0542. [Original source: Grizzard, Jr. and Hoth, *The Papers of George Washington*, Vol. 12, 596.]

57 "To George Washington from Colonel Theodorick Bland, 11 December 1777," *Founders Online*, National Archives, https://founders.archives.gov/documents/Washington/03-12-02-0541. [Original source: Grizzard, Jr. and Hoth, *The Papers of George Washington*, Vol. 12, 594–96.]; Founders Online also includes a note that FOL Bland seemed to be referring to "Bevin's" Ford on the Schuylkill River, roughly halfway between Matson's and Swedes fords. Jonathan Robertson (1745–1825) was a blacksmith who lived near the falls of the Schuylkill in Lower Merion Township, Philadelphia (now Montgomery) County. (Robertson became Superintendent of the Delaware and Schuylkill Canal Company in the 1790s.) Bevin's Ford must have been a minor ford across the Schuylkill River because it can rarely be found in any writings from 1777 or today. Nevertheless, it is also believed to be spelled as "Bevan's" Ford after the Bevan family that owned property in Gulph Mills on the banks of the Schuylkill.

58 "From George Washington to Lund Washington, 11 December 1777 [letter not found]," *Founders Online*, National Archives, https://founders.archives.gov/documents/Washington/03-12-02-0543. [Original source: Grizzard, Jr. and Hoth, *The Papers of George Washington*, Vol. 12, 597.]

59 "To George Washington from Lund Washington, 24 December 1777," *Founders Online*, National Archives, https://founders.archives.gov/documents/Washington/03-12-02-0646. [Original source: Grizzard, Jr. and Hoth, *The Papers of George Washington*, Vol. 12, 698–700.]

60 "From Benjamin Franklin to Thomas Walpole, 11 December 1777," *Founders Online*, National Archives, https://founders.archives.gov/documents/Franklin/01-25-02-0202. [Original source: Willcox, *The Papers of Benjamin Franklin*, Vol. 25, 272–73.]

61 "Nini Medallion of Benjamin Franklin | the Franklin Institute," fi.edu, March 8, 2014, https://fi.edu/en/science-and-education/collection/nini-medallion-benjamin-franklin.

62 Some 11,500 Americans died on British prison ships and in New York prisons, more than the 4,300 killed in the American armed forces during the entire Revolutionary War. Prison Ships Speech, National Society of the Sons of the American Revolution.

63 "The American Commissioners: Instructions to John Thornton [11 December 1777]," *Founders Online*, National Archives, https://founders.archives.gov/documents/Franklin/01-25-02-0199. [Original source: Willcox, *The Papers of Benjamin Franklin*, Vol. 25, 269–71.]

Chapter 4: The Army is on the Move Again, December 12

1 "Norristown, PA | Official Website," n.d. Norristown.org. Accessed February 1, 2024. https://norristown.org.
2 Laurens, *Correspondence*, 96–97.
3 Angell, *Journal*, December 12.
4 Wild, *Journal*, 30.
5 Armstrong, *Diary*, 256.
6 Brigham, *Diary*, 15.
7 Dearborn, *Journal*, 111.
8 Waldo, *Diary*, 305.
9 McMichael, *Diary*, 157.
10 A. E. Zucker, "THE BROGLIE INTRIGUE." In *General de Kalb, Lafayette's Mentor* (Chapel Hill, NC: University of North Carolina Press, 1966), 53: 94–107. http://www.jstor.org/stable/10.5149/9781469658759_zucker.11.
11 Footnote 3, "General Orders, 12 December 1777," *Founders Online*, National Archives, https://founders.archives.gov/documents/Washington/03-12-02-0544. [Original source: Grizzard, Jr. and Hoth, *The Papers of George Washington*, Vol. 12, 592–99.]

12 William Howe, *William Howe Orderly Book, March 9, 1776–May 1, 1778* (University of Michigan, 1776), https://quod.lib.umich.edu/h/howew/howew.0001.001/1.
13 Andre, *Journal*, 130–31.
14 "General Orders, 12 December 1777," *Founders Online*, National Archives, https://founders.archives.gov/documents/Washington/03-12-02-0544. [Original source: Grizzard, Jr. and Hoth, *The Papers of George Washington*, Vol. 12, 592–99.]
15 Subaltern is defined as any officer [in the British army] below the rank of captain. "Subaltern Noun—Definition, Pictures, Pronunciation and Usage Notes | Oxford Advanced Learner's Dictionary at OxfordLearnersDictionaries.com." Oxfordlearnersdictionaries.com, 2024, https://www.oxfordlearnersdictionaries.com/definition/english/subaltern.
16 Washington, General Orders, December 12, 1777.
17 "City of Reading, PA," n.d., www.readingpa.gov. https://www.readingpa.gov.
18 "From George Washington to William Shippen, Jr., 12 December 1777," *Founders Online*, National Archives, https://founders.archives.gov/documents/Washington/03-12-02-0548. [Original source: Grizzard, Jr. and Hoth, *The Papers of George Washington*, Vol. 12, 602.]
19 Robert F. Haggard, "The Nicola Affair: Lewis Nicola, George Washington, and American Military Discontent during the Revolutionary War," *Proceedings of the American Philosophical Society: Held at Philadelphia for Promoting Useful Knowledge* 146 (2) (2002): 139–69.
20 Ibid.
21 "General Orders, 12 December 1777," *Founders Online*, National Archives, https://founders.archives.gov/documents/Washington/03-12-02-0544. [Original source: Grizzard, Jr. and Hoth, *The Papers of George Washington*, Vol. 12, 597–99.]
22 "To George Washington from Henry Laurens, 12 December 1777," *Founders Online*, National Archives, https://founders.archives.gov/documents/Washington/03-12-02-0545. [Original source: Grizzard, Jr. and Hoth, *The Papers of George Washington*, Vol. 12, 599–600.]
23 Ford, *Journal of the Continental Congress*, 1010–11.
24 Ford, *Journal of the Continental Congress*, 1013–15.
25 Pennsylvania Archives, 86–87.
26 Pennsylvania Archives, 85.
27 "The American Commissioners to Lord North, 12 December 1777," *Founders Online*, National Archives, https://founders.archives.gov/documents/Franklin/01-25-02-0203. [Original source: Willcox, *The Papers of Benjamin Franklin*, Vol. 25, 273–76.]
28 Ibid.
29 "Dumas to the American Commissioners, 12 December 1777," *Founders Online*, National Archives, https://founders.archives.gov/documents/Franklin/01-25-02-0204. [Original source: Willcox, *The Papers of Benjamin Franklin*, Vol. 25, 276–78.]

Chapter 5: The March into Gulph Mills, December 13

1 Also called Matsunk, which referred to the Swedish settlement on those west banks of the Schuylkill. Dr. G. W. Holstein, "Swedes' Ford and Surroundings." *Bulletin of the Historical Society of Montgomery County* IV (1910): 73–77.
2 Smyth, "Matson's Ford," 62–72. https://archive.org/details/historicalsketch04hist.
3 The Editors of Encyclopedia Britannica, "St. Lucia's Day | History, Traditions, & Facts," in *Encyclopedia Britannica*, January 14, 2019, https://www.britannica.com/topic/St-Lucias-Day.
4 There is a plaque at Old Swede's Church noting that Washington visited on December 13, 1777 after crossing the Schuylkill and seeing a light on in the church. See also https://

www.mainlinemedianews.com/2009/07/01/upper-merion-steeped-in-history-at-old-swedes-church/; and https://www.kophistory.org/washington-visits-christ-church/.
5   Orderly Book, Richard Platt, December 12, 1777.
6   "General Orders, 13 December 1777," *Founders Online*, National Archives, https://founders.archives.gov/documents/Washington/03-12-02-0549. [Original source: Grizzard, Jr. and Hoth, *The Papers of George Washington*, Vol. 12, 602–3.]
7   Armstrong, *Diary*, 256–57.
8   Albigence Waldo, "Valley Forge, 1777–1778. Diary of Surgeon Albigence Waldo, of the Connecticut Line," 21 (January) (1897): 299–323. https://ia601907.us.archive.org/1/items/jstor-20085750/20085750.pdf.
9   Dearborn, *Journal*, 111.
10 Angell, *Diary*, December 13.
11 Wild, *Diary*, 30.
12 Brigham, *Diary*, 15.
13 Ewald, *Diary*, 110. https://archive.org/details/EwaldsDIARYOFTHEAMERICANWAR/page/n143/mode/2up.
14 William Bradford Reed, *Life and Correspondence of Joseph Reed*, Vol. 1 (Philadelphia: Lindsay & Blackiston, 1847): 354–55.
15 "Thursday's Post from the London Gazette," *Leeds Intelligencer*, Vol. 24, No. 1243, January 27, 1778. Cornwallis, who set sail for England on December 16, arrived in England on January 18, 1778. He then gave Howe's letter to Germain, as reported in "Thursday's Post From the London Gazette," in the January 27, 1778 edition of the *Leeds Intelligencer* newspaper. Howe's perspective of these battles and the state of the Revolutionary War at the time is fascinating. The paper also goes on to explain how other residents in England viewed the war, along with a very detailed description of how Cornwallis was welcomed with all pageantry and excess by the King and other British royalty at St. James Palace on January 19. Id., article titled, "London, January 20."
16 "Thursday's Post from the London Gazette," *Leeds Intelligencer*, Vol. 24, No. 1243, January 27, 1778.
17 Ibid.
18 Howe, General Orders, December 13, 1777.
19 *Pennsylvania Archives*, 89.
20 Ibid.
21 Anna M. Holstein, *Swedish Holsteins in America from 1644 to 1892* (Norristown, PA: Anna M. Holstein, 1892), 26, 46–47. https://www.archive.org/details/swedishholsteins00hols.
22 Holstein, *Swedish Holsteins*, 48–49. Anna Holstein was the sister of Mrs. John Hughes, Sr.
23 Ibid, 49–50.
24 "Washington's War Tents," www.amrevmuseum.org, n.d., https://www.amrevmuseum.org/washington-s-war-tents. Washington's war tent is permanently displayed at the Museum of the American Revolution in Philadelphia.
25 See Application of Poplar Lane, National Register of Historic Places Inventory—Nomination Form.
26 See E. Pinkowski, *Washington's Officers Slept Here, Historic Homes of Valley Forge and Its Neighborhood* (Philadelphia, 1959), 159.
27 Holstein, *Swedish Holsteins*, 46–47.
28 Pennsylvania Historical and Museum Commission, *The WPA Guide to Philadelphia* (Philadelphia: University Of Pennsylvania Press, 1988), 676, Map of Jaunts to the Environs of Valley Forge, Compiled by the Federal Writers Project of the Commonwealth of Pennsylvania.

29 Baker, "The Camp by the Old Gulph Mill," 414–29.
30 See Chapter 12, herein, Gulph Mills During the Valley Forge Encampment.
31 John Corr, "Sturdy Old House Retains Flavor of Its History," *Philadelphia Inquirer*, August 8, 1993.
32 Holstein, *Swedish Holsteins*, 28–29.
33 Ibid, 23–24.
34 Howard DeHaven Ross, *History of the de Haven Family* (1894; repr., New York, NY: The Pandick Press, 1929), 9.
35 Ibid, 23.
36 Ibid, 11–18; Lisa Belkin, "213 YEARS after LOAN, UNCLE SAM IS DUNNED (Published 1990)," *New York Times*, May 27, 1990, https://www.nytimes.com/1990/05/27/us/213-years-after-loan-uncle-sam-is-dunned.html.
37 Holstein, *Swedish Holsteins*, 29.
38 Samuel Brecht, "Valley Forge & the Schwenkfelders," *The Exile Herald* 13, no. 1 (April 1936).
39 Supplee, "Gulph Mills and Rebel Hill," 18–20.
40 "History," Gulph Mills Civic Association, accessed February 10, 2024, http://gulphmillscivicassoc.weebly.com/history.html.
41 Sheilah Vance, "Valley Forge's Threshold: The Encampment at Gulph Mills," *Journal of the American Revolution* (November 5, 2019). https://allthingsliberty.com/2019/11/valley-forges-threshold-the-encampment-at-gulph-mills/; Sheilah Vance, *Six Days in December: General George Washington's and the Continental Army's Encampment on Rebel Hill, December 13–19, 1777* (Paoli, PA: The Elevator Group, 2011).
42 Paul David Nelson, *William Alexander, Lord Stirling* (Tuscaloosa, AL: University of Alabama Press, 2003), 213; "To George Washington from Major General Stirling, 23 December 1777," *Founders Online*, National Archives, https://founders.archives.gov/documents/Washington/03-12-02-0634. [Original source: Grizzard, Jr. and Hoth, *The Papers of George Washington*, Vol. 12, 691–92.]
43 No individual letters or writing from Monroe during this period of the Revolutionary War have been found.
44 Nelson, *William Alexander, Lord Stirling*, 123. There are no known existing writings of James Monroe while he was encamped on Rebel Hill with Stirling.
45 Henry Woodman, *The History of Valley Forge* (1920), 68, www.google.com/books/edition/The_History_of_Valley_Forge/eFdKAAAAYAAJ?hl=en.
46 This information was found in Mapping West Philadelphia Landowners in October 1777, a project posted by University of Pennsylvania Archives, maps.archives.upenn.edu.
47 This is the area that was developed in the 1990s by John S. Trinsey as the new Rebel Hill/Lemington Way development.
48 "The Conway Cabal." n.d., www.ushistory.org. Accessed February 2, 2024. https://ushistory.org/march/other/cabal2.htm; "Conway Cabal." George Washington's Mount Vernon. Mount Vernon. 2019. https://www.mountvernon.org/library/digitalhistory/digital-encyclopedia/article/conway-cabal/.
49 Andrew A. Zellers, -Fredrich, "General Thomas Conway: Cabal Conspirator or Career Climber," October 29, 2018, allthingsliberty.org.
50 The Conway Cabal, ushistory.org; "Thomas Conway | American Revolution, Continental Army, Pennsylvania | Britannica." n.d. www.britannica.com. https://www.britannica.com/biography/Thomas-Conway#ref27008.
51 Jamie Slaughter, "Frederick the Great," George Washington's Mount Vernon, 2023, https://www.mountvernon.org/library/digitalhistory/digital-encyclopedia/article/frederick-the-great/.

52 "Conway Cabal," George Washington's Mount Vernon, 2019, https://www.mountvernon.org/library/digitalhistory/digital-encyclopedia/article/conway-cabal/.
53 "From George Washington to Brigadier General Thomas Conway, 5 November 1777," *Founders Online*, National Archives, https://founders.archives.gov/documents/Washington/03-12-02-0118. [Original source: Grizzard, Jr. and Hoth, *The Papers of George Washington*, Vol. 12, 129–30.]
54 "To George Washington from Brigadier General Thomas Conway, 5 November 1777," *Founders Online*, National Archives, https://founders.archives.gov/documents/Washington/03-12-02-0119. [Original source: Grizzard, Jr. and Hoth, *The Papers of George Washington*, Vol. 12, 130–31.]
55 James Thomas Flexner, *Washington: The Indispensable Man* (New York: Little, Brown and Company, 1974), 113.
56 "To George Washington from Brigadier General Thomas Conway, 16 November 1777," *Founders Online*, National Archives, https://founders.archives.gov/documents/Washington/03-12-02-0266. [Original source: Grizzard, Jr. and Hoth, *The Papers of George Washington*, Vol. 12, 276–77.]
57 Note 3, "From George Washington to John Parke Custis, 14 November 1777," *Founders Online*, National Archives, https://founders.archives.gov/documents/Washington/03-12-02-0235. [Original source: Grizzard, Jr. and Hoth, *The Papers of George Washington*, Vol. 12, 249–50.]
58 Conway to Washington, November 16, 1777.
59 Ford, *Journal of the Continental Congress*, 1023–24.
60 Ibid, 1023–26.
61 "Arthur Lee to Franklin and Silas Deane, 13 December 1777," *Founders Online*, National Archives, https://founders.archives.gov/documents/Franklin/01-25-02-0207. [Original source: Willcox *The Papers of Benjamin Franklin*, Vol. 25, 280.]
62 "Joseph Priestley, "Discoverer of Oxygen National Historic Chemical Landmark," n.d. American Chemical Society. Accessed February 2, 2024. http://www.acs.org/content/acs/en/education/whatischemistry/landmarks/josephpriestleyoxygen.html.
63 "To Benjamin Franklin from Joseph Priestley, 13 December 1777," *Founders Online*, National Archives, https://founders.archives.gov/documents/Franklin/01-25-02-0208. [Original source: Willcox, *The Papers of Benjamin Franklin*, Vol. 25, 281.]

Chapter 6: Hardships at the Gulph, December 14

1 Waldo, *Diary*, 306.
2 *Pennsylvania Archives*, 92–93.
3 Dearborn, *Journal*, 111.
4 Armstrong, *Diary*, 257.
5 W. Edmunds Claussen, *The Revolutionary War Years in Berks, Chester and Montgomery County* (Boyertown, PA: Gilbert Printing Company, 1973), 162.
6 Brigham, *Diary*, 15.
7 Wild, *Journal*, 30.
8 Ibid, 91.
9 "Extract of a Letter, Written by a Captain of Light Horse in the Southern Department, to His Friend in Connecticut," *Continental Journal & Weekly Advertiser,* January 29, 1778.
10 Ibid.

ENDNOTES • 201

11 "General Orders, 14 December 1777," *Founders Online*, National Archives, https://founders.archives.gov/documents/Washington/03-12-02-0550. [Original source: Grizzard, Jr. and Hoth, *The Papers of George Washington*, Vol. 12, 603.]

12 "Headquarters' Orderly Book." n.d. National Park Service, Valley Forge National Historical Park, Pennsylvania. Accessed February 2, 2024. https://www.nps.gov/vafo/learn/history/culture/hq_orderly_book.htm. Another source states that the protocol for transmitting Washington's orders was that Washington gave his orders to the Major General of the Day, who then gave them to the Adjutant General, who dictated them to the brigade majors, aides-de-camp, or staff officers of the brigadier generals, then the brigadier generals gave the orders to their brigades and regiment adjutants, who then gave the orders to their regiment's orderlies and first sergeants, who then gave the orders to the captains and their companies. Harry Schenawolf, "Washington's Staff during the American Revolutionary War: Major General of the Day," *Revolutionary War Journal*, February 18, 2015, https://revolutionarywarjournal.com/washingtons-major-general.

13 "Founders Online: Home." n.d. Founders.archives.gov. https://www.founders.archives.gov/.

14 Library of Congress. "About This Collection | George Washington Papers | Digital Collections | Library of Congress." 2015. https://www.loc.gov/collections/george-washington-papers/about-this-collection/.
"Early American Orderly Books, 1748–1817 Reel Listing." n.d. Cengage. Accessed February 2, 2024. https://assets.cengage.com/gale/psm/3073000R.pdf.

15 "Early American Orderly Books, 1748–1817 Reel Listing." 6, Reel 5, No. 55. n.d. Cengage. Accessed February 2, 2024. https://assets.cengage.com/gale/psm/3073000R.pdf. This is a finding aid to the orderly books on microfilm at the Library of Congress, Manuscript Room.

16 Washington General Orders, *Founders Online*, December 12 and 13, 1777.

17 "From George Washington to Richard Peters, 14 December 1777," *Founders Online*, National Archives, https://founders.archives.gov/documents/Washington/03-12-02-0554. [Original source: Grizzard, Jr. and Hoth, *The Papers of George Washington*, Vol. 12, 607–9.]

18 "From George Washington to Richard Peters, 14 December 1777," *Founders Online*, National Archives, https://founders.archives.gov/documents/Washington/03-12-02-0554. [Original source: Grizzard, Jr. and Hoth, *The Papers of George Washington*, Vol. 12, 607–9.]

19 General Orders, 20 November 1777," *Founders Online*, National Archives, https://founders.archives.gov/documents/Washington/03-12-02-0324. [Original source: Grizzard, Jr. and Hoth, *The Papers of George Washington*, Vol. 12, 327–28.]

20 https://www.mountvernon.org/library/digitalhistory/digital-encyclopedia/article/adam-stephen-ca-1721-1791/

21 Washington to Peters, December 14, 1777.

22 "From George Washington to Henry Laurens, 14–15 December 1777," *Founders Online*, National Archives, https://founders.archives.gov/documents/Washington/03-12-02-0553. [Original source: Grizzard, Jr. and Hoth, *The Papers of George Washington*, Vol. 12, 604–7.]

23 Washington to Laurens, December 14, 1777.

24 "From George Washington to General William Howe, 14 December 1777," *Founders Online*, National Archives, https://founders.archives.gov/documents/Washington/03-12-02-0552. [Original source: Grizzard, Jr. and Hoth, *The Papers of George Washington*, Vol. 12, 603–4.] For descriptions of the contents of Burgoyne's letter see "Burgoyne to Washington," November 25 and "Washington to Burgoyne," December 17.

25 "To George Washington from the Board of War, 14 December 1777 [letter not found]," *Founders Online*, National Archives, https://founders.archives.gov/documents/Washington/03-12-02-0551. [Original source: Grizzard, Jr. and Hoth, *The Papers of George Washington*, 603.]

26 "From George Washington to the Board of War, 22 December 1777," *Founders Online*, National Archives, https://founders.archives.gov/documents/Washington/03-12-02-0607. [Original source: Grizzard, Jr. and Hoth, *The Papers of George Washington*, Vol. 12, 665–66.]
27 "To George Washington from Lieutenant Colonel Isaac Sherman, 14 December 1777," *Founders Online*, National Archives, https://founders.archives.gov/documents/Washington/03-12-02-0555. [Original source: Grizzard, Jr. and Hoth, *The Papers of George Washington*, Vol. 12, 610.]
28 Editors of Encyclopedia Britannica, "Jan Ingenhousz," Encyclopedia Britannica. Accessed February 2, 2024. https://www.britannica.com/biography/Jan-Ingenhousz.
29 Greek Particles are a class of words, some of them conjunctions, some adverbs, some both at once, which are used freely in the Greek language to make clear certain relations between ideas; see dcc.dickinson.edu, Dickinson College Commentaries. Also defined as words that have a grammatical function but have little meaning on their own; see pressbooks.pub.
30 "To Benjamin Franklin from Ingenhousz, 14 December 1777," *Founders Online*, National Archives, https://founders.archives.gov/documents/Franklin/01-25-02-0212. [Original source: Willcox, *The Papers of Benjamin Franklin*, Vol. 25, 286–90.]
31 Ibid.
32 Ibid.
33 Howard Gest, *A "Misplaced Chapter" in the History of Photosynthesis Research; the Second Publication (1796) on Plant Processes by Dr Jan Ingen-Housz, MD, Discoverer of Photosynthesis*. (Netherlands: Kluwer Academic Publishers, 1997). https://www.life.illinois.edu/govindjee/history/articles/GestOnIngenhousz_missing.pdf.
34 Ingenhouz to Franklin, December 14, 1777.

Chapter 7: The Army Settles Down, December 15

1 Weekly Return of Brigadier General Varnum's Brigade, December 15, 1777, Library of Congress, Manuscript Room, Microfilm Frame # 000020, Varnum, James M. (James Mitchell), 1748–1789. James M. Varnum and John Stark papers, 1777–1780. 1 item. 1 microfilm reel. Local shelving no.: MMC-2283Microfilm 17,360-1N-1P; https://lccn.loc.gov/mm78083238.
2 The next Weekly Return of Varnum's Brigade was December 22 from Valley Forge, and it showed 1,463 soldiers total, with 830 present and fit for duty.
3 Waldo, *Diary*, 307–8.
4 Armstrong, *Diary*, 257.
5 Dearborn, *Diary*, 111.
6 Washington stayed in his tent at Valley Forge for a few days until he rented a house from Deborah Hewes, who had rented the house from her relative, Isaac Potts. Continental law at the time forbade the army mandating that citizens accommodate them in their homes. "Washington's Headquarters (Isaac Potts House)," American Battlefield Trust, accessed February 12, 2024, https://www.battlefields.org/visit/heritage-sites/washingtons-headquarters-isaac-potts-house.
7 J. Laurens, *Diary*, 93–94.
8 Angell, *Diary*, December 15, 1777.
9 Wild, *Journal*, 30.
10 Brigham, *Diary*, 15.
11 Andre, *Journal*, 131.

12 Parker, *Correspondence*, 49.
13 https://www.battlefields.org/learn/biographies/robert-morris
14 Shirley L. Green, *Revolutionary Blacks: Discovering the Frank Brothers, Freeborn Men of Colors, Soldiers of Independence* (Yardley, PA: Westholme Publishing, 2023).
15 "Pennsylvania—An Act for the Gradual Abolition of Slavery." n.d. Battlefield Trust. Accessed February 5, 2024. https://www.battlefields.org/learn/primary-sources/pennsylvania-act-gradual-abolition-slavery-1780.
16 Buck, *History of Montgomery County*, 41; see also David Montalvo, "A Brief History of Slavery and Freedom in Pennsylvania and Montgomery County." Presented at the Presentation, King of Prussia Historical Society, September 14, 2019. https://www.kophistory.org/archive/files/MANUSCRIPT/ShortEnslavedinPA&MontCo.pdf. Pennsylvania is noted as having 3,707 enslaved persons and 6,531 free African Americans.
17 Benjamin Quarles, *The Negro in the American Revolution* (Chapel Hill, NC: University of North Carolina Press, 1996, 1961), 58. The book provides an excellent examination of the role of African Americans in the Revolutionary War, the war's dichotomy with slavery, and the actions of the various state governments, federal government, Washington, and other Continental Army officers in this regard. [Note: 1961 was the original publication date; it was republished in 1961.]
18 Margaret Denise Dennis, *Bristol Budd Sampson: Patriot of the American Revolution* (La Plume, PA: Keystone Press Publishing, 2023). Sampson was blind later in life, and he applied for the Revolutionary War era pensions that were made available to disabled veterans of the war in 1818. Sampson and his wife, Phoebe Perkins Sampson, lived in northeast Pennsylvania at the time with his in-laws. Sampson made a 400-mile journey to Connecticut, on foot, to obtain affidavits from his commanding officer attesting to his service. His efforts were successful, and he received the pension for the rest of his life. He passed away in 1848 and is buried in the Perkins-Dennis Cemetery, which is the family cemetery of his wife, on the Historic Dennis Farm in Kingsley, Pennsylvania. Phoebe later received a widow's pension and a land grant. The Dennis farm is on the National Register of Historic Places.
19 Denise Dennis, "African American Dennis Ancestors Who Fought in the Revolutionary War," interview by Sheilah Vance, 2024.
20 Quarles, *The Negro in the American Revolution*, 61–62, 57–58.
21 Ibid, 55–56.
22 *Continental Journal and Weekly Advertiser*, Boston, MA. "Massachusetts Legislature," January 8, 1778.
23 "George Washington's Mount Vernon." George Washington's Mount Vernon, 2019. https://www.mountvernon.org/library/digitalhistory/digital-encyclopedia/article/william-billy-lee/.
24 John Blair Linn, History of Centre and Clinton Counties, Pennsylvania (1883); Potter's Mill Store Ledger, November 8, 1790.
25 Cadwalader's ownership of enslaved persons is detailed in the excellent resource Penn and Slavery Project, which shows which of the University of Pennsylvania's early trustees and faculty owned enslaved persons. It includes information about such other Revolutionary War-era Pennsylvania patriots as General James Potter, Benjamin Franklin, and Continental Congress delegate Joseph Reed. "Early Trustees—Slave Ownership," pennandslaveryproject.org, accessed February 25, 2024, https://pennandslaveryproject.org/exhibits/show/slaveownership/earlytrustees.
26 Woodman, *History of Valley Forge*, 67. Woodman also recalls a tale regarding a man named Phineas, who was enslaved on Woodman's grandfather's farm in the Valley Forge area in fall 1777. Woodman wrote that Hessian soldiers went to his grandfather's farm. "I allude to a black man, a slave of my grandfather, named Phineas, generally called 'Phin,' for be it known that

at the time slavery existed in Pennsylvania, and Friends, of whom my grandfather was one, as well as others, held them in unconditional servitude." Woodman noted that Phin ran and got the family gun when he saw the Hessians coming and then hid in a sinking hole or cave for several days to defend himself from the enemy. "The place of his retreat was afterwards called by my father, 'Phin's Fort.'" Ibid, 41.

27 Woodman, *History of Valley Forge*, 67; DeKalb took over Weedon's command. Woodman described DeKalb as "tall of stature and very erect for a person of his years, being more than sixty years of age, having been forty years in the Prussian Service." Ibid.
28 Woodman, *History of Valley Forge*, 50–51.
29 Baker, *Camp by the Old Gulph Mill*, 426.
30 Holstein, *Swedish Holsteins*, 264, 414. The author also visited the Pennsylvania Historical Society and reviewed the original documents to which Holstein referred.
31 "LTC Isaac Hughes (1747–1782)—Find a Grave..." n.d. www.findagrave.com. Accessed February 5, 2024. https://www.findagrave.com/memorial/13056639/isaac-hughes.
32 Isaac Hughes Will, Historical Society of Pennsylvania.
33 Charles Henry Browning, *Welsh Settlement of Pennsylvania* (Philadelphia, PA: W. J. Campbell, 1912), 163–67, 490; "John Bevan of Welsh Tract & Mi—Genealogy.com." n.d. www.genealogy.com. Accessed February 5, 2024. https://www.genealogy.com/forum/surnames/topics/bevan/139/.
34 Montalvo, "Slavery and Freedom in Pennsylvania and Montgomery County," 5.
35 Montalvo, "Slavery and Freedom in Pennsylvania and Montgomery County," 12; *Pennsylvania Gazette*, May 11, 1749.
36 Gary Nash, "Agrippa Hull: Revolutionary Patriot—BlackPast." BlackPast. July 2, 2008. https://www.blackpast.org/african-american-history/agrippa-hull-revolutionary-patriot/.
37 Noah Lewis, "Edward Hector Research Documentation—Edward 'Ned' Hector—Black Revolutionary War Hero," Accessed February 5, 2024. https://www.nedhector.com/edward-hector-research-documentation/.
38 Noah Lewis, "Pennsylvania's African American Revolutionary War Hero, Ned Hector, During the Gulph Mills Encampment," Interview by Sheilah Vance.
39 "Patriots of African Descent Monument (U.S. National Park Service)," n.d., www.nps.gov. https://www.nps.gov/places/patriots-african-descent-monument.htm.
40 "General Orders, 15 December 1777," *Founders Online*, National Archives, https://founders.archives.gov/documents/Washington/03-12-02-0556. [Original source: Grizzard, Jr. and Hoth, *The Papers of George Washington*, Vol. 12, 610–11.]
41 Platt, Orderly Book, December 15, 1777.
42 "Orders to Commissaries and Quartermasters, 15 December 1777," *Founders Online*, National Archives, https://founders.archives.gov/documents/Washington/03-12-02-0558. [Original source: Grizzard, Jr. and Hoth. *The Papers of George Washington,* Vol. 12, 611–12.]
43 "From George Washington to Henry Laurens, 14–15 December 1777," *Founders Online*, National Archives, https://founders.archives.gov/documents/Washington/03-12-02-0553. [Original source: Grizzard, Jr. and Hoth, *The Papers of George Washington*, Vol. 12, 604–7.]
44 *Pennsylvania Archives*, 98.
45 *Pennsylvania Archives*, 94.
46 Ibid.
47 Ford, *Journal of the Continental Congress*, 932–35.
48 *Journal of the House of Delegates of Virginia*. 1827 Edition. Vol. October 1777 Session: 80.
49 "To Benjamin Franklin from ―――― Boudet, 15 December 1777: résumé," *Founders Online*, National Archives, https://founders.archives.gov/documents/Franklin/01-25-02-0213. [Original source: Willcox, *The Papers of Benjamin Franklin*, Vol. 25, 291.]

Chapter 8: Tents Arrive, Skirmishes with the British, and the Army Waits, December 16

1. "The Articles of Confederation, 1777 | Gilder Lehrman Institute of American History." n.d. www.gilderlehrman.org. https://www.gilderlehrman.org/history-resources/spotlight-primary-source/articles-confederation-1777.
2. John P Kaminski et al., *The Documentary History of the Ratification of the Constitution and the Bill of Rights*, Volume 38, 2022.
3. "Extract of a Letter from a Gentleman at Camp, on Schuylkill, Dated Dec. 17, 1777," *The Continental Journal and Weekly Advertiser*, January 22, 1778.
4. Waldo, *Diary*, 308.
5. Elijah Fisher, *Elijah Fisher's Journal While in the War for Independence*. Edited by William Lapham (Augusta, ME: Press for Badger & Manley, 1880). https://ia801305.us.archive.org/3/items/cu31924032740478/cu31924032740478.pdf. Fisher was a private in the 4th Massachusetts Regiment at the time; he was assigned to Washington's Life Guards from 1778 to 1780.
6. Armstrong, *Diary*, 257.
7. Dearborn, *Journal*, 111.
8. Wild, *Journal*, 30.
9. Brigham, *Diary*, 16.
10. *Pennsylvania Archives*, 99.
11. See Chapter 3, The Battle of Matson's Ford.
12. "Benjamin Tallmadge." n.d. George Washington's Mount Vernon. https://www.mountvernon.org/library/digitalhistory/digital-encyclopedia/article/benjamin-tallmadge.
13. "To George Washington from Major Benjamin Tallmadge, 16 December 1777," *Founders Online*, National Archives, https://founders.archives.gov/documents/Washington/03-12-02-0565. [Original source: Grizzard, Jr. and Hoth, *The Papers of George Washington*, Vol. 12, 618–19.]
14. *Pennsylvania Archives*, 100–2.
15. "General Orders, 16 December 1777," *Founders Online*, National Archives, https://founders.archives.gov/documents/Washington/03-12-02-0561. [Original source: Grizzard, Jr. and Hoth, *The Papers of George Washington*, Vol. 12, 613–14.]
16. Ibid, note.
17. Ibid, note. (Muhlenberg's Orderly Book, 35: 299; See also Weedon's Orderly Book, 157.)
18. Richard Platt, Orderly Book, November 12 to December 16, 74; accessed Library of Congress, Microfilm; Orderly Book 55.
19. Clark, a member of Virginia's 8th Regiment, was one of Washington's first spymasters. "A New Nation's First Spies." n.d. www.intelligence.gov. https://www.intelligence.gov/evolution-of-espionage/revolutionary-war/new-nations-first-spies.
20. "From George Washington to Major John Clark, Jr., 16 December 1777," *Founders Online*, National Archives, https://founders.archives.gov/documents/Washington/03-12-02-0562. [Original source: Grizzard, Jr. and Hoth, *The Papers of George Washington*, Vol. 12, 614.]
21. Ibid.
22. Ibid. John Fitzgerald, a native of Ireland, was a Virginia merchant from Alexandria and a friend of George Washington. He was a captain in the 3rd Virginia Regiment. In 1776, Washington appointed him as an aide-de-camp when an opening on his staff arose in October 1776. He provided the evidence to stamp out the Conway Cabal. Carlos Briceno, "'From the Archives'—Aide-De-Camp Colonel John Fitzgerald." The Basilica of Saint Mary. October 20, 2023. https://stmaryoldtown.org/aide-de-camp-colonel-john-fitzgerald.

23 Ibid.
24 Laurens, *Correspondence*, 94. Full transcript of Laurens's correspondence of December 15 is in Chapter 7 previous.
25 Marquis de Lafayette, *Memoirs, Correspondence and Manuscripts of General Lafayette. Published by His Family*. (New York, NY: Columbia College, 1837). https://www.gutenberg.org/cache/epub/8376/pg8376-images.html.
26 Lafayette, *Memoirs*, December 16, 1777.
27 Ibid.
28 Angell, *Diary*, December 16.
29 Andre, *Journal*, 131.
30 "Lieutenant General Charles Cornwallis—Yorktown Battlefield Part of Colonial National Historical Park (U.S. National Park Service)." n.d. www.nps.gov. Accessed February 3, 2024. https://www.nps.gov/york/learn/historyculture/cornwallis.htm.
31 Ewald, *Diary*, 110.
32 Ford, *Journals of the Continental Congress*, 1029–31. This report, in the writing of Joseph Jones, is in the Papers of the Continental Congress, No. 33, folio 87. The letter of the Committee to Washington, dated December 16, is in the Washington Papers, Vol. 91, folio 108.
33 "To Benjamin Franklin from Henry Grand, 16 December 1777," *Founders Online*, National Archives, https://founders.archives.gov/documents/Franklin/01-25-02-0219. [Original source: Willcox, *The Papers of Benjamin Franklin*, Vol. 25, 298.]
34 "To Benjamin Franklin from Silas Deane, 16 December 1777," *Founders Online*, National Archives, https://founders.archives.gov/documents/Franklin/01-25-02-0218. [Original source: Willcox, *The Papers of Benjamin Franklin*, Vol. 25, 296–97.]
35 "John Young to the American Commissioners, 16 December 1777," *Founders Online*, National Archives, https://founders.archives.gov/documents/Franklin/01-25-02-0217. [Original source: Willcox, *The Papers of Benjamin Franklin*, Vol. 25, 295–96.]

Chapter 9: Washington Announces the Move to Winter Quarters, December 17

1 Due to delays in communications during that time, Washington was not aware that French King Louis XVI that day had made the decision to officially recognize and support the new United States.
2 "General Orders, 17 December 1777," *Founders Online*, National Archives, https://founders.archives.gov/documents/Washington/03-12-02-0566. [Original source: Grizzard, Jr. and Hoth, *The Papers of George Washington*, Vol. 12, 620–21.]
3 Bauermeister, *Revolution in America*, 146.
4 Platt, Orderly Book, December 17, 1777.
5 Orderly Book: Philip Van Courtland's Second New York Regiment of 1777, Pennsylvania, Library of Congress, Early American Orderly Books, No. 56.20.
6 Van Courtland Orderly Book, December 17, 1777.
7 Dearborn, *Journal*, 111.
8 Armstrong, *Diary*, 257.
9 Angell, *Diary*, December 17, 1777.
10 Paul Brigham, "A Revolutionary Diary of Capt. Paul Brigham, Nov. 19, 1777 to Sept. 4, 1778." Edited by Edward Hoyt. *Vermont History* 34 (1) (1966): 15–16.

11 Parker, *Correspondence*, December 17, Frame 51.
12 "No Title," *The Pennsylvania Ledger or the Philadelphia Market Day Advertiser*, December 17, 1777.
13 "William Heath–1911 Encyclopedia Britannica," StudyLight.org, April 14, 2024, https://www.studylight.org/encyclopedias/bri/w/william-heath.html.
14 Ford, *Journal of the Continental Congress* 9, 1032; "To George Washington from Henry Laurens, 17 December 1777," *Founders Online*, National Archives, https://founders.archives.gov/documents/Washington/03-12-02-0571. [Original source: Grizzard, Jr. and R. Hoth, *The Papers of George Washington*, Vol. 12, 625.]
15 "To George Washington from Major General William Heath, 17 December 1777," *Founders Online*, National Archives, https://founders.archives.gov/documents/Washington/03-12-02-0570. [Original source: Grizzard, Jr. and R. Hoth, *The Papers of George Washington*, Vol. 12, 624–25.]
16 "To George Washington from Steuben, 6 December 1777," *Founders Online*, National Archives, https://founders.archives.gov/documents/Washington/03-12-02-0519. [Original source: Grizzard, Jr. and R. Hoth, *The Papers of George Washington*, Vol. 12, 567–68.]
17 Ibid.
18 Stockwell, "Baron von Steuben," https://www.mountvernon.org/library/digitalhistory/digital-encyclopedia/article/baron-von-steuben/. Once Von Steuben arrived at the camp of the Continental Army in Valley Forge in February 1778, he transformed the Continental Army by instituting military discipline through a manual of orders and drills, similar to those he was under when he served in the Prussian Army. Von Steuben would go on to be called the Drillmaster at Valley Forge. His drills and order made the Continental Army a much better one when they marched out of the encampment on June 19, 1778.
19 Note 1, "To George Washington from Steuben, 6 December 1777," *Founders Online*, National Archives, https://founders.archives.gov/documents/Washington/03-12-02-0519. [Original source: Grizzard, Jr. and R. Hoth, *The Papers of George Washington*, Vol. 12, 567–68.]; citing the Library of Congress, George Washington Papers. Mary Stockwell, "Baron von Steuben," https://www.mountvernon.org/library/digitalhistory/digital-encyclopedia/article/baron-von-steuben/.
20 "To George Washington from the Continental Navy Board, 17 December 1777," *Founders Online*, National Archives, https://founders.archives.gov/documents/Washington/03-12-02-0568. [Original source: Grizzard, Jr. and R. Hoth, *The Papers of George Washington*, Vol. 12, 622.]
21 Note 1, Ibid.
22 "To George Washington from Major Morgan Alexander, 17 December 1777," *Founders Online*, National Archives, https://founders.archives.gov/documents/Washington/07-01-02-0019. [This document from *The Papers of George Washington* is original to the digital edition. It was added on July 4, 2020.]
23 *Pennsylvania Archives*, 104.
24 Ford, *Journal of the Continental Congress*, 102–3.
25 Pennsylvania Archives, 106.
26 "The American Commissioners to the Committee for Foreign Affairs, 18 December 1777," *Founders Online*, National Archives, https://founders.archives.gov/documents/Franklin/01-25-02-0227. [Original source: Willcox, *The Papers of Benjamin Franklin*, Vol. 25, 305–9.]
27 Archives.gov, Treaty of Alliance with France (1778).

28 Jean Bouvier, "Anne-Robert-Jacques Turgot, Baron de l'Aulne | French Economist," in *Encyclopedia Britannica*, March 14, 2019, https://www.britannica.com/biography/Anne-Robert-Jacques-Turgot-baron-de-lAulne.

29 "To Benjamin Franklin from Anne-Robert-Jacques Turgot, Baron de l'Aulne, 17 [December?] 1777," *Founders Online*, National Archives, https://founders.archives.gov/documents/Franklin/01-25-02-0224. [Original source: Willcox, *The Papers of Benjamin Franklin*, Vol. 25, 302–3.]

30 Note 4, "To Benjamin Franklin from Charles Millon, 17 December 1777: résumé," *Founders Online*, National Archives, https://founders.archives.gov/documents/Franklin/01-25-02-0223. [Original source: Willcox, *The Papers of Benjamin Franklin*, Vol. 25, 301–2.]

31 "To Benjamin Franklin from Charles Millon, 17 December 1777: résumé," *Founders Online*, National Archives, https://founders.archives.gov/documents/Franklin/01-25-02-0223. [Original source: Willcox, *The Papers of Benjamin Franklin*, Vol. 25, 301–2.]

32 "From Thomas Jefferson to John Adams, 17 December 1777," *Founders Online*, National Archives, https://founders.archives.gov/documents/Jefferson/01-02-02-0038. [Original source: Julian P. Boyd, ed., *The Papers of Thomas Jefferson*, Vol. 2, *1777–18 June 1779* (Princeton: Princeton University Press, 1950), 120–21.]

Chapter 10: Thanksgiving, December 18

1 Ford, *Journal of the Continental Congress*, Vol. 9, 854–55; "Religion and the Founding of the American Republic," n.d., Library of Congress. https://www.loc.gov/exhibits/religion/rel04.html.

2 "The First Thanksgiving of the United States," n.d. Accessed February 4, 2024. https://thanksgiving.org/wp-content/uploads/2016/06/The-First-Thanksgiving-of-the-United-States.pdf.

3 Ames Robbins, "The Anti-Washington Cabal," *National Review*. November 26, 2008. https://www.nationalreview.com/2008/11/anti-washington-cabal-james-s-robbins/.

4 Dearborn, *Journal*, 118.

5 Armstrong, *Diary*, 251.

6 Wild, *Diary*, 30.

7 Angell, *Diary*, December 18, 1777.

8 Brigham, *Journal*, 16.

9 Waldo, *Diary*, 308.

10 Joseph Plumb Martin was identified as the author of the book *A Narrative of Some of the Adventures, Dangers and Sufferings of a Revolutionary Soldier*. History.com Editors. "Joseph Plumb Martin." HISTORY. March 8, 2010. https://www.history.com/topics/american-revolution/joseph-plumb-martin; Joseph Plumb Martin, *A Narrative of Some of the Adventures, Dangers and Sufferings of a Revolutionary Soldier*. Glazier, Masters & Co., 1830. https://www.google.com/books/edition/A_Narrative_of_Some_of_the_Adventures_Da/ZbdcAAAAcAAJ?hl=en.

11 Martin, *Narrative*, 73–75.

12 "From George Washington to Israel Evans, 13 March 1778," *Founders Online*, National Archives, https://founders.archives.gov/documents/Washington/03-14-02-0134. [Original source: David R. Hoth, ed., *The Papers of George Washington*, Revolutionary War Series, Vol. 14, *1 March 1778–30 April 1778* (Charlottesville: University of Virginia Press, 2004), 169.]

13 Israel Evans, *A Discourse, Delivered, on the 18th Day of December, 1777, the Day of Public Thanksgiving, Appointed by the Honourable Continental Congress, by the Reverend Israel Evans, A.M. Chaplain to General Poor's Brigade: And Now Published at the Request of the General and*

Officers of the Said Brigade, to Be Distributed among the Soldiers, Gratis (Lancaster, PA: Francis Bailey, 1778), 2009. https://quod.lib.umich.edu/e/evans/N12491.0001.001?view=toc.
14 Evans, *Discourse*, 14–15.
15 Ibid, 17–18.
16 Ibid.
17 "The First Thanksgiving of the United States." n.d. Accessed February 4, 2024. https://thanksgiving.org/wp-content/uploads/2016/06/The-First-Thanksgiving-of-the-United-States.pdf.
18 Timothy Dwight. *A Sermon, Preached at Stamford, in Connecticut, upon the General Thanksgiving, December 18th, 1777* (Norwich: Green & Spooner, 1778). https://quod.lib.umich.edu/e/evans/n12490.0001.001.
19 David Avery, and Internet Archive. *The Lord Is to Be Praised for the Triumphs of His Power. A Sermon, Preached at Greenwich, in Connecticut, on the 18th of December 1777. ... By David Avery. ... 1778. Internet Archive.* https://archive.org/details/bim_eighteenth-century_the-lord-is-to-be-praise_avery-david_1778.
20 "General Orders, 18 December 1777," *Founders Online*, National Archives, https://founders.archives.gov/documents/Washington/03-12-02-0573. [Original source: Grizzard, Jr. and Hoth, *The Papers of George Washington*, Revolutionary War Series, Vol. 12, 626–28.]
21 "General Orders, 15 December 1777," *Founders Online*, National Archives, https://founders.archives.gov/documents/Washington/03-12-02-0556. [Original source: Grizzard, Jr. and Hoth, *The Papers of George Washington*, Vol. 12, 610–11.]
22 Ibid.
23 Orderly Book, Lt. Col. Joseph Storer, York County, Massachusetts Regiment, December 18, 1777, Library of Congress, Manuscript Room, Early American Orderly Books, #47.
24 Orderly Book, Capt. Peter Brown's Company of the Philadelphia Militia Artillery, #54, 175pp.
25 To George Washington from Joseph Galloway, 18 December 1777," *Founders Online*, National Archives, https://founders.archives.gov/documents/Washington/03-12-02-0575. [Original source: Grizzard, Jr. and Hoth, *The Papers of George Washington*, Vol. 12, 630.]; See Note 1, Grace Gowden, a daughter of Pennsylvania Supreme Court justice Lawrence Growden, married Galloway.
26 "To George Washington from Colonel John Gunby, 18 December 1777," *Founders Online*, National Archives, https://founders.archives.gov/documents/Washington/03-12-02-0576. [Original source: Grizzard, Jr. and Hoth, *The Papers of George Washington*, Vol. 12, 631–32.]
27 "To Benjamin Franklin from Pageant veuve Rivaud, 18 December 1777: résumé," *Founders Online*, National Archives, https://founders.archives.gov/documents/Franklin/01-25-02-0234. [Original source: Willcox, *The Papers of Benjamin Franklin*, Vol. 25, 315.]
28 "To Benjamin Franklin from Doerner, 18 December 1777," *Founders Online*, National Archives, https://founders.archives.gov/documents/Franklin/01-25-02-0232. [Original source: Willcox, *The Papers of Benjamin Franklin*, Vol. 25, 312–13.]
29 "To Benjamin Franklin from the Duchesse de Deux-Ponts, 18 December 1777," *Founders Online*, National Archives, https://founders.archives.gov/documents/Franklin/01-25-02-0233. [Original source: Willcox, *The Papers of Benjamin Franklin*, Vol. 25, 313–15.]

Chapter 11: The Army Leaves the Gulph and Marches to Valley Forge, December 19

1 Storer, Orderly Book, December 18.
2 Fisher, *Journal*, 7.

3. Lilley P is a pie made from the jelly of a Gilly flower, a clove-scented pink carnation. Karen Hess, *Martha Washington's Booke of Cookery and Booke of Sweetmeats: Being a Family Manuscript, Curiously Copied by an Unknown Hand Sometime in the Seventeenth Century, Which Was in Her Keeping from 1749, the Time of Her Marriage to Daniel Custis, to 1799, at Which Time She Gave It to Eleanor Parke Custis, Her Granddaughter, on the Occasion of Her Marriage to Lawrence Lewis* (New York: Columbia University Press, 1995).
4. Armstrong, *Diary*, 258.
5. Dearborn, *Diary*, 112.
6. Laurens, *Correspondence*, 97.
7. Martin, *Narrative*, 75.
8. Angell, *Diary*, December 19, 1777.
9. Nancy K. Loane, *Following the Drum Women at the Valley Forge Encampment*, 1st ed. (Washington, DC: Potomac Books, 2009), 3, 117.
10. Brigham, *Diary*, 16.
11. Wild, *Diary*, 30.
12. McMichael, *Diary*, 157.
13. Washinton Irving, *Washington Irving, the Life of Washington*, Vol. 3 (New York, NY: Thomas Y. Crowell and Company, 1865), 306–8.
14. Irving, 306–8; it must be noted, however, that Washington Irving's book completely skips over the Gulph Mills Encampment.
15. Anthony Wayne Papers, Historical Society of Pennsylvania.
16. Harry Emerson Wildes, *Anthony Wayne, Trouble Shooter of the American Revolution* (Greenwood, 1970), 148–49.
17. Ewald, *Diary*, 110–11.
18. Platt, Orderly Book, December 19, 1777.
19. John Thomas Scharf, *History of Delaware: 1609–1888* (Philadelphia, PA: L. J. Richards & Co., 1888).
20. "From George Washington to George Read, 19 December 1777," *Founders Online*, National Archives, https://founders.archives.gov/documents/Washington/03-12-02-0582. [Original source: Grizzard, Jr. and Hoth, *The Papers of George Washington*, Vol. 12, 639–40.]
21. "From George Washington to George Read, 19 December 1777," *Founders Online*, National Archives, https://founders.archives.gov/documents/Washington/03-12-02-0582. [Original source: Grizzard, Jr. and Hoth, *The Papers of George Washington*, Vol. 12, 639–40.]
22. "From George Washington to Patrick Henry, 19 December 1777," *Founders Online*, National Archives, https://founders.archives.gov/documents/Washington/03-12-02-0579. [Original source: Grizzard, Jr. and Hoth, *The Papers of George Washington*, Vol. 12, 636–37.]
23. "To George Washington from Brigadier General Casimir Pulaski, 19 December 1777," *Founders Online*, National Archives, https://founders.archives.gov/documents/Washington/03-12-02-0581. [Original source: Grizzard, Jr. and Hoth, *The Papers of George Washington*, Vol. 12, 637–39.]
24. "To George Washington from Major General John Armstrong, 19 December 1777," *Founders Online*, National Archives, https://founders.archives.gov/documents/Washington/03-12-02-0577. [Original source: Grizzard, Jr. and Hoth, *The Papers of George Washington*, Vol. 12, 632–34.]
25. "To George Washington from Major John Clark, Jr., 19 December 1777," *Founders Online*, National Archives, https://founders.archives.gov/documents/Washington/03-12-02-0578. [Original source: Grizzard, Jr. and Hoth, *The Papers of George Washington*, 635–36.]
26. *Pennsylvania Archives* 1777, 107–8.

27 *Pennsylvania Archives*, 107–18.
28 Ford, *Journal of the Continental Congress*, 1036. The Continental Congress minutes reflect in the Resolution "that Gen. Washington, be [further] informed that, in the opinion of Congress, the State of New Jersey demands, in a peculiar degree, the protection of the armies of the United States so far as the same can possibly be extended, consistent with the safety of the army and the general welfare; as that state lies open to attack from so many quarters, and the struggles which have been made by the brave and victorious inhabitants of that State, in defence of the common cause, cannot fail of exposing them to the particular resentment of a merciless enemy."
29 "Dumas to the American Commissioners, 19 December 1777," *Founders Online*, National Archives, https://founders.archives.gov/documents/Franklin/01-25-02-0235. [Original source: Willcox, *The Papers of Benjamin Franklin*, Vol. 25, 315.] Note 6 cites Wharton, Diplomatic Correspondence, n. 451.
30 "To Benjamin Franklin from [Benjamin Sowden], 19 December 1777," *Founders Online*, National Archives, https://founders.archives.gov/documents/Franklin/01-25-02-0239. [Original source: Willcox, *The Papers of Benjamin Franklin*, Vol. 25, 317–20.]
31 Ibid.
32 "To Benjamin Franklin from ——— de Reynaud, 19 December 1777: résumé," *Founders Online*, National Archives, https://founders.archives.gov/documents/Franklin/01-25-02-0238. [Original source: Willcox, *The Papers of Benjamin Franklin*, Vol. 25, 317.]; British General William Howe's older brother, Richard, was the Commander of the Royal Navy in America. William R. Griffith, "The Howe Brothers in North America," American Battlefield Trust. April 13, 2020. https://www.battlefields.org/learn/articles/howe-brothers-north-america.
33 Aubrey Anderson, "Historic Valley Forge: The Overhanging Rock at Gulph Mills." www.ushistory.org. December 19, 1924. https://www.ushistory.org/valleyforge/history/rock.html. The Hanging Rock was also known as the "Overhanging Rock." The Hanging Rock became the most famous symbol of the Gulph Mills Encampment. In 1893, the Pennsylvania Sons of the Revolution put a mural on a large, rough memorial stone to symbolize the Hanging Rock as a representation of the Gulph Mills Encampment. The marker said, "The main Continental Army commanded by George Washington encamped in this immediate vicinity from December 13–19, 1777, before going into winter quarters in Valley Forge." Mrs. Aubrey Anderson, who owned the land on which the Hanging Rock is located, donated the Hanging Rock to the Valley Forge Historical Society in 1924 so that the rock would be preserved. Later that year, the Valley Forge Historical Society dedicated the rock as a memorial to the Gulph Mills Encampment.

There used to be a freshwater fountain that flowed out of Hanging Rock. It was fed by a natural spring that originated near the summit of Rebel Hill. In 1953, the Gulph Mills Civic Association put a plaque directly on Hanging Rock which read, "To the soldiers of the Continental Army who passed this Spring. Gulph Mills Civic Association, 1953." The spring was capped off when the Pennsylvania Department of Transportation built a high-speed rail line that ran near the top of the Hanging Rock and when townhouses were built at the top of Rebel Hill.

In 1962, the memorial stone was rededicated, when it was moved to Executive Estates Park in Gulph Mills. Also in 1962, The Friends of Valley Forge put a marker directly on Hanging Rock, which read, "George Washington and the American Army passed under this rock on the march to Valley Forge on December 19, 1777."

The Hanging Rock was cut back significantly over the years because trucks kept running into it. The local community and local historical societies fought successfully for years against the Pennsylvania Department of Transportation's efforts to seriously cut back the Rock. In 1997, they successfully got the Hanging Rock listed on the National Register of Historic Places after one major battle to scale back or even remove the rock. National Archives Catalog. "Registration Form, Pennsylvania SP Hanging Rock, National Register for Historic Places," September 1997. https://catalog.archives.gov/id/71995725?fbclid=IwZXh0bgNhZW0CMTAAAR0GxTm-2D9oi2SNgj8Gfvrq7NcTdIdln9xINYRCTGnMZ3_SbPhmWhrZDk0E_aem_wnnJphSe1S-C8uywJpz_wlg

However, the Hanging Rock was cut back again in 2021 when PennDOT reconfigured Gulph Road and routed it away from the Rock. Local historical societies worked with Penn Dot to use the stones of the original fountain to construct a new memorial, which was installed in 2022. The new memorial is at the intersection of Upper Gulph, South Gulph, and Old Gulph Roads, right across the street from the former picket post, which is now a restaurant.

William Trego's painting *March to Valley Forge* is of Washington and his army marching down Gulph Road, past the Hanging Rock. You can see the outlines of the Gulph Mill, which was down the street from the rock, in the background. Trego's painting was inspired by Washington Irving's writings about the march to Valley Forge.

Today, the physical Hanging Rock is a shadow of its former self. Yet, its significance has grown even larger over time.

Chapter 12: Gulph Mills During the Valley Forge Encampment

1. Menu from the Picket Post Restaurant, by Hanging Rock, early 1960s. The restaurant now located there is called Savona.
2. See Chapter 5 for descriptions of where the generals' quarters were located during the Gulph Mills Encampment.
3. Ed Pinkowski, *Washington's Officers Slept Here, Historic Homes of Valley Forge and Its Neighborhood* (Philadelphia: Sunshine Press, 1953), 98–105.
4. "To George Washington from Captain Henry Lee, Jr., 9 January 1778," *Founders Online*, National Archives, https://founders.archives.gov/documents/Washington/03-13-02-0156. [Original source: Edward G. Lengel, ed., *The Papers of George Washington*, Revolutionary War Series, Vol. 13, *26 December 1777–28 February 1778*, Charlottesville: University of Virginia Press, 2003, 190–91.]
5. Radnor Friends Meeting | Religious Society of Friends," n.d. Accessed February 4, 2024. https://radnorquakers.net. The Radnor Meeting House was for area Quakers. It also served as a headquarters, hospital, and picket for the Continental Army at various points during the Philadelphia Campaign.
6. Note, "To George Washington from Captain Henry Lee, Jr., 9 January 1778," *Founders Online*, National Archives, https://founders.archives.gov/documents/Washington/03-13-02-0156. [Original source: Lengel, *The Papers of George Washington*, Vol. 13, 190–91.]
7. Colonel Morgan commanded a picket post in Villanova, Radnor Township, on the grounds of a 400-foot hill called Camp Woods. Franklin Burns, "New Light on the Encampment of the Continental Army at Valley Forge: December 19, 1777–June 21, 1778," *Tredyffrin Easttown Historical Society History Quarterly* 2, no. 3 (July 1939): 59–74, https://www.tehistory.org/hqda/html/v02/v02n3p075.html.
8. "General Orders, 10 January 1778," *Founders Online*, National Archives, https://founders.archives.gov/documents/Washington/03-13-02-0162. [Original source: Lengel, *The Papers of George Washington*, Vol. 13, 194–95.]
9. "General Orders, 10 January 1778," *Founders Online*, National Archives, https://founders.archives.gov/documents/Washington/03-13-02-0162. [Original source: Lengel, *The Papers of George Washington*, Vol. 13, 194–95.]

10 "General Orders, 12 January 1778," *Founders Online*, National Archives, https://founders.archives.gov/documents/Washington/03-13-02-0172. [Original source: Lengel, *The Papers of George Washington*, Vol. 13, 204–5.]

11 John Ferling, "Thomas Jefferson, Aaron Burr and the Election of 1800." Smithsonian.com. November 2004. https://www.smithsonianmag.com/history/thomas-jefferson-aaron-burr-and-the-election-of-1800-131082359/.

12 Ibid.

13 MacDonald P. Jackson, *Who Wrote "The Night before Christmas"?: Analyzing the Clement Clarke Moore vs. Henry Livingston Question* (Jefferson, North Carolina: McFarland & Company, Inc., Publishers, 2016).

14 Note 3, "From George Washington to Colonel Henry Beekman Livingston, 16 April 1778," *Founders Online*, National Archives, https://founders.archives.gov/documents/Washington/03-14-02-0487. [Original source: Hoth, *The Papers of George Washington*, Vol. 14, 533.]

15 Franklin Burns, "New Light on the Encampment of the Continental Army at Valley Forge: December 19, 1777–June 21, 1778," *Tredyffrin Easttown Historical Society History Quarterly* 2, no. 3 (July 1939): 59–74, https://www.tehistory.org/hqda/html/v02/v02n3p075.html.

16 National Archives, War Department Collection of Revolutionary War Records, n.d., https://catalog.archives.gov/search-within/422?q=gulph.

17 "Case Files of Pension and Bounty-Land Warrant Applications Based on Revolutionary War Service, Ca. 1800–Ca. 1912," National Archives Catalog, n.d., https://catalog.archives.gov/id/300022; Application W18379.

18 Lacey, *Memoirs*, 110.

19 Lacey, *Memoirs*, 110–11.

20 "General Orders, 1 May 1778," *Founders Online*, National Archives, https://founders.archives.gov/documents/Washington/03-15-02-0001. [Original source: Lengel, *The Papers of George Washington*, Vol. 15, 1.]

21 Ibid.

22 Ibid, Note. There was a Baptist church and another building used as a schoolhouse on Matson's Ford Road and the intersection of Gulph Road.

23 Ibid, Note.

24 "From George Washington to Major General Lafayette, 18 May 1778," *Founders Online*, National Archives, https://founders.archives.gov/documents/Washington/03-15-02-0152. [Original source: Lengel, *The Papers of George Washington*, Vol. 15, 151–54.]

25 Ibid. The notes on the letter From Washington to Lafayette give a very good description of the Battle of Barren Hill.

26 Mary Stockwell, "Marquis de Lafayette." George Washington's Mount Vernon. 2022. https://www.mountvernon.org/library/digitalhistory/digital-encyclopedia/article/marquis-de-lafayette/.

27 "Richard Kidder Meade," n.d. George Washington's Mount Vernon. Accessed February 10, 2024. https://www.mountvernon.org/library/digitalhistory/digital-encyclopedia/article/richard-kidder-meade/.

28 Note 3, "From George Washington to Brigadier General William Smallwood, 23 May 1778," *Founders Online*, National Archives, https://founders.archives.gov/documents/Washington/03-15-02-0207. [Original source: Lengel, *The Papers of George Washington*, Vol. 15, 206–7.]

29 Ibid.

30 "General Orders, 7 June 1778," *Founders Online*, National Archives, https://founders.archives.gov/documents/Washington/03-15-02-0356. [Original source: Lengel, *The Papers of George Washington*, Vol. 15, 338–44.]

31 "To George Washington from John Johnston, 9 June 1778," *Founders Online*, National Archives, https://founders.archives.gov/documents/Washington/03-15-02-0380. [Original source: Lengel, *The Papers of George Washington*, Vol. 15, 366–68.]
32 Ibid.
33 Ibid.
34 "General Orders, 16 June 1778," *Founders Online*, National Archives, https://founders.archives.gov/documents/Washington/03-15-02-0431. [Original source: Lengel, *The Papers of George Washington*, Vol. 15, 410–12.]

Appendix

1 Source: "From George Washington to Henry Laurens, 10 December 1777," *Founders Online*, National Archives, https://founders.archives.gov/documents/Washington/03-12-02-0538. [Original source: Grizzard, Jr. and Hoth, *The Papers of George Washington*, Vol. 12, 591–93.]
2 Source: Worthington Ford, editor, *Journal of the Continental Congress*, Vol. 9, 1014–15, Washington, DC: Government Printing Office, 1907; Washington made a similar proclamation for the same purpose in his General Orders on December 20, 1777, the second day of the Valley Forge Encampment. See "General Orders, 20 December 1777," *Founders Online*, National Archives, https://founders.archives.gov/documents/Washington/03-12-02-0584. [Original source: Grizzard, Jr. and Hoth, *The Papers of George Washington*, Vol. 12, 641–44.]
3 Source: *Pennsylvania Archives*, Vol. 6, 104, 105.
4 Source: "The American Commissioners to the Committee for Foreign Affairs, 18 December 1777," *Founders Online*, National Archives, https://founders.archives.gov/documents/Franklin/01-25-02-0227. [Original source: Willcox, *The Papers of Benjamin Franklin*, Vol. 25, 305–9.]
5 Source: "To George Washington from Brigadier General Casimir Pulaski, 19 December 1777," *Founders Online*, National Archives, https://founders.archives.gov/documents/Washington/03-12-02-0581. [Original source: Grizzard, Jr. and Hoth, *The Papers of George Washington*, Vol. 12, 637–39.]

Bibliography

Ament, George. "Page 4—US, Revolutionary War Pensions, 1800–1900." Fold3. Accessed February 21, 2024. https://www.fold3.com/image/11020345/ament-george-page-4-us-revolutionary-war-pensions-1800-1900.
American Battlefield Trust. "Brandywine." Accessed February 14, 2024. https://battlefields.org/learn/revolutionary-war/battles/brandywine.
American Battlefield Trust. "John Sullivan." n.d. https://www.battlefields.org/learn/biographies/john-sullivan.
American Battlefield Trust. "Pennsylvania—an Act for the Gradual Abolition of Slavery, 1780." Accessed February 5, 2024. https://www.battlefields.org/learn/primary-sources/pennsylvania-act-gradual-abolition-slavery-1780.
American Battlefield Trust. "Robert Morris," July 27, 2017. https://www.battlefields.org/learn/biographies/robert-morris.
American Battlefield Trust. "Washington's Headquarters (Isaac Potts House)." Accessed February 12, 2024. https://www.battlefields.org/visit/heritage-sites/washingtons-headquarters-isaac-potts-house.
American Chemical Society. "Joseph Priestley, Discoverer of Oxygen National Historic Chemical Landmark." Accessed February 2, 2024. http://www.acs.org/content/acs/en/education/whatischemistry/landmarks/josephpriestleyoxygen.html.
American Revolutionary War 1775 to 1783. "Battle of White Marsh—American Revolutionary War." Accessed February 6, 2024. https://revolutionarywar.us/year-1777/battle-white-marsh/#:~:text=Casualties%20-%20American%20casualties%20were%20estimated%20to%20be.
Anderson, Aubrey. "Historic Valley Forge: The Overhanging Rock at Gulph Mills." www.ushistory.org, December 19, 1924. https://www.ushistory.org/valleyforge/history/rock.html.
Andre, John. *Major Andre's Journal*. Edited by Henry Cabot Lodge. Vol. 1. Boston, MA: The Bibliophile Society, 1903. https://babel.hathitrust.org/cgi/pt?id=osu.32435024928012&seq=236.
Angell, Israel. *The Diary of Colonel Israel Angell Commanding Officer, 2nd Rhode Island Regiment, Continental Army*. Edited by Norman Desmarais and Edward Field. Providence, RI: Preston and Rounds Company, 1899. https://digitalcommons.providence.edu/cgi/viewcontent.cgi?article=1000&context=primary.
Armstrong, Samuel. "From Saratoga to Valley Forge: The Diary of Lt. Samuel Armstrong." Edited by Joseph Boyle. *The Pennsylvania Magazine of History and Biography* CXXI, no. 3 (1997).
Avery, David, and Internet Archive. *The Lord Is to Be Praised for the Triumphs of His Power. A Sermon, Preached at Greenwich, in Connecticut, on the 18th of December 1777 ... By David Avery ... 1778*. Internet Archive, 1778. https://archive.org/details/bim_eighteenth-century_the-lord-is-to-be-praise_avery-david_1778.
Baker, William. "The Camp by the Old Gulph Mill." *Pennsylvania Magazine of History and Biography* 17, no. 4 (1893): 414–29. http://www.jstor.org/stable/20083558.

Barker, Charles R. "The Gulph Mill." *Pennsylvania Magazine of History and Biography*, April 1, 1929, 168–83. https://journals.psu.edu/pmhb/article/view/28158.

Baurmeister, Carl Leopold. *Revolution in America*. Translated by Bernhard Uhlendorf. New Brunswick, NJ: Rutgers University Press, 2003. https://archive.org/details/revolutioninamer00baur/page/139/mode/2up.

Belkin, Lisa. "213 YEARS after LOAN, UNCLE SAM IS DUNNED (Published 1990)." *New York Times*, May 27, 1990. https://www.nytimes.com/1990/05/27/us/213-years-after-loan-uncle-sam-is-dunned.html.Bertram, Michael, ed. "The Revolutionary War." *Tredyffrin Easttown Historical Society Quarterly Archives* 44, no. 1 & 2, The History of Tredyffrin Township (2007): 22–26. https://www.tehistory.org/hqda/html/v44/v44n1+2p022.html.

Boudinot, Elias. *Journal or Historical Recollections of American Events during the Revolutionary War*. Philadelphia: F. Bourquin, 1890.

Bouvier, Jean. "Anne-Robert-Jacques Turgot, Baron de l'Aulne | French Economist." In *Encyclopædia Britannica*, March 14, 2019. https://www.britannica.com/biography/Anne-Robert-Jacques-Turgot-baron-de-lAulne.

Brandywine Battlefield. "Battle of Brandywine – Brandywine Battlefield Park Associates." Accessed February 12, 2024. https://brandywinebattlefield.org/battle.

Brecht, Samuel. "Valley Forge & the Schwenkfelders." *The Exile Herald* 13, no. 1 (April 1936).

Briceno, Carlos. "'From the Archives'—Aide-De-Camp Colonel John Fitzgerald." The Basilica of Saint Mary, October 20, 2023. https://stmaryoldtown.org/aide-de-camp-colonel-john-fitzgerald.

Brigham, Paul. "A Revolutionary Diary of Capt. Paul Brigham, Nov. 19, 1777 to Sept. 4, 1778." Edited by Edward Hoyt. *Vermont History* XXXIV, no. 1 (1966).

Browning, Charles Henry. *Welsh Settlement of Pennsylvania*. Philadelphia, PA: W. J. Campbell, 1912.

Buck, William Joseph. *History of Montgomery County within the Schuylkill Valley*. Norristown, PA: E. L. Acker, 1859.

Burns, Franklin. "New Light on the Encampment of the Continental Army at Valley Forge: December 19, 1777—June 21, 1778." *Tredyffrin Easttown Historical Society History Quarterly* 2, no. 3 (July 1939): 59–74. https://www.tehistory.org/hqda/html/v02/v02n3p075.html.

Cengage. "Early American Orderly Books, 1748–1817 Reel Listing." Accessed February 2, 2024. https://assets.cengage.com/gale/psm/3073000R.pdf.

Claussen, W. Edmunds. *The Revolutionary War Years in Berks, Chester and Montgomery County*. Boyertown, PA: Gilbert Printing Company, 1973.

Conshohocken HS. "About Conshohocken | Conshohocken Historical Society." Accessed February 6, 2024. https://www.conshohockenhistoricalsociety.org/about-conshohocken.

Conshohocken Register. Conshohocken, PA: Recorder Publishing Company, 1920.

Continental Journal & Weekly Advertiser. "Extract of a Letter, Written by a Captain of Light Horse in the Southern Department, to His Friend in Connecticut." January 29, 1777.

Corr, John. "Sturdy Old House Retains Flavor of Its History." *Philadelphia Inquirer*, August 8, 1993.

Dearborn, Henry. *Journals of Henry Dearborn, 1776–1783*. J. Wilson & Son, 1887.

DeHaven Ross, Howard. *History of the de Haven Family*. Fourth Edition. 1894. Reprint, New York, NY: The Pandick Press, 1929.

Dennis, Denise. "African American Dennis Ancestors who Fought in the Revolutionary War." Interview by Sheilah Vance, February 6, 2024.

Dennis, Margaret Denise. *Bristol Budd Sampson: Patriot of the American Revolution*. La Plume, PA: Keystone Press Publishing, 2023.

digital.americanancestors.org. "Samuel Armstrong Diary Original Pages." Accessed February 15, 2024. https://digital.americanancestors.org/digital/collection/p15869coll22/id/1225/rec/1.

Dwight, Timothy. *A Sermon, Preached at Stamford, in Connecticut, upon the General Thanksgiving, December 18th, 1777*, 2007. https://quod.lib.umich.edu/e/evans/n12490.0001.001.

Early American orderly books, 1748–1817 [microform]. New Haven, CT: Research Publications, 1977. 19 microfilm reels; 35mm. Local shelving no.: Microfilm 21,211; https://lccn.loc.gov/82205170.

Editors. "Jan Ingenhousz." Britannica. *Encyclopedia Britannica*. December 4, 2023. Accessed February 2, 2024. https://www.britannica.com/biography/Jan-Ingenhousz.

Evans, Farrell. "America's First Black Regiment Gained Their Freedom by Fighting against the British." HISTORY, February 3, 2021. Accessed August 18, 2024. https://www.history.com/news/first-black-regiment-american-revolution-first-rhode-island.

Evans, Israel. *A Discourse, Delivered, on the 18th Day of December, 1777, the Day of Public Thanksgiving, Appointed by the Honourable Continental Congress, by the Reverend Israel Evans, A.M. Chaplain to General Poor's Brigade: And Now Published at the Request of the General and Officers of the Said Brigade, to Be Distributed among the Soldiers, Gratis*. 1778. Reprint, Lancaster, PA: Francis Bailey, 2009. https://quod.lib.umich.edu/e/evans/N12491.0001.001?view=toc.

Ferling, John. "Thomas Jefferson, Aaron Burr and the Election of 1800." Smithsonian. Smithsonian.com, November 2004. https://www.smithsonianmag.com/history/thomas-jefferson-aaron-burr-and-the-election-of-1800-131082359/.

fi.edu. "Nini Medallion of Benjamin Franklin | the Franklin Institute," March 8, 2014. https://fi.edu/en/science-and-education/collection/nini-medallion-benjamin-franklin.

Fisher, Darlene Emmert. "Social Life in Philadelphia during the British Occupation." *Pennsylvania History: A Journal of Mid-Atlantic Studies* 37, no. 3 (1970): 237–60. https://www.jstor.org/stable/27771875.

Fisher, Elijah. *Elijah Fisher's Journal While in the War for Independence*. Edited by William Lapham. Augusta, ME: Press for Badger & Manley, 1880. https://ia801305.us.archive.org/3/items/cu31924032740478/cu31924032740478.pdf.

Flexner, James Thomas. *Washington: The Indispensable Man*. New York: Little, Brown and Company, 1974.

Fold3. "US, Revolutionary War Pensions, 1800–1900." Accessed February 24, 2024. https://www.fold3.com/publication/467/us-revolutionary-war-pensions-1800-1900.

Ford, Worthington, ed. *Journal of the Continental Congress*. Vol. IX. Washington, DC: Government Printing Office, 1907.

founders.archives.gov. "Founders Online: Home," n.d. https://www.founders.archives.gov/.

George Washington's Mount Vernon. "Benjamin Tallmadge," n.d. https://www.mountvernon.org/library/digitalhistory/digital-encyclopedia/article/benjamin-tallmadge.

George Washington's Mount Vernon. "Conway Cabal." Mount Vernon, 2019. https://www.mountvernon.org/library/digitalhistory/digital-encyclopedia/article/conway-cabal/.

George Washington's Mount Vernon. "William (Billy) Lee." Mount Vernon, 2019. https://www.mountvernon.org/library/digitalhistory/digital-cncyclopedia/article/william-billy-lee/.

George Washington's Mount Vernon. "John Cadwalader," n.d. https://www.mountvernon.org/library/digitalhistory/digital-encyclopedia/article/john-cadwalader/.

George Washington's Mount Vernon. "Richard Kidder Meade." Accessed February 10, 2024. https://www.mountvernon.org/library/digitalhistory/digital-encyclopedia/article/richard-kidder-meade/.

George Washington's Mount Vernon. "Adam Stephen (ca. 1721–1791)." Mount Vernon 2024. Accessed August 18, 2024. https://www.mountvernon.org/library/digitalhistory/digital-encyclopedia/article/adam-stephen-ca-1721-1791/.

Germain, Edward St. "Pierre-Augustin Caron de Beaumarchais Biography & Facts." AmericanRevolution.org. Accessed April 17, 2024. https://www.americanrevolution.org/pierre-augustin-caron-de-baumarchais-biography/.

greatseal.com. "E Pluribus Unum—History of Motto Carried by Eagle on Great Seal," n.d. https://greatseal.com/mottoes/unum.html.

greatseal.com. "Out of Money, One—Symbols of Unity on State and Continental Currency." Accessed January 29, 2024. https://greatseal.com/unity/money.html.

Green, Shirley L. *Revolutionary Blacks: Discovering the Frank Brothers, Freeborn Men of Colors, Soldiers of Independence*. Westholme Publishing, 2023.

Griffith, William. "The Howe Brothers in North America." American Battlefield Trust, April 13, 2020. https://www.battlefields.org/learn/articles/howe-brothers-north-america.

Griswold, Rufus, W. William Simms, and Edward Ingraham. *Washington and the Generals of the American Revolution*. 2nd ed. Vol. I and II. Philadelphia, PA: E. Meeks, 1885. Pdf. https://www.loc.gov/item/14020937/.

Gulph Mills Civic Association. "History." Accessed February 10, 2024. http://gulphmillscivicassoc.weebly.com/history.html.

Haggard, Robert F. "The Nicola Affair: Lewis Nicola, George Washington, and American Military Discontent during the Revolutionary War." *Proceedings of the American Philosophical Society: Held at Philadelphia for Promoting Useful Knowledge* 146, no. 2 (January 1, 2002): 139–69.

Hale, Edward, and Edward Hale, Jr. *Franklin in France*. Boston, MA: Roberts Brothers, 1887.

Head, David. "Hessians." George Washington's Mount Vernon. Mount Vernon, 2019. https://www.mountvernon.org/library/digitalhistory/digital-encyclopedia/article/hessians/.

Hess, Karen. *Martha Washington's Booke of Cookery and Booke of Sweetmeats: Being a Family Manuscript, Curiously Copied by an Unknown Hand Sometime in the Seventeenth Century, Which Was in Her Keeping from 1749, the Time of Her Marriage to Daniel Custis, to 1799, at Which Time She Gave It to Eleanor Parke Custis, Her Granddaughter, on the Occasion of Her Marriage to Lawrence Lewis*. New York: Columbia University Press, 1995.

History.com Editors. "Joseph Plumb Martin." HISTORY, March 8, 2010. https://www.history.com/topics/american-revolution/joseph-plumb-martin.

history.state.gov. "Milestones: 1776–1783— Office of the Historian," n.d. https://history.state.gov/milestones/1776-1783/secret-committee.

Holstein, Anna M. *Swedish Holsteins in America from 1644 to 1892*. Norristown, PA: Anna M. Holstein, 1892. https://www.archive.org/details/swedishholsteins00hols.

Holstein, Dr. G. W. "Swedes' Ford and Surroundings." *Bulletin of the Historical Society of Montgomery County* IV (1910): 73–77.

Hopkinson, Joseph. *Hail Columbia*, 1789. https://www.loc.gov/item/ihas.200000008.

Howe, William. *William Howe Orderly Book, March 9, 1776 – May 1, 1778*. University of Michigan, 1776. https://quod.lib.umich.edu/h/howew/howew.0001.001/1.

hsmcpa.org. "The History of Montgomery County—Historical Society of Montgomery County, PA." Accessed February 14, 2024. https://hsmcpa.org/index.php/learn/the-history-of-montgomery-county.

Irving, Washington. *The Works of Washington Irving: Life of George Washington*. New York, NY: G. P. Putnam and Sons, 1895.

Irving, Washinton. *Washington Irving, the Life of Washington*. Vol. III. New York, NY: Thomas Y. Crowell and Company, 1865.

Jackson, MacDonald P. *Who Wrote "The Night before Christmas"?: Analyzing the Clement Clarke Moore vs. Henry Livingston Question*. Jefferson, North Carolina: McFarland & Company, Inc., Publishers, 2016.

Jan. 8, 1778, Continental Journal and Weekly Advertiser, Boston, MA. "Massachusetts Legislature" January 8, 1778.

Journal of the House of Delegates of Virginia. Vol. October 1777 Session, 1827.

Kaminski, John P, Thomas H. Linley, Elizabeth M. Schoenleber, et al. *The Documentary History of the Ratification of the Constitution and the Bill of Rights Volume XXXVIII*, 38, 2022.

Kaminski, John, Gaspare Saladino, Richard Leffler, et al., eds. *The Documentary History of the Ratification of the Constitution Digital Edition.* Charlottesville, VA: University of Virginia Press, 2009.
Kapp, Friedrich. *The Life of John Kalb.* Applewood Books, 2009.
Lacey, John and John Armstrong. "Memoirs of Brigadier-General John Lacey of Pennsylvania." *The Pennsylvania Magazine of History and Biography* 25, no. 1 (1902): 101–11. https://www.jstor.org/stable/20086016?seq=10.
Lafayette, Marquis de. *Memoirs, Correspondence and Manuscripts of General Lafayette. Published by His Family.* New York, NY: Columbia College, 1837. https://www.gutenberg.org/cache/epub/8376/pg8376-images.html.
Laurens, John and William Gilmore Simms. *The Army Correspondence of Colonel John Laurens in the Years 1777–8.* New York, NY: The Bradford Club, 1867.
Leeds Intelligencer, Vol. XXIV, No. 1243. "Thursday's Post from the London Gazette." January 27, 1778.
Lewis, Noah. "Edward Hector Research Documentation—Edward 'Ned' Hector—Black Revolutionary War Hero Nedhector@Aol.com / 610-352-4372." Edward "Ned" Hector: Black Revolutionary War Hero. Accessed February 5, 2024. https://www.nedhector.com/edward-hector-research-documentation/.
———. "Ned Hector, Pennsylvania's African American Revolutionary War Hero, What Was His Role During the Gulph Mills Encampment?" Interview by Sheilah Vance, February 7, 2024.
Library of Congress. "About This Collection | George Washington Papers | Digital Collections | Library of Congress." The Library of Congress, 2015. https://www.loc.gov/collections/george-washington-papers/about-this-collection/.
Library of Congress. "Religion and the Founding of the American Republic," n.d. https://www.loc.gov/exhibits/religion/rel04.html.
Library of Congress. "Revolutionary War: The Turning Point, 1776–1777 | the American Revolution, 1763–1783 | U.S. History Primary Source Timeline | Classroom Materials at the Library of Congress | Library of Congress," n.d. https://www.loc.gov/classroom-materials/united-states-history-primary-source-timeline/american-revolution-1763-1783/revolutionary-war-turning-point-1776-1777.
Library of Congress. "The American Revolution | Timeline | Articles and Essays | George Washington Papers | Digital Collections | Library of Congress." Accessed January 28, 2024. https://www.loc.gov/collections/george-washington-papers/articles-and-essays/timeline/the-american-revolution.
Library of Congress. "The Province of New Jersey, Divided into East and West, Commonly Called the Jerseys." Accessed January 28, 2024. https://www.loc.gov/item/74692515.
Linn, John Blair. *History of Centre and Clinton Counties, Pennsylvania,* 1883.
Loane, Nancy K. *Following the Drum Women at the Valley Forge Encampment.* 1st ed. Washington, DC: Potomac Books, 2009.
Lower Merion Historical Society. "Inns, Restaurants, and Hotels." Accessed January 31, 2024. https://lowermerionhistory.org/home/full-text/lower-merion-and-narberth-postcards/inns-restaurants-hotels/.
Lower Merion Historical Society. "John Roberts of the Mill." Accessed January 30, 2024. https://lowermerionhistory.org/home/full-text/schmidt-collection/john-roberts-of-the-mill/.
loyalist.lib.unb.ca. "Papers: 1760–1795 | the Loyalist Collection." Accessed February 13, 2024. https://loyalist.lib.unb.ca/node/4519.
Marshall, John. *The Life of George Washington.* 1805. Reprint, New York, NY: Derby & Jackson, 1860.

Marshall, John. *The Life of George Washington*. Project Gutenberg. Vol. II, 2006. https://www.gutenberg.org/files/18592/18592-h/18592-h.htm#CHAPTER_IX.

Martin, Joseph Plumb. *A Narrative of Some of the Adventures, Dangers and Sufferings of a Revolutionary Soldier*. Glazier, Masters & Co., 1830. https://www.google.com/books/edition/A_Narrative_of_Some_of_the_Adventures_Da/ZbdcAAAAcAAJ?hl=en

McDonald, Bob. "Thro Mud & Mire into the Woods." Revwar75.com, 2024. https://www.revwar75.com/library/bob/smith2.htm.

McGuire, Thomas J. *Battle of Paoli*. Mechanicsburg, PA: Stackpole Books, 2006.

McGuire, Thomas J. *The Philadelphia Campaign Volume I: Brandywine and the Fall of Philadelphia*. Mechanicsburg, PA: Stackpole Books, 2006.

McGuire, Thomas J. *The Philadelphia Campaign Volume II: Germantown and the Roads to Valley Forge*. Mechanicsburg, PA: Stackpole Books, 2007.

McMichael, James. "Diary of Lieutenant James McMichael, of the Pennsylvania Line, 1776–1778." *The Pennsylvania Magazine of History and Biography* 16, no. 2 (1892): 129–59. https://www.jstor.org/stable/20083473.

Montalvo, David. "A Brief History of Slavery and Freedom in Pennsylvania and Montgomery County." Presented at the Presentation, King of Prussia Historical Society, September 14, 2019. https://www.kophistory.org/archive/files/MANUSCRIPT/ShortEnslavedinPA&MontCo.pdf.

Muhlenberg, Henry Melchior. *The Journals of Henry Melchior Muhlenberg*. Translated by Theodore Tapput and John W. Doberstein. Vol. 3. Philadelphia, PA: Muhlenberg Press, 1958. https://babel.hathitrust.org/cgi/pt?id=mdp.39015011394700&seq=130.

Nash, Gary. "Agrippa Hull: Revolutionary Patriot—BlackPast." BlackPast, July 2, 2008. https://www.blackpast.org/african-american-history/agrippa-hull-revolutionary-patriot/.

National Archives. "The American Revolution," July 22, 2019. https://www.archives.gov/research/military/american-revolution.

National Archives Catalog. "Case Files of Pension and Bounty-Land Warrant Applications Based on Revolutionary War Service, Ca. 1800–Ca. 1912," n.d. https://catalog.archives.gov/id/300022.

National Archives Catalog. "Registration Form, Pennsylvania SP Hanging Rock, National Register for Historic Places," September 1997. https://catalog.archives.gov/id/71995725?fbclid=IwZXh0bgNhZW0CMTAAAR0GxTm2D9oi2SNgj8Gfvrq7NcTdIdln9xINYRCT-GnMZ3_SbPhmWhrZDk0E_aem_wnnJphSe1SC8uywJpz_wlg.National Archives, War Department Collection of Revolutionary War Records, n.d. https://catalog.archives.gov/search-within/422?q=gulph.

National Constitution Center. "America's First Rock Star: Benjamin Franklin in France," December 17, 2015. https://constitutioncenter.org/blog/americas-first-rock-star-benjamin-franklin.

National Constitution Center. "Pennsylvania Constitution (1776) | the National Constitution Center," n.d. https://constitutioncenter.org/the-constitution/historic-document-library/detail/pennsylvania-constitution.

National Park Service, Valley Forge National Historical Park, Pennsylvania. "Headquarters' Orderly Book." Accessed February 2, 2024. https://www.nps.gov/vafo/learn/history/culture/hq_orderly_book.htm.

Nelson, Paul David. *William Alexander, Lord Stirling*. University of Alabama Press, 2003.

norristown.org. "Norristown, PA | Official Website." Accessed February 1, 2024. https://norristown.org.

Nudd, Jean. "Using Revolutionary War Pension Files to Find Family Information, Genealogy Notes." *Prologue Magazine*. Accessed January 31, 2024. https://www.archives.gov/publications/prologue/2015/summer/rev-war-pensions.html.

onlineonly.christies.com. "The First National Thanksgiving, Continental Congress, 1777 | Christie's." Accessed February 4, 2024. https://onlineonly.christies.com/s/fine-printed-books-manuscripts-including-americana/first-national-thanksgiving-36/99809.

Orderly Book, Col. Philip van Cortland's 2nd New York Regiment of 1777, 55; accessed Library of Congress, Microfilm; Orderly Book 56.2.

Orderly Book, Lt. Col. Joseph Storer, York County, Massachusetts Regiment, 76; accessed Library of Congress, Microfilm; Orderly Book 47.

Orderly Book, Peter Brown's Company of the Philadelphia Militia Artillery, 175; accessed Library of Congress, Microfilm; Orderly Book 54.

Orderly Book, Richard Platt, November 12 to December 16, 1777, 74; accessed Library of Congress, Microfilm; Orderly Book 55.

Oxfordlearnersdictionaries.com. "Subaltern Noun – Definition, Pictures, Pronunciation and Usage Notes | Oxford Advanced Learner's Dictionary at OxfordLearnersDictionaries.com," 2024. https://www.oxfordlearnersdictionaries.com/definition/english/subaltern.

Parker, James. *James Parker's Journal of His Experiences during the Revolutionary War*, 1777, 49–52.

Parton, James. *The Life and Times of Aaron Burr*. Edited by Ellen Parton. Vol. I. 1855. Reprint, Boston, MA: Houghton Mifflin Co., 1892. https://archive.org/details/lifeandtimesaar06partgoog/page/n20/mode/2up.

Peckham, Howard H. *The Toll of Independence: Engagements & Battle Casualties of the American Revolution*. Editorial: Chicago; London: The University Of Chicago Press, 1974.

pennandslaveryproject.org. "Early Trustees · Slave Ownership." Accessed February 25, 2024. https://pennandslaveryproject.org/exhibits/show/slaveownership/earlytrustees.

Pennsylvania Archives. Vol. VI. Philadelphia, PA: Joseph Severns & Co., 1853.

Pennsylvania Historical and Museum Commission. *The WPA Guide to Philadelphia*. Philadelphia: University of Pennsylvania Press, 1988.

Pinkowski, E. *Washington's Officers Slept Here, Historic Homes of Valley Forge and Its Neighborhood*. Sunshine Press, 1959.

Potter's Mill Store Ledger, November 8, 1790.

Powerlibrary.org. "Revolutionary War Pension Files and Related Accounts, 1785–1809 | Psa," 2024. https://digitalarchives.powerlibrary.org/psa/islandora/object/psa%3Arwpfra.

Quarles, Benjamin. *Negro in the American Revolution*. 1961. Reprint, Chapel Hill, NC: University of North Carolina Press, 1996.

"Radnor Friends Meeting | Religious Society of Friends." Accessed February 4, 2024. https://radnorquakers.net.

Reed, John. "The Fight on Old Gulph Road." *Bulletin of the Historical Society of Montgomery County* XV, no. 1 and 2 (1966): 32–36.

Reed, William Bradford. *Life and Correspondence of Joseph Reed*. Vol. I. Philadelphia: Lindsay & Blackiston, 1847.

Revolutionary War US. "Battle of Matson's Ford—American Revolutionary War." Accessed January 30, 2024. https://revolutionarywar.us/year-1777/battle-matsons-ford.

Robbins, James. "The Anti-Washington Cabal." National Review, November 26, 2008. https://www.nationalreview.com/2008/11/anti-washington-cabal-james-s-robbins/.

Roberts, Richard. "Peter 'Johann Peter' Samsel (1734–1777)—Find A..." www.findagrave.com, July 20, 2012. https://www.findagrave.com/memorial/93936585/peter-samsel.

Robertson, Archibald. *Archibald Robertson, Lieutenant General Royal Engineers: His Diaries and Sketches in America, 1762–1780*. Edited by Harry M. Lydenberg. 1930. Reprint, New York, NY: New York Public Library, 1971. https://babel.hathitrust.org/cgi/pt?id=mdp.39015019750978&seq=11.

Roos, Dave. "How John Marshall Expanded the Power of the Supreme Court." HISTORY, November 30, 2021. http://www.history.com/news/supreme-court-power-john-marshall.Scharf, John Thomas. *History of Delaware: 1609–1888*. Philadelphia, PA: L. J. Richards & Co., 1888.

Schaffel, Kenneth. "The American Board of War, 1776–1781." *Military Affairs* 50, no. 4 (1986): 185–89. https://doi.org/10.2307/1988008.

Schenawolf, Harry. "Washington's Staff during the American Revolutionary War: Major General of the Day." *Revolutionary War Journal*, February 18, 2015. https://revolutionarywarjournal.com/washingtons-major-general.

Simes, Thomas. *A Treatise on the Military Science*, 1780.

Slaughter, Jamie. "Frederick the Great." George Washington's Mount Vernon, 2023. https://www.mountvernon.org/library/digitalhistory/digital-encyclopedia/article/frederick-the-great/.

Smyth, S. Gordon. "Matson's Ford." *Bulletin of the Historical Society of Montgomery County* IV (1910): 62–72. https://archive.org/details/historicalsketch04hist.

Smyth, S. Gordon. "The Gulph Hills in the Annals of the Revolution." *Historical Sketches of Montgomery County* 3 (1905): 171–74.

State.gov. "Buildings of the Department of State—Buildings—Department History—Office of the Historian," 2023. https://history.state.gov/departmenthistory/buildings/section1.

Stockwell, Mary. "Baron von Steuben." George Washington's Mount Vernon, n.d. https://www.mountvernon.org/library/digitalhistory/digital-encyclopedia/article/baron-von-steuben/.

Stockwell, Mary. "Marquis de Lafayette." George Washington's Mount Vernon, 2022. https://www.mountvernon.org/library/digitalhistory/digital-encyclopedia/article/marquis-de-lafayette/.

StudyLight.org. "William Heath—1911 Encyclopedia Britannica," April 14, 2024. https://www.studylight.org/encyclopedias/bri/w/william-heath.html.

Supplee, M. Regina. "Gulph Mills and Rebel Hill." *Bulletin of the Historical Society of Montgomery County* 6 (1947): 17.

Teamer, S. Paul. "The Welsh Tract." *TEHS Quarterly Archives (Tredyffrin Easttown Historical Society)* 2, no. 1 (January 1939): 19–24. https://www.tehistory.org/hqda/html/v02/v02n1p019.html.

The Conshohocken Register. Recorder Publishing Co., 1920.

The Continental Journal and Weekly Advertiser. "Extract of a Letter from a Gentleman at Camp, on Schuylkill, Dated Dec. 17, 1777." January 22, 1778.

The Editors of Encyclopedia Britannica. "Lydia Barrington Darragh | American War Heroine." In *Encyclopedia Britannica*, 2019. https://www.britannica.com/biography/Lydia-Barrington-Darragh.

The Editors of Encyclopedia Britannica. "St. Lucia's Day | History, Traditions, & Facts." In *Encyclopedia Britannica*, January 14, 2019. https://www.britannica.com/topic/St-Lucias-Day.

"The First Thanksgiving of the United States." Accessed February 4, 2024. https://thanksgiving.org/wp-content/uploads/2016/06/The-First-Thanksgiving-of-the-United-States.pdf.

The Pennsylvania Ledger or the Philadelphia Market Day Advertiser. "No Title." December 17, 1777.

The Hughes Family Papers, Courtesy of The Historical Society of Pennsylvania, Philadelphia, Pennsylvania.

Thoms, Herbert. "Albigence Waldo, Surgeon." *Annals of Medical History* 10, no. 4 (December 1, 1928): 486–97. https://www.ncbi.nlm.nih.gov/pmc/articles/PMC7940074/.

ThoughtCo. "American Revolution: Major General John Sullivan." Accessed February 11, 2024. https://www.thoughtco.com/major-general-john-sullivan-2360602#:~:text=Receiving%20a%20commission%20as%20a%20brigadier%20general%2C%20Sullivan.

University Archives and Records Center. "James Irvine." Accessed January 28, 2024. https://archives.upenn.edu/exhibits/penn-people/biography/james-irvine/.

Ushistory.org. "Biography of General Henry Knox," 2019. https://www.ushistory.org/valleyforge/served/knox.html.

Vance, Sheilah. *Becoming Valley Forge*. Paoli, PA: The Elevator Group, 2016.

Vance, Sheilah. "Valley Forge's Threshold: The Encampment at Gulph Mills—Journal of the American Revolution." *Journal of the American Revolution*, November 5, 2019. https://allthingsliberty.com/2019/11/valley-forges-threshold-the-encampment-at-gulph-mills/.

BIBLIOGRAPHY • 223

Vance, Sheilah. *Six Days in December: General George Washington's and the Continental Army's Encampment on Rebel Hill, December 13–19, 1777.* Paoli, PA: The Elevator Group, 2011.

Varnum, James M. (James Mitchell), 1748–1789. James M. Varnum and John Stark papers, 1777–1780. 1 item. 1 microfilm reel. Local shelving no.: MMC-2283 Microfilm 17,360-1N-1P; https://lccn.loc.gov/mm78083238.

Von Ewald, Johann. *Diary of the American War: A Hessian Journal.* Edited and translated by Joseph Philips Tustin. New Haven: Yale University Press, 1979. https://archive.org/details/EwaldsDIARYOFTHEAMERICANWAR/page/n143/mode/2up.

Waldo, Albigence. "Valley Forge, 1777–1778. Diary of Surgeon Albigence Waldo, of the Connecticut Line." Vol. 21, No. 3 (January 1, 1897): 299–323. https://ia601907.us.archive.org/1/items/jstor-20085750/20085750.pdf.

Walker, Harriet J., and JSTOR. *Revolutionary Soldiers Buried in Illinois. Internet Archive.* Journal of the Illinois State Historical Society (1908–1984), 1916. https://archive.org/details/jstor-40194379.

Wharton, Anne. "Thomas Wharton, Jnr." *Pennsylvania Magazine of History and Biography* 5, no. 4 (1881): 426–39. https://jstor.org/stable/20084522.

Whittemore, Charles P., *A General of the Revolution: John Sullivan of New Hampshire*, New York: Columbia University Press, 1961.

Wild, Ebenezer. *The Journal of Ebenezer Wild (1776–1781).* Cambridge: John Wilson and Son, University Press, 1891. https://babel.hathitrust.org/cgi/pt?id=chi.56986164&seq=1.

Wildes, Harry Emerson. *Anthony Wayne, Trouble Shooter of the American Revolution.* Greenwood, 1970.

Woodman, Henry. *The History of Valley Forge*, 1920. www.google.com/books/edition/The_History_of_Valley_Forge/eFdKAAAAYAAJ?hl=en.

www.amrevmuseum.org. "Washington's War Tents," n.d. https://www.amrevmuseum.org/washington-s-war-tents.

www.britannica.com. "Thomas Conway | American Revolution, Continental Army, Pennsylvania | Britannica," n.d. https://www.britannica.com/biography/Thomas-Conway#ref27008.

www.delcopa.gov. "History—at a Glance—Delaware County, Pennsylvania," n.d. https://www.delcopa.gov/departments/history.html.

www.findagrave.com. "LTC Isaac Hughes (1747–1782)—Find a Grave..." Accessed February 5, 2024. https://www.findagrave.com/memorial/13056639/isaac-hughes.

www.genealogy.com. "John Bevan of Welsh Tract & Mi—Genealogy.com." Accessed February 5, 2024. https://www.genealogy.com/forum/surnames/topics/bevan/139/.

www.gilderlehrman.org. "The Articles of Confederation, 1777 | Gilder Lehrman Institute of American History," n.d. https://www.gilderlehrman.org/history-resources/spotlight-primary-source/articles-confederation-1777.

www.hmdb.org. "A Revolutionary River Historical Marker." Accessed January 30, 2024. https://www.hmdb.org/m.asp?m=203794.

www.intelligence.gov. "A New Nation's First Spies," n.d. https://www.intelligence.gov/evolution-of-espionage/revolutionary-war/new-nations-first-spies.

www.merriam-webster.com. "Definition of TORY," n.d. https://www.merriam-webster.com/dictionary/Tory.

www.nps.gov. "Lieutenant General Charles Cornwallis—Yorktown Battlefield Part of Colonial National Historical Park (U.S. National Park Service)." Accessed February 3, 2024. https://www.nps.gov/york/learn/historyculture/cornwallis.htm.

www.nps.gov. "Patriots of African Descent Monument (U.S. National Park Service)," n.d. https://www.nps.gov/places/patriots-african-descent-monument.htm.

www.readingpa.gov. "City of Reading, PA." Accessed February 1, 2024. https://www.readingpa.gov.

www.ushistory.org. "Biography of General Baron Johan DeKalb," n.d. https://www.ushistory.org/valleyforge/served/dekalb.html.

www.ushistory.org. "Biography of General Chevalier Louis Lebegue DePresle Duportail," n.d. https://www.ushistory.org/valleyforge/served/duport.html.

www.ushistory.org. "The Conway Cabal." Accessed February 2, 2024. https://ushistory.org/march/other/cabal2.htm.

www.ushistory.org. "US History." Accessed January 28, 2024. https://ushistory.org/valleyforge/served/Armstrong2.html.

In *A "Misplaced Chapter" in the History of Photosynthesis Research; the Second Publication (1796) on Plant Processes by Dr Jan Ingen-Housz, MD, Discoverer of Photosynthesis*. Netherlands: Kluwer Academic Publishers, n.d. https://www.life.illinois.edu/govindjee/history/articles/GestOnIngenhousz_missing.pdf.

n.d. Fold3, US, Pennsylvania Revolutionary War Battalions and Militia Index, 1775–1783. Accessed February 24, 2024. https://www.fold3.com/publication/1162/us-pennsylvania-revolutionary-war-battalions-and-militia-index-1775-1783.

Zucker, A. E. "THE BROGLIE INTRIGUE." In *General de Kalb, Lafayette's Mentor*, 53:94–107. University of North Carolina Press, 1966. http://www.jstor.org/stable/10.5149/9781469658759_zucker.11.

Index

Adams, John, 134
Adams, Samuel, 135–36
African American soldiers, 98–100, 102
Alexander, Major General William, 2–4, 76
American Commissioners, 4, 6, 51–52, 56, 63–64, 77, 80, 119–21, 131–34, 160, 162, 178
American Philosophical Society, 12, 58, 79
Andre, Major John, 31, 57, 98, 116
Angell, Israel, 41, 54, 67, 95, 97, 116, 123, 138, 150
Armstrong, Lieutenant Samuel, 39, 55, 83, 97, 108, 123, 136, 150
Armstrong, Major General John, 4, 10–12, 62, 67, 69, 83–84, 88, 111–12, 157–58, 168–69

Barren Hill, 158, 166, 170
Beaumarchais, Pierre Augustin Caron de, 180
Bevan, Richard, 101–2
Black Horse Inn, 31–32, 34
Bland, Colonel Theodorick, 39, 50
Boudinot, Elias, 20, 70–71
Brandywine, Battle of, 6, 8, 45, 74, 102, 111, 117, 136, 155
Bridgeport, 23
Brigham, Captain Paul, 41, 55, 68, 84, 98, 108, 123, 138, 151
Bucks County, 31, 45, 47, 112
Burgoyne, General William, 52, 90–91, 102, 116, 124–26, 135–36, 140–41, 161, 178
Burr, Aaron, 164–66

Cadwalader, Brigadier General John, 10–13, 69, 100
camp women, 151

Chester County, 7–9, 23, 37, 50, 75, 112, 122, 155
Christmas, 66, 75, 166
Clark, Major General John, 3, 114–15, 145, 158–59
clothing, 4, 12–13, 15–16, 28, 58, 60–62, 79, 88, 104–5, 139, 150–51, 156, 180
Committee for Foreign Affairs, 131, 178
Committee of Correspondence, 72
Conshohocken, 23, 102
    West, 23
Conshohocken Hills, 32, 48, 64, 90, 162, 170
Continental Congress, 1, 3, 9, 10, 22–23, 26–28, 31, 37, 59, 61–62, 71, 77–78, 89–91, 97–98, 103–6, 112, 114, 117, 119, 121, 126, 128–31, 135–38, 152, 155, 160–61, 175, 178
    Camp Committee (CCCC), 10–11, 17–18, 21–23, 59
Continental money, 26, 100, 130
Cornwallis, Lieutenant General Lord Charles, 20–21, 28, 31–33, 37, 41–44, 47, 56–57, 68–70, 90, 97, 107, 116–17

Darragh, Lydia, 19–20
Deane, Silas, 4, 6, 63, 80, 119, 126, 133, 162, 178, 180
Dearborn, Lieutenant Colonel Henry, 40, 55, 67, 83, 97, 108, 123, 136, 150
defile, 42, 90, 162–63
DeHaven, 65, 73–75
De Kalb, Major General Johann, 3, 5, 10, 14, 56, 149
Delaware County, 25
Delaware River, 5, 9, 26, 155

Dickinson, Brigadier General Philemon, 49
Duportail, Brigadier General Louis, 3, 4, 10, 13, 25, 146
Dutch, 64, 92, 160 *see also* Holland

enslaved persons, 51, 72, 98–102 *see also* slavery
enslaver, 99, 102, 151 *see also* slavery
Evans, Rev. Israel, 139–40
Ewald, John, 42, 68, 117, 152

Fort Mercer, 10–11, 27, 128
Fort Mifflin, 11, 27, 90, 128
Founders Online, 87, 113, 115, 154
France, 5, 8, 27, 5–52, 56, 63, 77–78, 80, 92–93, 106, 115, 119–20, 121–22, 127, 131–34, 146, 156, 160, 162, 169, 178–79 *see also* French Alliance
Franklin, Benjamin, 4, 8, 13, 51–52, 58, 63, 72, 80, 92–93, 106, 119, 126, 131, 133–34, 146–47, 160–62, 178, 180
Frank, William and Ben, 98
Frederick William II, King of Prussia, 14, 23, 77, 126–27
French Alliance, 169

Germantown, 9, 18, 48, 88–89, 109–12, 117, 136, 152, 158
Germantown Road, 18, 20, 109–12
General Orders, 33, 36, 49, 57, 66, 86–88, 103, 113, 121, 123, 141–43, 154, 164, 169, 171–72
Glover, General John, 24, 86, 149, 164
Greene, Major General Nathanael, 3, 5, 10, 13, 14, 24, 66, 98, 145, 149
Grey, Charles "No Flint," 21, 31, 57, 170
Gulf, the (or Gulph), 152, 162, 169, 171
Gulph Mills, 3, 7, 19, 24–25, 30–34, 36–37, 41, 44–45, 47–50, 56, 65–67, 69, 71–80, 81–84, 88, 93, 95–103, 106, 107–9, 112, 114–15, 117, 123–24, 127, 136, 139, 142–45, 149–51, 154–56, 161–62, 163–72
Gulph Road, 29, 31–35, 73–75, 161–63

Hanging Rock, 73, 76, 161–62
Harrison, Lieutenant Colonel Robert Hanson, 3, 10

Harriton, 31–32, 34
Hector, Ned, 102
Holland, 64, 160 *see also* Dutch
Holstein, Anna, 65, 73, 100
Holstein, Matthias, 23, 65, 73, 100
Howe, Admiral Richard, 161
Howe, General William, 1, 13, 17, 19–21, 26–27, 41, 43, 49, 51, 57, 69–70, 84, 86, 91, 98, 105, 116–17, 125–26, 155, 161, 170, 173
Hughes, Isaac, 72–74, 100–1
Hughes, John, 72–73, 100–1
Hull, Agrippa, 102
Huntington, Colonel Jedidiah, 24, 39, 123, 145, 164
huts, 4–6, 8–10, 55, 66–67, 71, 97, 108, 115–16, 122, 136–37, 141–43, 150, 152, 154–55, 163–64

Ingenhousz, Jan, 92–93
Invalid Brigade, 58, 79
Irvine, Brigadier General James, 3, 5, 63, 71, 84, 111, 173

Jackson, Henry, 125, 166–67, 169–72
Jefferson, President Thomas, 134, 164–65
Jerseys, 5, 9, 24–26, 49, 58, 59, 69–70, 117, 128, 160, 177
Johnston, John, 31, 171–72

Kidder Meade, Richard, 164, 171
King of Prussia Historical Society, 65, 81, 162
Knox, Brigadier General Henry, 3, 6, 10–11, 14, 23

Lacey, John, 31, 34–36, 45, 47, 168–69
Lafayette, Major General Marquis de, 3, 6, 10–11, 14, 56, 66, 75, 89, 115–16, 146, 149, 156, 170
Lancaster, 3, 5–7, 9, 10, 31, 61, 70–71, 139, 151, 160, 168
Lancaster Road, 24–25, 31, 32, 34, 42, 50, 163
Laurens, Henry, 27, 37–39, 59, 89–91, 97, 104, 126, 136
Laurens, John, 37, 53, 115, 150
Lee, Arthur, 63–64, 80, 125, 133, 162, 178, 180

Lee, William, 100
Livingston, Colonel Henry Beekman, 166
Long Island, 47
    Battle of, 2, 3, 21
Louis Auguste XVI, King of France, 4, 121, 130–33, 162
Lower Merion, 7, 23, 31, 73 *see also* Upper Merion
Lutterloh, Henry Emanuel, 3, 6

map, 33, 76
Marshall, John, 40–41
Martin, Joseph Plumb, 138–39, 150
Matson's Ford, 6, 23, 25, 29–47, 49, 50, 53, 56–57, 73, 90, 102, 109, 117, 168, 170
    Battle of, 29–47, 68–70, 90, 102, 109, 117, 168
Maxwell, Brigadier General William, 3, 6–7, 10–11, 15, 24, 103, 164
McMichael, Lieutenant James, 41, 55, 151
Merion *see* Lower Merion, Upper Merion
Middle Ferry, 30–32, 34, 41, 50, 57, 68
Monroe, James, 76
Montgomery County, 29, 33, 99
Montgomery County Historical Society, 29
Morgan, Daniel, 21, 27, 166–67, 171
Muhlenberg, Brigadier General Peter, 3, 7, 10, 15, 24, 47–49, 73, 113–13, 164, 172
Muhlenberg, Reverend Henry, 47
musket, 32, 44–45, 165, 168

Netherlands, the *see* Dutch, Holland
New York, 8, 11, 47, 70, 87, 102, 116–17, 125, 128, 145, 165–66, 170, *see also* Long Island
Nelson, Jr., Brigadier General Thomas, 26–27

Oneida Indian Nation, 170
Orderly Books, 54, 69, 73, 86–88, 103, 113–14, 123, 143–45, 154, 164

Paoli, 9, 50, 61, 136
Paris, 51, 119, 133
Parker, James, 43, 98, 123–24
Pennsylvania General Assembly, 59, 61, 105, 121
Pennsylvania Supreme Executive Council, 160, 162

Philadelphia, 3, 5–11, 15–18, 19–24, 30–34, 37–38, 40, 44, 47–49, 53, 57–59, 67, 69–70, 75–76, 79, 83–85, 88, 101–9, 112, 114–18, 123, 128 29, 136, 145–46, 152, 156, 158, 161–62, 168, 173, 175
Philadelphia County, 23, 45, 57, 72–73, 112
picket, 30–34, 50, 73–74, 110–11, 158, 163–70, 172
Platt, Major Richard, 54, 87–88, 103, 113–14, 123, 145, 154
Plymouth Meeting, 45
Plymouth Whitemarsh, 23
Poor, Brigadier General Enoch, 3, 7, 10–11, 15, 24, 139, 149, 164
Potter, Brigadier General James, 3, 7, 8, 11, 15, 20, 24–25, 29–37, 39–42, 42, 45, 50, 56, 57, 68–69, 71, 84, 90, 100, 109, 112, 122, 158–59, 168–69
Prince Negro, 99
provisions, 4, 20–21, 26, 32, 38, 42, 55–56, 58–59, 66, 86, 88, 91, 103, 105, 112, 118, 125, 129, 138, 150–51, 157, 159, 164, 175, 177
Pulaski, Brigadier General Casimir, 3, 8, 10, 146, 157, 181

Quaker, 7, 19, 32, 53, 102, 129–30, 159

Radnor, 19, 25, 32, 56, 76, 164, 166, 171
Rambo, 23, 65, 76–77
Rebel Hill, 72–76, 162–63
Reed, General Joseph, 7, 8, 11, 15, 29, 68–70, 85, 89, 92
resolutions, 59, 106, 118, 175
Rhode Island, 5, 9, 11, 27, 41–42, 90, 97–99, 116, 126, 150
river road, 66, 72
Robertson, Lieutenant General Archibald, 28, 42, 50, 57
Royal Engineers, 28, 42

Sampson, Bristol Budd, 99
Schuylkill River, 3, 5–6, 8, 23–26, 30, 39, 41, 47, 53, 65, 68, 85, 90, 102, 128, 152, 163
slave *see* enslaved persons
slavery, 98–99, 102, 141 *see also* enslaved persons, enslaver

Smallwood, Brigadier General William, 3, 9–11, 16, 155–56, 170–71
Spain, 131–33, 178–80
Spanish, 56, 131
Storer, Joseph, 113–14, 143–45
Sturgis, Jonathan, 73–74, 163
Sullivan, Major General John, 3, 9–11, 16, 24, 32–39, 56, 123, 136, 143, 149, 154, 156
Supplee, 75–76
Swedeland, 23
Swedesburg, 23–25, 65, 72
Swedes Ford, 23, 32–33, 36, 38, 40–41, 46, 49, 53, 83, 88

tents, 21–22, 40–42, 55, 66, 75, 107–9, 111, 113–17, 119–20, 136, 151, 154, 157
Thanksgiving, 122, 134, 135–47
Tilghman, Tench, 169–71

Upper Merion, 23, 25, 29, 31, 37, 53, 65, 73, 79, 83, 101, 166 see also Lower Merion

Valley Forge, 2, 4, 20, 29, 37, 70, 73–75, 96–97, 100, 102, 115, 122–41, 143–45, 149–58, 160–62, 163–74, 176, 180
Varnum, Brigadier General James, 3, 9–11, 16, 24, 87, 95–96, 98–99, 114, 123, 164
Vergennes, Comte (Count) de, 127
Villanova, 166
Von Steuben, Baron Friedrich, 126–27, 146

Waldo, Albigence, 39–40, 55, 67, 81–82, 96, 108, 113, 138
Walpole, Thomas, 51–52

Washington, George, 1–13, 16–18, 19–23, 25–33, 36 41, 44, 45, 47, 49–54, 57–59, 66, 69, 71–75, 77–78, 81–82, 84–92, 95, 97, 99–104, 107, 109, 111–18, 121–33, 135–36, 139–46, 151–72
   letters from, 17, 26–27, 51–52, 59–60, 81, 88–89, 91, 115, 125–26, 139, 155–56, 173
   letters to, 8, 11–12, 31, 90, 125, 146, 157
Wayne, Brigadier General Anthony, 3, 9–12, 16–17, 32, 37, 40, 59–62, 145, 149, 152–53
Weedon, Brigadier General George, 3, 9–11, 16, 24, 66, 87, 100, 123, 154
Wharton, Thomas, 29–30, 34, 36, 51, 60–62, 68, 70–71, 82, 84, 105, 109, 111–12, 159
Whig, 69, 105, 129, 130, 158, 177
whiskey, 51, 55, 66, 83
Whitemarsh, 1, 3, 11, 18, 19–30, 37, 40–41, 44–45, 47–48, 53, 57, 59, 62, 68–71, 75, 84, 90, 92, 96, 109, 111–12, 117, 124, 157–58, 166, 170
Wild, Lieutenant Ebenezer, 42, 84, 97, 108, 137, 151
Wilkerson, General James, 77–78
Wilmington, 3, 5–10, 26, 31, 128, 155–56, 171, 177
women, 19, 20, 100, 108, 116, 150, 151 see also camp women
Woodford, Brigadier General William, 3, 10–11, 17, 24, 164

York, 3, 45, 47, 70, 77, 89, 98, 113, 136, 143–44, 160, 176, 178